Coming of Age
in the 21st Century

ALSO BY MARY FROSCH

Coming of Age Around the World
(Faith Adiele and Mary Frosch, editors)

Coming of Age in America
(Mary Frosch, editor)

Coming of Age
in the
21st Century

Growing Up in America Today

EDITED BY MARY FROSCH

THE NEW PRESS

NEW YORK
LONDON

Requests for permission to reproduce selections from this book should be mailed to:
Permissions Department, The New Press, 120 Wall Street, 31st floor,
New York, NY 10005

Published in the United States by The New Press, New York, 2008
Distributed by Perseus Distribution

LIBRARY OF CONGRESS CATALOGING-IN-PUBLICATION DATA

Coming of age in the 21st century: growing up in America today / edited by Mary Frosch.
p. cm.
ISBN 978-1-59558-055-9 (pbk.)
1. Adolescence—Literary collections. 2. Minority teenagers—United States—Literary
collections. 3. American literature—Minority authors. I. Frosch, Mary.
PS509.M5C67 2008
813.008'920693—dc22

2008024671

The New Press publishes books that promote and enrich public discussion and
understanding of the issues vital to our democracy and to a more equitable world.
These books are made possible by the enthusiasm of our readers; the support of a
committed group of donors, large and small; the collaboration of our many partners
in the independent media and the not-for-profit sector; booksellers, who often hand-sell
New Press books; librarians; and above all by our authors..

www.thenewpress.com

Printed in the United States of America

4 6 8 10 9 7 5

For Thomas, Daniel, and Jonathan—always.

Contents

Contents

DISCOVERING RELATIONSHIPS

Preface

Octavio Paz, in his great essay *The Labyrinth of Solitude*, wrote, "All of us, at some moment, have had a vision of our existence as something unique, untransferable and very precious. This revelation almost always takes place during adolescence. Self-discovery is above all the realization that we are alone: it is the opening of an impalpable, transparent wall—that of our consciousness—between the world and ourselves." Though Paz wrote these words in the 1960s, they seem particularly relevant today, as we look out on an American landscape that has in so many ways lost its innocence, relying on disaster to bring together groups that might otherwise remain unknown and essentially invisible to one another, and that may well once again scatter into that unknown and separate invisibility once the disaster becomes old news.

When I put together the first *Coming of Age in America* collection that was published in 1994, I was struck by the power of the common threads that bound together our very different struggles of growing up. While I continue to believe in those common threads, and even to believe that a few of these threads exist in coming-of-age stories and experiences throughout the world, I also see that perhaps the most common of these threads is the notion of solitude, a feeling of aloneness that can be both positive and negative. In the post-9/11, post–Oklahoma City, post-Columbine, post-Katrina world of twenty-first-century America, in Matthew Shepherd's America, we have learned the shocking cost of aloneness as well as the healing power of stories. We need these stories of the struggle to locate, name, and share aloneness now more than ever; we need them to remember what we can be, and we need them to transform the negative connotation of aloneness into its more imaginative possibilities.

In collecting these short stories, fiction excerpts, and memoir pieces, I was able to stick mainly to works published since the first *Coming of Age in America*. These stories for the twenty-first-century focus on the times and places in which coming-of-age-moments are most likely to occur: in the expanded notion of the family, fraught with secrecy and conflict; between school and home, where education becomes a means of avoidance and flight as well as confrontation; in crises precipitated by all sorts of loss; in relationships meant to redefine our notion of identity.

Ironically, I had started this project before Ellen Reeves at The New Press contacted me about working on *Coming of Age Around the World* with Faith Adiele, a writer whose story "Fire: An Origin Tale" I had already chosen for this anthology. My collaboration with Faith helped to shape my vision; I began to see coming of age as a state of mind that could occur both earlier than adolescence and later than the teenage years, and I began to see how much outside circumstances influenced the onset and development of this state. My sons, children when I first began doing anthologies, were now men—writers, both; they also contributed to the way that I continued to think about coming of age. I noted that though they were both "men" chronologically, they represented a generation that took coming of age with an edge, wrestling with its challenges long after the metaphoric second hand told them that their time was up. Perhaps the issues they grappled with were not as obvious as (and therefore more dangerous than) the issues of former generations.

The stories that I found for this anthology are less philosophical than the ones that inhabit my first anthology—but they stab at deeper and more complicated truths, offering many troubling observations and unresolved endings. In the time between the first anthology and this one, great changes occurred in my own life, no doubt influencing the way I came to see the world. My mother and father-in-law died, and those events brought on another stage in my coming of age, belated though it was. It therefore was not a total surprise to find that, in casting my nets wide, I uncovered many more compelling stories about absent or dead parents—beautifully catalogued in Lan Samantha Chang's "The Eve of the Spirit Festival" and in Danzy Senna's "Triad"—and the impact of this experience on the surviving generation. Families have also come to redefine themselves and moments of crisis to include not only the inevitable experiences of absence and death, but that experience of aloneness, of how we can be absent or dead to ourselves, as seen in the story of Larry Blank in Lowenthal's "Ordinary Pain." In those moments we turn away from the power of truth in favor of a more temporarily palatable fiction, a condition that ZZ Packer's Dina comes to understand all too well in "Drinking Coffee Elsewhere."

In this collection, examples of racism and homophobia still abound (sometimes providing unique opportunities for disclosure, as in Emily Raboteau's "Mrs. Turner's Lawn Jockeys," and self recognition, as in David Levithan's "The Alumni Interview" and ZZ Packer's "Drinking Coffee Elsewhere"), but here a more subtle and egregious all-purpose xenophobia seems to have settled into stories reflecting American culture—even if we don't care to acknowledge its presence—the kind that is subtly recorded in Don Lee's "Casual Water" and in Akhil Sharma's "Surrounded by Sleep." In these stories, withdrawal into familiar and comfortable patterns of either contempt for or disregard of the strange and different tears families asunder or drives individuals, often already estranged from larger communities, even further from the fragile attachments that anchor them.

For many of these protagonists, conflict has become a way of life. George Tucker understands this phenomenon only too well, as he shows in "How I Learned to Fly," a story that employs a form of magical realism to embody the narrator's desire to get his mind around what his father is doing in the Gulf War. Today's wars are not governed by the draft, making them more insular and polarizing; antiwar efforts no longer belong exclusively to college campuses and self-proclaimed activists. In fact, protesting seems to be an anachronism, left over from a time when superpowers determined our fears and actions. Now our wars are televised, making them both closer and more distant. But conflict can also come in the form of a teacher's attitude toward a writing assignment, as Lois-Ann Yamanaka demonstrates in her excerpt from *Wild Meat and the Bully Burgers*. It can appear in the desire of first-generation "Americans" to reject every identification with the cultures of their parents, who came to America to provide something more for their children but did not count on the outcome of that equation: a hybrid identity. Mary Chen-Johnson, Abraham Rodriguez Jr., Lan Samantha Chang, Akhil Sharma, and Carmit Delman tell these stories.

Generations do not always reach across divides to help each other, as we see in Mary Chen-Johnson's "Knuckles," William Henry Lewis's "Shades," and Abraham Rodriguez's "The Boy Without a Flag." Sometimes, self-revelation comes at too high a cost, demonstrated in all of the stories in this anthology's "Crisis" section—the only section title also appearing in the first *Coming of Age in America*. For the most part, the stories in the "Crisis" section deal with irreparable loss—the kind where self-delusion becomes part of a destructive process that erodes hope altogether.

But then there are the moments in which hope manages to find an eloquent breakthrough or a hilarious voice: Yamanaka's Lovey writing her obituary in standard English lyrically infused by Hawaiian Pidgin; Seth Kantner's Cutuk, taking ownership of his solitary quest for manhood for the first time; Junot Diaz's would-be lover offering wry, self-deprecating quips to cover his helplessness; young Carmit Delman, munching on a burnt but delicious chapati; Sherman Alexie's Victor, whose education defies his own expectations; Louise Erdrich's narrator revising a tragic family saga for his father so that he can emerge from his alcoholic stupor and begin to live. Older legends—such as La Llorona, the weeping woman tale that inspires Alma Luz Villanueva to confront her young protagonist with the most vulnerable and fearful part of her life—can make us stronger, reminding us that crisis itself is a familiar state, not breaking news, and that it can call forth our hidden power to heal ourselves and move forward.

Perhaps it was Faith Adiele and Louise Erdrich who turned me, finally, in the direction of this hidden power, this hope. In their stories—which I was sure I wanted to use from the moment I read them—the absolute aloneness experienced by youth approaching adulthood offers opportunities to reflect and transform something sad or even hopeless into a vessel of beauty. Though these experiences do not necessarily offer the happy ending that we might have expected or longed for a few decades ago, they do provide something richer, darker, and more significant and fine. Whether enduring and surviving transitions between school and home, between generations or individuals that may or may not share a common bond, between the sometimes murky distinctions that differentiate truth and fiction, and between the fictions that we create and the hope that we imagine through these fictions, these stories represent coming of age in the twenty-first-century. So in Paz's concept of aloneness, in our adolescent awareness of that transparent wall of solitude that separates us from, yet makes us citizens of, the world, we now come of age, conscious of who we are and who we might yet strive to be.

—Mary Frosch
July 2007
Santa Monica, California

Acknowledgments

I would like to thank Ellen Reeves and Jennifer Rappaport of The New Press; Ellen, especially, envisioned my three anthologies—the original *Coming of Age in America, Coming of Age Around the World* (co-edited by Faith Adiele), and this one—as a worthwhile series. Ellen also introduced me to Faith as a co-editor—though I had already discovered her wonderful writing on my own. Many years ago, Dawn Davis was my first editor at The New Press and convinced me that collecting stories was something that I could do; it's time to thank her for that push.

I could not have completed this work without the saintly offices of Frederick T. Courtright of The Permissions Company, who put up with the many changes and substitutions I made with great forbearance and patience. He has been a pleasure to work with on this anthology as well as on *Coming of Age Around the World.*

Much of my work for this anthology was done in the Santa Monica Public Library, both at its temporary quarters and at its beautiful, new, state-of-the-art facility. I only wish that every city had a library like this one, with terrific collections and librarians who wish you well and want to be helpful.

And now for the usual suspects: thanks go to my students, past and present, who keep me thinking and reading, and my colleagues in The Spence School English Department, who command an impressive knowledge of the latest and best in reading and writing; to my dear friend Michèle Krauthamer, whose influence on the way that I think spans the years and the coasts; to my ladies-who-read models whose intellectual curiosity became my own—my aunt Alice Woodrow, my mother-in-law, Annette Frosch, and my late mother, Jane Calvin.

Last and most important, I owe everything to my husband, Thomas, and my two sons, Daniel and Jonathan, writers all. Daniel insisted that I read Junot Diaz and William Henry Lewis, each of whose work appears in this anthology, and Jonathan's compelling vision of literature—its beauty, its power, and its message—is permanently ensconced in my head, forcing me to see and read differently. Thomas Frosch never wavers for a moment in his loving support and understanding of my endeavors; because he is, I feel that I can do this work.

Families Are Not
All Alike

The mythology of the traditional family is examined in this group of stories in which fathers may be mostly absent or often prove to be disturbing presences, and in which adolescents are left to grapple with new information, secrets, and unfamiliar circumstances without much adult help. How these adolescents interpret and navigate their worlds tells us much about their strengths and uniqueness and, at the same time, offers us a new conception of what constitutes a family.

FIRE: AN ORIGIN TALE

by Faith Adiele

This memory piece, in which the author learns "the true story" of her birth fifteen months before the catastrophic eruption of Mount Saint Helens in May 1980, at first seems like an account of a small, almost humorous family rift when juxtaposed with the most destructive volcanic event in the history of the United States. Yet Adiele brilliantly sets her story against this event-to-come, using it as the lens through which we are to read the past, both Adiele's own and the geographic past that changed completely after the landscape-altering debris avalanches. The volcano's toll—57 dead, 250 homes destroyed, 47 bridges gone, 15 miles of railways and 185 miles of highways obliterated, and a brand new landscape created—somehow mirrors the toll that the story of Adiele's mother, the first in her family of Scandinavian immigrants to go to college, takes on her daughter as she reveals long-hidden secrets about her relationship with Adiele's Nigerian father. As Adiele presses for a revelation, her family history becomes a story that she no longer trusts either for its comforts and joys or for its frictions and doubts. Her name, Faith, must shepherd her through a new world of knowledge, just as her impending birth once saved her mother.

Since Adiele fashions her story as a creation myth, she refers to northwest Native American tales having to do with the etiology of

Mount Saint Helens. She also laces her memory piece with destructive images from the past, such as the bombing of Hiroshima and Nagasaki, and the repressive atmosphere of 1960s Sunnyside, Washington, the small town that resembles Hawthorne's Salem despite its cheerful name. There, Adiele's mother returns to raise her half-African child. The question becomes, how has Faith—the concept and the name—been shaped, and the answer takes us back to the beginning: through fire.

Adiele, a professor of creative writing at the University of Pittsburgh, is the subject/writer of My Journey Home, *a PBS documentary about her Nigerian-Nordic heritage. She also won the PEN Beyond Margins Award for* Meeting Faith, *her travel memoir about coming of age in Thailand, and edited, with Mary Frosch,* Coming of Age Around the World: A Multicultural Anthology.

You may wish to compare this piece with Louise Erdrich's "The Shawl" for its devastating envisioning of the past (though in Erdrich's story, the son provides a new, more positive reading of that past for his haunted father). It can also be compared to Susan Perabo's "Some Say the World," a story in which fire symbolizes both destruction and renewal in an unending cycle, and to Alma Luz Villanueva's "La Llorona/Weeping Woman," in which a young girl attempts to discover the ongoing unhappiness among the different generations of women in her family through a mythological figure.

I'm nearly sixteen years old before I learn the true story of my birth. It is the spring of 1979, fifteen months before snowcapped Mount Saint Helens will wake up a few hundred miles away and create a new country; seventeen years after my teenage mother lay down on the floor of her father's house and contemplated suicide. I can picture her in 1962 with her apple cheeks and light brown ponytail, lying flat against the gray carpet, looking too brunette to be Scandinavian and much younger than her nineteen years. She might have been wearing a sleeveless blue cotton smock, the patch pockets stuffed with half-used tissues, and a mannish pair of black glasses. Those droopy blue eyes of hers, so deceptively sleepy, would have been wide open for once. Seventeen years later, except for the short bowl haircut swirled with cowlicks, she looks exactly the same.

Time has stopped in the living room of our tiny house. It's as if my mother's silence has cast a spell that descends over us like the ash when Mount Saint Helens erupts, turning cars and flowerbeds silver. We will have to wear surgical masks outside, just like at the Annual Portland Rose Festival to the south, thousands of spectators and beauty queens waving to each other from behind white paper cones. But for now, my mother contemplates the ceiling, and the cats on the roof fall asleep, whiskered chins upturned in the shade of the honeysuckle vine.

Bound by the spell of her silence, no one on Gregory Avenue moves. Next door, Mr. Graham turns to stone in the midst of his prized hybrid teas and floribunda. Across the street, Tommy the Plumber stalls, tattoos motionless in the hairy forests of his arms and legs and chest. At the end of the street, the boys on the high school wrestling team—state champions for three years straight—slump, drooling, onto gym mats, while next door at my mother's junior high, three kids smoking joints topple over on the football field.

The entire town of Sunnyside, Washington—where according to the Chamber of Commerce, the sun shines 360 days a year—holds its breath. At the feedlot near the sign welcoming visitors to SUNNYSIDE—HOME OF ASTRONANT BONNIE DUNBAR, the milk-faced Herefords and polled Angus stand vacant-eyed and slack-jawed, just like when the volcano blows. In the tiny business district, the Rotarians and Kiwanis and Elks and Eagles stop singing in mid-song; the neon warrior on the awning of the Safari Lounge watches his spear and shield blink and fizzle out; and the Golden Pheasant Chinese restaurant actually closes.

The blond kids up on Harrison Hill drift in their blue swimming pools, while Mexican workers doze on ladders in the sooty fruit orchards, their burlap bags slipping to the ground. Nothing much was happening to start with at the big Catholic and Mormon and Episcopalian and Methodist and Baptist and Presbyterian churches, but in the tiny new churches that are continually forming and separating at any time of day—so many that Sunnyside is in the *Guinness Book of World Records*—the congregations begin to snore in their folding chairs.

This hush, while I wait for my mother to call the true tale of my origins up from hibernation, carries out of town, past Old Doc Querin's big animal practice, past the huge Dutch dairies with their tin-roofed barns, past fields strung high and beaded with hops. It wafts along the restricted road to the Hanford Nuclear Reservation, which did the plutonium finishing for the bombs dropped on Hiroshima and Nagasaki, and where people say that strange, new insects breed in the chalky limestone. It floats by the Moore farm with its collapsing barn and twelve kids, the Kludas farm with its narrow lambing shed and single giant son, and my grandparents' farm wedged in between. For once the woodpecker attacking their trees is quiet, enjoying the bright pink blossoms on the thorny Hawthorn, the heart-shaped leaves of the Catalpa, the drooping Weeping Willow. The silence winds along the irrigation ditch to the asparagus fields at the tiny airport, the same fields where my mother walked barefoot in 1962, the soil damp between her toes, and considered killing herself and her unborn child.

"I need the form that shows you have custody of me," I repeat, in case my mother didn't hear me. A permission slip for a study program in Mexico rests on the sofa cushion between us.

A few minutes ago, when I announced that the study program required the signatures of both parents—unless one can prove sole custody—my mother grunted, setting the spell. Now her eyes contemplate the ceiling, blue specks beneath a field of gently waving cowlicks.

I wait. It is 1979, my sophomore year of high school, the moment for which I have been raised. From our monthly United Nations Day dinners where my mother and I dress in makeshift *rebosas* and saris and dashikis and make optimistic stabs at crêpes and *piroshki* and *kimchee* from the Time-Life international cookbooks series, to the home curriculum she designs for me from her college anthropology textbooks, to our mispronounced mutterings over the *kinara* ("*Umoja* means 'unity' . . .")

and the *Haggadah* ("We were slaves of Pharaoh . . .") and the *shahāda*
("There is no god but God . . ."), my mother has been preparing me for
this. It is to be my first trip out of North America—the escape from
Sunnyside she never quite managed herself. The only thing standing in
the way is my father's signature.

"I'll get the custody agreement." I offer, holding out a pen. Program
enrollment to Mexico is on a first come–first served basis. "Where is it?"

Anything having to do with my father, who lives overseas, is a bit of
a mystery. He and my mother divorced when I was still a baby, and in
time she returned to her hometown and he to his. His photograph—a
college man with close-cropped curls, thick glasses matching hers, and a
green wool overcoat—hangs above my bed. Occasionally I write to him,
and his affectionate replies drag themselves in months later. I know
what he looks like and I know his handwriting. I know that he loves me
very much. I just can't remember ever having seen him.

If I think about this, I'm a bit bewildered. I believe that, no matter
how young I was when he left, I should remember my father. At least
the sharp bouquet of Lux soap, the scratch of green wool against my
cheek, the rich bass of his full-throated laugh, the lush Rs of his accent.
He is, after all, the only one in the family like me. The only one who is
black.

Being black matters. It was the reason for the trouble. Though my
mother's story is sparse, always the same information presented in the
exact same words, she has always been forthcoming about the trouble.
For years I've watched her bee-stung lips twist into tight shapes as she
describes how my grandfather demanded that she stop seeing my father,
a Nigerian graduate student. How, when she refused, he forced her to
transfer to another college hundreds of miles away.

It was 1961, a moment of firsts. My father was the first in his family
to come to the West; my mother was the first in her family of Scandinavian immigrants to go to college. "I was wild about it," she confesses,
eyes gleaming. "All those books—I thought I had died and gone to
heaven!" Her freshman year she met my father, and they became the
first interracial couple on campus. This among ten thousand college
students.

After my mother was sent away, my parents met in secret and were married at the Seattle courthouse one Saturday. "I wore a pale green princess-style dress with matching jacket like Jackie Kennedy might have worn—only much cheaper," she says, smile firmly in place, "and your grandfather immediately disowned me." Without his support, she was forced to drop out of college and banned from ever going home or seeing her mother and brother.

The newlyweds were broke. The apartment swelled with international students who were also broke and who stopped by for dinners of vegetable curry and groundnut stew. I remember being poor—a chalky taste like scorched kidney beans—and I remember the stew, my mother's wooden spoon swirling peanut butter into tomato sauce—a vivid, oily spiral of red and brown. I remember murmured discussions about Cuba and Vietnam lasting late into the night, backed by Bob Dylan's whine or smooth African Highlife on the hi-fi. I remember the scent of vanilla drifting from the coffee table and the squish of warm wax between my fingertips as I caught candle drips before being chased off to bed. I don't remember my father.

After politics, my parents' great loves were movies and dancing. I know little else. But if we are riding the bus and pass a former hangout of theirs, or if I come across a photograph of one of their friends, my mother dusts off a memory and presents it to me. "Your poppie used to like this place," she might say, or "That girl was dating a West African too, and once we double-dated." She chooses these anecdotes carefully, sparingly, as if we are still poor.

I was born at Saint Elizabeth's Hospital in Spokane, Washington, in 1963. I don't know why Spokane, which is hundreds of miles from Seattle. I do know that my mother enjoyed being pregnant: sleepy, swollen, with a ready-made excuse to spend entire days reading. I can see her seventeen years ago, propped against the sofa bed of their tiny apartment, stacks of history textbooks and news magazines and dime-store mysteries covering every inch of the linoleum.

"Tell me again what the nurses said when they saw me for the first time," I demand.

She laughs, dog-earing a page of *The Guerrilla—And How to Fight*

Him and settling my head in her lap. On this last point she is always eloquent. The nurses had never seen a mixed baby before, she recounts, slim fingers working my curls. "They fussed over you for days. Everyone did. For years strangers stopped us in the street and gave you presents— pieces of candy, shiny dimes—old men who looked like they had nothing to give."

Despite the sun shining from my face, my parents divorced soon after, and my father returned to West Africa. We haven't seen him since.

Before we could afford to buy the Norse legends and African folktales that peopled my childhood, my mother wrote stories set in mythic African lands and illustrated them with her own watercolor paintings of wise queens and beautiful warrior princesses in pastel tunics. Every morning and evening she read aloud to me, creating different voices for each character. Sometimes, if she was tired from teaching, she lost a voice, and I would bolt upright, protesting. "*That's* not the right voice!"

"No?" she would say, blinking rapidly as she does when she's trying to think. "Was it higher?" She would try again. "*Dear Prince Amalu—*"

My eyes would widen in horror.

"Lower? Ahem, *Dear Prince—*"

"*No!*" I'd wail, hands trembling like leaves.

"Okay, pause for a minute." She would lean forward and enact her usual ritual—a sip of tepid water masquerading as tea, a quick blow of her nose, the unwrapping of a half-sucked cough drop, and the popping of it into her mouth.

Throughout all this, I would squirm. How could she take so long? How could she have forgotten this character who'd been living with us for days?

"Okay, let's see." She'd clear her throat and begin anew.

Not until she recaptured the correct voice—or invented a new one close enough to placate me—could I resume my curl in her lap, accept the narrative. Her own tale, however, she delivered in a detached, matter-of-fact tone.

"Who was at your wedding?" I'd ask periodically, hungry for the details of my origins. Some of my father's African classmates? What about her college roommate, the one who borrowed her nicest outfit, a sophisticated black cocktail dress with tiny buttons, and never returned it, despite my mother's increasingly bitter letters?

"Oh, no one really," she'd answer, glancing up from *Report from a Chinese Village*. "Just a pal of your poppie's and his girlfriend. I can't even remember their names."

I don't understand it. For years she labored to create the definitive family history, spending hours hunched over an old manual typewriter, clacking out family names and places and dates. She drew floor plans of childhood houses she remembered her mother and aunt describing. She pored over albums and scrapbooks and boxes of photographs. As with her anecdotes about my father, she was reductionist, a perfectionist. She chose photographs the same way she chose her memories—only the most representative and best preserved. History in her hands was finite. I wonder why major family events like my grandparents' wedding got a single photograph in the album. Did she have only one, or was it her rigid aesthetic taste?

The spring of 1979, the year before Mount Saint Helens decides to wake from her 123-year slumber, the self my mother has kept dormant these seventeen years creeps out of the past. The last time the mountain blew was 1857, the same year the U.S. Supreme Court decided that blacks were not citizens. And like the pressure now building beneath our feet, the Dred Scott case weakened the fault line between the Northern abolitionists and Southern slaveholders, four years later exploding into civil war.

Mount Saint Helens' very first outburst was the stuff of legends, an origin tale that also pitted brother against brother. According to the Klickitat, who call her *Tah-one-lat-cha* ("Fire Mountain"), and the Puyallup, who call her *Loowitlatka* or *Loowit* ("Lady of Fire"), and the Yakima, our local tribe, the mountain was a lovely, white-clad maiden with whom both sons of the Creator fell in love. They battled each other for her, causing the sun to darken and the earth to tremble. As they hurled molten rock back and forth, entire forests and villages disappeared in flames. Angered, the Creator turned one son into Mount Adams, the other into Mount Hood, and Loowit into the symmetrically beautiful Mount Saint Helens, perennially encased in ice and snow.

For three months in 1980, prior to the eruption, the ground beneath her will tremble—ten thousand quakes in seven weeks. A crater will yawn in her mouth, growing at a rate of six feet per day. Though geologists and biologists recognize the signs, they will ignore them. When at last Loowit succumbs to the pressure, the avalanche preceding the blast will splash water 850 feet high, temperatures will reach 1,000 degrees, and 500 million cubic yards of rock will be released in one of the largest volcanic explosions in North American history. The entire mountaintop will slide into the Toutle River Valley.

Two hundred miles away in Sunnyside, we will sit openmouthed before the television, watching thick white smoke curdle like brain matter against a blackened crater. We will hear the stunned cries of journalists and rescue workers. "It doesn't even look like the same country!" someone shouts into a radio. "I can't find any landmarks. It doesn't look like anyplace I've ever been before."

The Lady of Fire will forge an entirely new country. Before the explosion, Sunnyside is so dry that when it rains, school closes. When Loowit blows, the largest landslide in recorded history will level 230 square miles of forest in three minutes, wiping out entire populations of elk, deer, bear, and coyote. Glistening Spirit Lake, where my cousin Heidi and I crest through snow thaw, will become a bowl of mud, as will the Columbia River, going from a depth of forty feet to thirteen and stranding four dozen freighters in the process. The silvery ash will drift in a fifteen-mile-high column all the way here to southeast Washington. By noon, ash will be falling in Idaho. In two weeks, it will circle the globe. After that, rain in Sunnyside becomes normal and school is never canceled.

The spring before our geography irrevocably changes, my mother breaks the spell that holds us to the living room sofa. "Well," she says, rubbing her temple with the same hand that now holds the permission slip to Mexico, "can you keep a secret?" She half-grins.

I bite the insides of my mouth to keep from smiling back. This must be big, bigger even than my first trip abroad. I nod, as chill as mountain runoff. "Sure."

"Well . . ." she begins, tilting her head to the side and looking a bit like me when caught rifling her drawers for old photographs and letters. "I can't prove sole custody because"—she pauses—"your father and I were never divorced." She gives me an amused, expectant look.

After a minute I ask, "What do you mean—did Dad die?" Even as I say it, I suspect it can't be the explanation. My father writes to me, after all. And though I haven't heard from him in five years, as we learned following his three-year silence during the Nigerian civil war, as we will learn a mere three weeks after Loowit blows when horsetail rushes and fireweed pop up through the still-smoldering ash, followed by a scurry of pocket gophers and ground squirrels, rebirth is always possible.

My mother shakes her head, and unbidden, The Question arises from childhood memory, where it dozes fitful, ever near. I can feel it rumble through my stomach, force its way into my head as clearly as if I am on the playground, surrounded by a crowd of children who have just seen my mother's white skin for the first time and won't stop asking. "Is that your real mom?"

"Uh-huh" is my reply, rushing to head off the inevitable barrage of questions. I shut down my mind and chant my answer like a nursery rhyme: "My father is black. He's darker than me. My mother is white. Black and white together make brown." I present my arm for inspection. "See?"

Sometimes the scowls relax, the play resumes. There is frequently one who doubts. "Nuh-*uh*," he or she insists, balled hands against Toughskin-clad hips, as if this were high noon at the O.K. Kiddie Corral. "She can't be your real mom." Pale eyes squint through potential holes in my story. Then, the drawled challenge: "Where's your *real* mom?"

Suddenly it's *The Big Country*, and I'm Gregory Peck, Eastern navy captain turned rancher, raised to reason. I flail, repeating my claim to my mother, tender-footed and at a loss out here in the Western territories. Only a grown-up can save me. But when they arrive, it's often clear that the parents have no more idea than their offspring how I could possibly be my mother's child. Herding my challenger away, they glance back over their shoulders, as if the question of my origins is somehow unspeakable.

When I'm lucky, my mother herself appears, cowlicks crackling and baby cheeks aflame as she marches, all five-feet-two of her, up to full-grown men and jeering teenagers. "Do you have something to say to my daughter?" she roars, loud as any natural phenomenon. She stands on tiptoe and jabs a finger in their faces. They could be big as Burl Ives, Gregory Peck's *Big Country* nemesis, or belligerent as Chuck Conners, his rotten son; she doesn't care.

Kids "too young to know any better" get hugged. "Hey, hey," she says, kneeling on the asphalt, dimpled arms firmly encircling her captive. "What's going on here?"

By now Gregory Peck and Chuck Conners are both wailing, snot streaking our faces. Through my tears I watch her pink cheeks, her mouth working close to the kid's ear. I never hear what she says, other than her prerelease signal—"Okay?"—more statement than query.

The stranger's son or daughter nods, Toughskins tensed to flee and yet surely relieved, too, to have the unexplainable explained by someone so certain of right and wrong.

At times even I wonder about my origins. For all her efforts to create our definitive history, there are no photographs of my parents' wedding in the family album, none of my mother pregnant, and none of me as a newborn. There is a lone snapshot of me taken before the age of seven months: a blurry infant in light blue, teetering on a bed I do not recognize. I see little resemblance to the buttery-colored baby my mother claimed I had been, the newborn whose sloping forehead and masses of wavy hair looked "just like a Mayan or Egyptian princess." Whenever I demand proof of this previous incarnation, she explains wistfully that they could not afford a camera. By the time they got one, my forehead had rounded out and my hair tightened into curls. But that was fine, too, according to her.

Back rigid against the sofa, I now unfurl The Question onto my tongue. Though I am nearly sixteen, it drags in my throat. "So . . . I'm adopted?"

My mother whips her head from side to side. "No, no, no. I'm just saying that your poppie and I were never married." A faint smile lurks around the corners of her mouth.

Not married! My best friend Cheryl will undoubtedly add this to her list of why my mother and I are going to Everlasting Hellfire—first being my refusal to accept Jesus as my personal savior and second my inability to get my mother to vote Republican. I can see her now asking her youth group to take a break from playing rock records backward in the church basement in an attempt to detect messages from Satan, so that they can spend an afternoon praying for my bastard soul.

I grin, mildly titillated by my parents' unconventionality. Here at last are the romance and drama of my origins. I sit back, eager to hear the rest.

My mother explains that the last time she saw my father was June 1962, his final secret visit to Seattle, during which they broke up. A few months later, she discovered she was pregnant. They made some gestures toward reconciliation, but my father was on his way to the East Coast for his doctorate and they soon realized it wouldn't work.

When my grandfather found out, he was furious, insisting that my mother get an abortion. She refused. *That* was the real reason he disowned her. The reason she had dropped to the living room floor after wandering barefoot in the asparagus fields. The reason I had been born in Spokane.

My mother cocks a brow and takes me by surprise: "That's where the home for unwed mothers was." She winces a bit, waits.

The home for unwed mothers? In a good origin tale, miraculous babes are found beneath garden leaves, nestled on riverbanks, even in the womb of a she-wolf, rarely in state-run institutions reeking of cabbage and shame. My mouth drops, and it occurs to me that she is making this whole thing sound easier than it was. This version may be more truthful, but it's still a story. Perhaps my mother's decision to have a mixed-race child alone was not a carefree slap in the face of convention after all. Perhaps—I try this idea on for the first time—she was not in control of her fate.

The image of my self-sufficient mother being hustled out of town in the middle of the night to give birth at some secret institution hundreds of miles from home is so foreign that I feel my mind withering. The scope of my questions shrinks to meet it. "How did you get pregnant?"

She confesses that she had been intentionally careless. "I think I knew we were breaking up," she confides, "and subconsciously I wanted a baby."

"What about Saint Elizabeth's?" Was Saint Elizabeth's a lie? And what of the nurses who vied to hold me, who had never seen such well-defined features in a newborn, such heavily lashed eyes, such a full rosebud mouth? Who had really been there as I took my first breath?

My mother assures me that both the nurses and Saint Elizabeth's were real. The only difference is that I had been born in the home's maternity ward. Saint Elizabeth's Hospital sent nurses and doctors to the home to oversee the deliveries. Together the two institutions collaborated on a procedure of secrecy. Saint Elizabeth's staff signed my birth certificate and registered my arrival with the hospital so that no record of my true birthplace would exist.

I hear this, and the mother I believe I know slips out of focus. I squint at her, as I might have squinted at myself on the playground, had I advanced such a tale. "What about your wedding outfit?" I have such a vivid image of the pale green suit and corsage that I've constructed a photograph of my mother the bride—pouty mouth, slim hand in a white glove, lacy sprig of baby's breath against a soft lapel. My father as groom is the same bespectacled graduate student who stares out from my bedroom wall. I imagine separate portraits hanging over my bed, almost touching in their cheap gilt frames. Until now I had not noticed never imagining my parents together in the same scene.

She laughs and tugs the loose curls at the back of my neck. Yes, the green suit was a real suit, a detail recalled from one of my father's visits.

My mother then teaches me how to lie: "It's always best to stay as close to the truth as possible," she says, as if she has not just spent sixteen years drilling the importance of honesty into me. I have been trained to return extra change to the penny, to raise my hand to confess wrongdoing, to resist the pressure of peers and authority figures alike.

She grimaces and gives her head a rueful shake. "I'm not a very good liar," she confesses. "I have such a poor memory."

I will later discover that my mother's poor memory spans most of my parents' breakup and the entire duration of her pregnancy. This is partly because her family kept her hidden like an insane aunt in the attic. No verbal or photographic record exists of her experience. Her recollection is a series of brief vignettes, fading into a broader, cloudy background like the constant rotation of a camera lens seeking focus.

And what she does remember is difficult to verify. "If you keep telling the same lies over and over," she warns me, "after a while you forget the truth."

My mother does not remember telling her parents she was pregnant. "But I remember roaming barefoot at dusk through the asparagus fields and contemplating suicide. Your grandfather was threatening to toss me into the street if I didn't get an abortion, and of course I didn't have any money of my own and neither did your poppie. He was the eldest of eleven and had been supporting himself on meager teaching fellowships for years." It was at this point that my nineteen-year-old mother fell to the floor of her father's house and resolved not to get up until she had decided once and for all what to do.

In 1979 as we sit on the sofa together, she gazes out the picture window at the spellbound landscape and recalls one of the few images that has stayed with her: a yellow farmhouse in a knot of trees, uncharacteristically empty. Her parents and brother had gone to town. My mother, who has always preferred solitude to companionship, had extended her arms and muddy feet as if making snow angels. The textured gray carpet had felt solid beneath her, the design swirling between her fingers. She'd stared up at the ceiling with its glitter flecks and reminded herself that she could be just as stubborn as her father.

She was lying on the floor of white, rural, Christian, soon-to-be-middle-class, pre–*Roe v. Wade* America. "And I had four options: illegal abortion, marriage, adoption, or death." She did not want a backstreet abortion and she did not want to marry my father. She rolled on her side, feeling the scratch of the carpet against her cheek.

Now her voice is light. "That left two options: have the baby and give it up for adoption, or kill us both."

Adoption wouldn't solve the problem of being destitute and having to drop out of college. Besides, in some secret recess of her mind she wished she could somehow keep the baby. "I worried, who would adopt a mixed-race baby?"

That left suicide.

Even at sixteen I know that my mother is not the kind of woman who considers suicide. For sixteen years she has been fierce, hugging tolerance into strangers' intolerant children, creating pastel-clad African queens to talk to me. Besides, there are simply too many books to read.

What nearly toppled my mother as she teetered on the edge of suicide was the fact that she wouldn't be able to finish college. College. The collective dream of her immigrant, just-leaving-working-class family— the collective dream of her entire dusty town, really. Her escape from life on the farm, from the *World's Record for Most Churches Per Capita, Small Town Division*, from 360 days of sun. Her release from a country where fathers packed their daughters away for life or married them off to sweaty farmboys at the end of a shotgun or paid strangers to fish around inside them with a rusting coat hanger.

As soon as my mother hefted death in one hand and thunked its roundness with her knuckle, everything fell into place. "It was all so simple." She shrugs, the mother I know returned to join us on the sofa. "The situation was not about suicide or shame or having no options. Money was the only thing holding me back from what I truly wanted— from college, from keeping the baby." Money and her father, wielding it like a weapon against her. "Money, nothing more."

And so she set herself free. "Let him disown me, I thought," she says, flipping her hands palms up. The ground as she got up off the floor of her father's house was solid beneath her feet. She would act without her father, without a husband, without anyone's approval. "I decided to have the baby, you."

Her voice drops, tender as a spring seedling. And it hits me, the message in my name. Despite fighting with my father and the entire town of Sunnyside over their staunch Christianity, despite claiming not to know why she chose the name—regardless of what she can or cannot remember—the evidence is there. It is the photograph she couldn't afford upon my arrival, the decision she made from her four options, the gift she prayed for—Faith.

There was, as to be expected, much more to the tale of my origins that my mother would reveal when I was older. The story of whom she called and what happened in the home. Still later would be the stories I had to uncover for myself. The rest of my name and what happened to my father. Who knows how much I would have been able to comprehend, had she been able to recall it, that spring day in 1979? I was sixteen, my primary concern getting to Mexico.

As if sensing this, my mother takes her arms from around me and offers to write a letter explaining that she is a single mother and have it notarized. I can give it, on the condition of secrecy, to the tour leader.

I frown. This is degrading. Why lie? Why give power to some unknown tour leader of undetermined discretion?

My mother turns to me. There will be no youth group praying for our souls in the church basement. "I confided in you," she stresses, "because you're old enough to know the truth, but you have to swear not to tell a soul; I could lose my job."

I protest. "C'mon, this is 1979. You've been teaching forever. No one cares."

"This is still Sunnyside," she replies. The town she had grown up in and tried to escape, then been cast out of. The town to which she eventually returned to raise me. A dip in the earth that resists each new decade with the fervor of the recently converted. A Christian holdout on the edge of the desert soon to be covered in 600,000 tons of volcanic ash. A mere forty-five minutes after the Lady of Fire blows, the sky will become black as night, and though it is only nine-thirty in the morning, all over Sunnyside, streetlights will sputter into light.

I have heard my mother's friends in the living room. I know that one teacher lost his job for lingering too long in the high school parking lot with a woman who was not his wife. Another found himself jailed after admitting his sexual orientation. Careers have been lost on more suspicion.

And so I inherit my mother's secret, continuing what is—though I do not know it then—a time-honored tradition among the women of our family. Neither of us has any way of knowing that this secret I force down my throat will turn out to be as bruising as the chunks of pumice that rain down from Loowit. My mother is mistaken—I am not old enough to know the truth. At least, not old enough to carry it, like my heavy, unpronounceable African name, out into the world alone.

Like any good creation myth, the true tale of my origins is deceptive. Upon first telling, it seems harmless enough. The major themes endure: My parents cared for each other and loved me; my mother managed alone. The only differences, I tell myself, are simple matters of legality and geography—the absence of a marriage certificate, a birth at a forgotten address across town. But beneath the thin crust of the earth we think we know, the new world shifts and steams.

GLOSSARY

Mount Saint Helens (4): part of the Cascade Range segment of the Pacific Ring of Fire that includes over 160 active volcanoes.

Bonnie Dunbar (5): born in Sunnyside and a graduate of Sunnyside High School, Dunbar became an astronaut in 1981 and is the veteran of five space flights.

Herefords (5): ancient breed of cattle kept in Western England for centuries, with medium frames and a distinct red body color with white markings.

polled Angus (5): solid black cattle originating in Scotland; "polled" refers to the fact that they do not grow horns.

Rotarians (5): nonpolitical, nonsectarian group whose members meet for "fellowship and service" and are culled from business and professions.

Kiwanis (5): first organization formed to promote business exchange and distribute Christmas baskets to the poor; originally defined as an "organization for men," but now accepts women as well.

Elks (5): American charitable and fraternal organization known as "The Benevolent & Protective Order of the Elks of the United States of America"; first established as a modest social club to elude New York City laws governing the opening hours of public taverns.

hops (6): flower used primarily as flavoring and a stability agent in beer as well as in herbal medicine.

Hiroshima/Nagasaki (6): On August 6, 1945, President Truman ordered atom bombs dropped on Hiroshima, Japan, followed on August 9 by the bombing of Nagasaki, the only instances of nuclear weapons used in warfare to date; on August 15, Japan surrendered to the Allied powers and World War II officially ended.

rebosas (6): Mexican shawls.

saris (6): traditional women's garments of the Indian subcontinent; very long strips of unstitched cloth used for wrapping.

dashikis (6): colorful men's garments widely worn in West Africa and which cover the top half of the body.

crêpes (6): thin, cooked French pancakes often made out of wheat flour.

piroshki (6): in Russian cuisine, small savory stuffed buns.

kimchee (6): a fermented Korean condiment made of seasoned vegetables.

kinara (6): special candleholder used during Kwanzaa.

Haggadah (7): meaning "telling," it contains the order of the Passover seder.

shahāda (7): Muslim creed meaning "to testify" or to "bear witness" in Arabic; it declares belief in the oneness of God and Mohammed as his final prophet.

Dred Scott case (10): In March 1857, the United States Supreme Court ruled that all blacks—free as well as slaves—were not and could never become citizens of the United States; it also ruled that slavery was permitted in all states and territories, overruling a previous decision that separated designated free states and territories from slave states. In the Dred Scott *v.* Sanford case, a slave who had lived in the free state of Illinois and then in the free territory of Wisconsin sued to maintain his freedom in Missouri, a slave state. Chief Justice Taney wrote that since Dred Scott was black, he wasn't a citizen and therefore had no right to sue the United States Government.

***The Big Country* (12):** a 1958 film directed by William Wyler, about the clash between an intellectual Eastern former sea captain and his Western action-oriented rivals.

***Roe v. Wade* (16):** a 1973 case that resulted in a landmark Supreme Court ruling about the right to privacy and granting the Constitutional right to abortion in the United States.

CASUAL WATER

by Don Lee

*Hidden dangers, potentially explosive and raw—the "casual wa-
ter" of the title—inhabit Don Lee's story about two boys abandoned first by their Filipino mother and then, intermittently and
arguably more cruelly, by their golf-obsessed Caucasian father.
Deeply imbedded racism, almost imperceptible but clearly a part of
the liberal, well-meaning culture in which they live, also governs
the way that the community treats the boys' attempt to live on their
own. High school graduation means that the eldest brother,
Patrick, can move on, though he still falls several months short of
being able to assume legal guardianship of his younger brother,
Brian. While Brian wants his brother Patrick to fulfill his dreams,
Brian is terrified about what this will mean for him. Lee's creation
of the subtle distinction between abandonment and departure resembles the difference between casual water and a water hazard in
the game of golf.*

*Set in a fictitious beach community in the San Francisco Bay
area, this story is rich with metaphors and symbols of loss and
threaded through with themes reflecting the challenge of living
with difference—not just a mother who cannot find her way into
American golf culture and a father who cannot let go of his dream,
but also children whose mixed race seems less challenging than
their living situation.*

*A third-generation Korean American and son of a career State
Department officer, Don Lee spent most of his childhood in Tokyo
and Seoul before attending UCLA and Emerson College. After
graduating with an MFA in creative writing and teaching at
Emerson for four years, Lee began working full-time at the literary
journal* Ploughshares, *where he eventually became editor. His
short story collection* Yellow, *from which this story is taken, won
awards from the American Academy of Arts and Letters and from
the Asian American Writers' Workshop. He is also the author of*
Country of Origin, *a novel which won an American Book
Award and the Edgar Award for Best First Fiction, and is about to
publish a new novel,* Wrack and Ruin. *Currently, he teaches creative writing at Macalester College in St. Paul, Minnesota.*

*Other stories included in this collection about sons trying to
compensate for absent fathers, or accommodate difficult fathers,
are William Henry Lewis's "Shades," Emily Raboteau's "Mrs.
Turner's Lawn Jockeys," Louise Erdrich's "The Shawl," Abraham
Rodriguez's "The Boy Without a Flag," George Tucker's "How I
Learned to Fly," and the excerpt from* Ordinary Wolves *by Seth
Kantner. In all of these stories, anger and loss are measured against
fears about the future.*

There was an airstrip a few miles down the coastal marsh, abandoned and accessible only by boat now, the road bridge washed out
by years of storms and erosion and neglect. Impractical as it was, Patrick
Fenny's father, Davis, a former P.G.A. golfer, was fond of using the
airstrip as a driving range, and Patrick and his little brother sometimes
accompanied him during the last two summers, when it had been unusually warm. They would stand on the rippling concrete, three hundred yards of cracked, potholed runway downwind from Davis, and
shag golf balls for him with baseball mitts.

Patrick, who was in high school, was the designated fielder, and
Brian, seven years his junior, served as backup. They'd watch the balls

sing through the thick, paludal air as if fired out of a cannon, like tracer bullets, just dots in the haze and fog, speeding toward them without trajectory. Of course, Patrick rarely caught any on the fly. The balls came too fast, bouncing down before he could get a bead on them, or they would tail just out of his reach. On the occasions when one was hit directly at him, he'd twist away on instinct, his glove held awkwardly in his stead. As much as he hated his father's reproofs ("Aw, you wuss"—said half-chuckled, half-disappointedly), it would have been disaster if he misjudged the ball, or equally painful if he caught the thing in the pocket of his mitt, which would leave his palm stinging for a week.

But last August, the last time they would go to the airstrip together, Patrick had a day which seemed to make up for all the misses, the endless puffing after balls that bounded past them, the hours of sweaty heat, the gnats and mosquitoes they forever had to wave aside with their gloves. He could do no wrong, flagging down everything that came near him. It was exhilarating, this sudden and perfect ability, and when Davis cracked his longest shot of the afternoon off the tee, a beautiful drive, straight and ascendant, Patrick would swear that he was locked on it from the beginning of its flight, that he could see the dimples of the ball, the brand Titleist, frozen in a slow whirl. He ran back, striding fast, covering impossible ground, and with a smooth swing of the arms and knee, leapt into the air, fully extended, almost horizontal. The ball smacked into the webbing of the glove, and Patrick, dropping to the concrete, was already remembering the sound of it, so sweet and true. He jogged back to Brian, laughing to himself—laughing because he knew it had been magnificent, that catch, and it had been so *easy*. For six and a half seconds, everything—the coordination of mind and body, time and place, the entire cosmos—had fallen into sync. He was nearly euphoric, and he knew that Brian, gawking at him, could intuit something intangibly special about the catch as well.

But they withheld their exultation, they waited, they looked to their father to see what he'd say. Davis, a wavering mirage at the end of the airstrip, faced them mutely. Then, slowly, he let his club drop out of his hand and took a step forward. He thrust both fists into the air and began howling. The boys started howling, too, and pretty soon father and sons were dancing and waving in celebration. At that moment, the two boys, motherless for so long, adored him with a purity akin to pain— this man whose approval they coveted, this man whose love they sought.

The following spring, in March, Davis abandoned them, and for nearly three months, Patrick kept the fact of his desertion secret, the knowledge weighing down on him, making him inwardly bitter and bereft and terrified. He told everyone that Davis had gone on the Nike Tour— a series of golf tournaments that made up a Triple-A minor league for the P.G.A.—which was partially true, and that he would return sometime soon, which wasn't exactly true, although it was what Patrick wanted to believe.

Patrick was graduating from high school—as the valedictorian, no less—and he was scheduled for induction into the Naval Academy in Annapolis, Maryland, on July 1. Here it was, the first week of June already, and he still didn't know what to do about his eleven-year-old brother, Brian, the pain-in-the-ass little shit whom he loved and had pretty much raised single-handedly, ever since their mother had repatriated to the Philippines eight years ago. Patrick was frozen with indecision. He couldn't take Brian with him to Annapolis—midshipmen weren't allowed to have dependents—and, in any case, still several months shy of his eighteenth birthday, he was ineligible to be Brian's legal guardian. And there were no relatives on Davis's side to speak of, no one still alive with whom they had kept in touch. If Patrick did anything, sought any kind of help or made the most innocent of inquires, he was sure that Brian would be put in foster care, a prospect Patrick dreaded, but knew was inevitable, and chose to deny, praying that his father would have a change of heart and return home before he went to Annapolis.

As it was, Brian decided things for him. On the last day of the school year, in his sixth-grade math class, he inexplicably slammed his head against his desk, splitting his forehead open. His teacher, Evelyn Yung, saw it happen. Throughout the class, she had noticed how quiet and subdued Brian was, and she had wondered why he seemed so sad, when the rest of the kids were giddy anticipating the onset of summer vacation. Then, as the final bell rang, as the other children sprang up, elated, Brian stayed in his chair, staring blankly at the wooden desktop, and, as Evelyn watched, he inhaled and stiffened upright—although she would remember perceiving the motion oppositely, as if he were coiling into a ball— and he flung his head, his entire torso, down. A sick thump sounded across the room, not loudly, but chilling somehow, causing his classmates to stop their delirious exodus and turn to Brian as he rose back up, exhibiting not a hint of pain or shock or mania, absolutely expressionless, as a gash on his skin bloomed apart and blood ran down his face.

Patrick was across town at Clothilde's Bistro, the new French restaurant in Rosarita Bay, prepping for the Friday dinner rush. It was a marked step up, this job as assistant chef, after years as a short-order fry cook at Rae's Diner, and he was lost in the rhythm of his work, marveling as he minced a shallot what a difference a good knife made, the precision-honed German blade slicing through the bulb and tapping against the cutting board as if nothing were there, when Sergeant Gene Becklund from the sheriff's office appeared next to him, looking stupidly lugubrious so at first Patrick assumed the worst. Patrick didn't like Becklund. He was humorless and by-the-book. Two summers ago, he'd arrested Patrick's father for drunk driving, but Davis had been acquitted at trial, which hadn't squared well with Becklund.

On the way to the clinic, Becklund asked questions: Where was their father? How long had he been gone? When was he expected back? How could he be reached? Patrick said he didn't really know. Davis was somewhere in the Midwest or South, and although he'd been checking in every few weeks, he hadn't called him since May.

"He just left you guys to fend for yourselves?" Becklund said.

"He left me some money," Patrick said. "It's not like I've never had to hold down the fort before." Becklund knew this. Everyone did. Davis had a reputation for taking off abruptly for days at a time, even weeks, and these little "business trips" were getting more frequent of late—trips he first claimed were part of a consulting job to help design a new golf course near Palm Springs, but were actually treks to small tournaments,

Davis going farther and farther afield to see if he could revive his competitive golf career.

At the clinic, Evelyn Yung was standing outside the room where a doctor was stitching Brian's forehead, and when she saw Patrick, she startled him by hugging him. Without meaning to, he sank into the smell and feel of her, her shampoo, her perfume, her moisturizer, her tiny waist and small, pointy breasts. She had been his elementary school math teacher as well, what seemed like many years ago, and he had had a profound crush on Miss Yung, but he had not spoken to her for quite a while, although he had heard rumors about her, about her and the man who stood behind him, Gene Becklund, married father of three, about their affair and Sally Becklund finding out and kicking him out of the house. When was that? Patrick tried to remember. What had happened? Were they still lovers? As he separated from Miss Yung's embrace, he watched her look at Becklund, watched Becklund look at her, but they betrayed nothing.

"He's going to be okay," she said. "The cut on his forehead, the doctor says it won't leave much of a scar, but he wouldn't talk to me, to anyone, he won't say anything at all."

"Can he leave after they finish?"

"I think so," she said. "Has something been going on at home? Has something been bothering him?"

"My dad's been away. I've been working a lot. Maybe he's been lonely."

"Lonely? It has to be more than that. He intentionally *hurt* himself. You didn't see it. It was horrifying."

The doctor came out into the hallway, and after a brief medical update, Patrick went into the treatment room alone. Brian was sitting on the gurney table, a large bandage on his forehead, blood caked on his T-shirt and jeans. He stared at his tennis shoes as he dangled and kicked his feet.

"Hey," Patrick said.

"Hey," Brian mumbled back, not lifting his head.

Patrick sat next to him. Together like this, there was no mistaking they were brothers. Although Patrick was thin, while Brian still had some prepubescent pudginess about him, they had the same chestnut-colored straight hair, sallow skin, sprinkle of freckles, and large, sloe eyes. They were good-looking boys, but there was an unsettling otherness about them, their blood mix unusual and somewhat antithetical: Irish, Scottish, Filipino, Malay, with, if Davis could be believed, a little bit of Ojibwa Indian thrown in.

Patrick palmed the top of Brian's head and tilted it back to examine the bandage. "Well, you pain-in-the-ass little shit," he said, "now look what you've done."

The next afternoon, Becklund brought a woman, Julie Fulcher, from the San Vicente County Department of Family and Children's Services, to the house. She was young and athletic-looking, which surprised Patrick, but the fact that she was there did not. Becklund again—by the book.

"You're really out in the middle of nowhere, aren't you?" she said.

They lived in a small three-bedroom rambler off Highway 1, on an access road that didn't have a name. The property was in the middle of the coastal marsh alongside a canal, and there was nothing within miles other than the abandoned airstrip. When Davis had bought the house, he had thought it a great investment; there had been plans for a big new development in the marshland. But Rosarita Bay's planning commission, pressured by environmental groups, had postponed the groundbreaking indefinitely. It turned out that one-fifth of all North American bird species could be found in the marsh, some of them endangered. "Goddamn snowy plovers," Davis would lament.

Julie Fulcher interviewed the boys together briefly, then took Brian aside to talk to him alone, leaving Patrick in the living room with Becklund.

"You could have given me some warning," Patrick said to him. "The place is a mess."

"Sorry. They like to operate that way," Becklund said. "Listen to me, Patrick. The Nike Tour's in Ohio this week, but your father's not there. He hasn't played in a single Nike tournament since January."

"He's not just playing Nike. He's doing other mini-tours. It all depends where he can get exemptions and enter."

"He didn't give you any details when he called last month?"

"We didn't talk long. He was in a rush."

"You know where he kept his records? Bank statements, credit card bills, things like that?"

"I think so," Patrick said, knowing precisely where they were. Over the last year, with his father increasingly negligent, Patrick had taken it upon himself to handle many of the bills—the utilities and the telephone and the everyday expenses—but Davis had withheld the larger financial matters from him. When he left in March, Patrick discovered—just as he'd suspected—that Davis had been in deep money trouble. He had a load of debt on a dozen credit cards, he'd let the family's Blue Cross coverage lapse, and he was way behind on his mortgage payments. The $5,000 he'd put in an envelope for Patrick—fifty crisp, new one-hundred-dollar bills—didn't make a dent in what they owed. The bank was preparing to foreclose on their property.

Fulcher came out of Brian's bedroom and asked Patrick to take a walk with her. Outside, she said, "Do you even get mail delivered here?"

"We have a P.O. box in town," he told her.

"It must be hard for Brian, being so isolated."

"He sees his friends," Patrick said. "He does sleepovers."

"But after school gets out, you and your father are usually working, right? He's alone all afternoon?"

"I spend time with him. I pick him up from school, and I make sure he's set up with a snack and his homework, and I make dinner for him and my dad to microwave before I leave."

They rounded the corner into the backyard. "Good God," Fulcher said, "what's that?"

It was a 1966 Piper Cherokee, a rusting heap of a seaplane without an engine or propeller, tied up to a tiny dock on the canal behind the house. Davis had bought it on a whim after many years of being harangued by Patrick about flying lessons. They never got around to refurbishing the plane beyond putting in two bucket seats from an old VW bug.

"You want to be a pilot at the Naval Academy, don't you?"

"You don't get into flight training until after you graduate, and even then it's a long shot, but yeah, that's what I want to do."

Fulcher stepped onto the dock and peered at the thirteen-foot Boston Whaler next to the seaplane. "You guys fish?"

"Sometimes."

"Did your father drink a lot?"

Patrick had expected the question. "You've been talking to Becklund."

"How much did he drink a day?"

"A couple of beers. He's not a drunk."

"Did he ever hit you or Brian? Ever threaten you?"

"No."

"He used a lot of rough language around you guys, didn't he?"

"What do you mean?"

"Is your nickname for Brian 'little shit'?"

Patrick stared at her. "You would be a lot better at your job," he said, "if you had a brain in your head."

After they finished dinner, Patrick moved to the sofa while his brother cleared away the plates. Brian scraped chicken bones into the cat's food bowl, opened the back door, and called into the dark, "Hey, Lucy. Come on, Lucy."

The cat scurried inside and began chomping on the bones.

"She might choke on those things, you know," Patrick said, glancing through the kitchen doorway.

"No, she won't," Brian said. He squatted down to pet the cat. "She's just going to take the meat off." He straightened up and ran the water in the sink. "Did you get some more detergent?"

Patrick flossed his teeth.

"Well, did you?"

"I forgot."

"You forgot? How am I going to wash the dishes, then?"

"Just leave them," Patrick told Brian. He heard him continuing to clatter plates in the sink. "Hey, I said leave them."

"Okay, okay," Brian said, shutting off the water. "I was just going to rinse."

It had become like this between them, their relationship one of accumulated resentments, bickering over the picayune—unfinished chores, noisy habits. An old married couple, Davis called them.

Brian picked up the cat and sat on the sofa. Absently, he spluttered a few bars of a song through smooched lips. He played trumpet in the elementary school band. He stopped suddenly and asked, "Are we Amerasian?"

Patrick looked at his brother. "Who told you that?"

"The woman. She asked if kids ever tease me because I'm Amerasian."

"We're not Amerasian," Patrick said. "That's what they call people whose mothers are Vietnamese."

"Was Mom a bargirl before she met Dad?"

"What are you talking about?"

"Billy Kim saw it in a movie. That's what they call hookers in the Philippines."

"She wasn't a hooker. She was in college and she worked as a secretary on the naval base. Billy Kim's full of shit." Patrick calmed himself, then said, "What else did the woman ask you?"

"She asked me if I know the difference between good touching and bad touching."

"Jesus," Patrick said. "She's a complete fucking idiot."

"Do you think Dad's going to come back before you leave for the Academy?"

"Sure he will. That's always been the plan," Patrick said, trying, as well, to convince himself. "He just wants to get in as many tournaments as possible—you know, while he still can. It's like his last hurrah."

"He didn't even say goodbye to me," Brian said. "He hasn't called when I've been around."

"I told you. You know how it is when he's on the road."

"If he doesn't come back," Brian said, "are they going to put me in a foster home?"

"No, that's ridiculous. He'll come back, and everything will be fine. Don't let that woman scare you." He waited for his brother to say more, but Brian sat still, stroking the cat. His hair was snagged on the corners of his bandage. "You need a haircut," Patrick told him.

Davis Fenny had not looked like a golfer. He was too fit, too stocked with muscle, ever to convince anyone that he could delicately chip out of the rough onto a short green, that he could do anything, for that matter, which required patience and restraint. He carried himself with the stand-up, bowlegged, bow-armed gait of a high school fullback or a Marine, both of which he'd been, and though he seemed amiable enough most of the time, one could never dismiss the sense that without provocation, he might fly off the handle: knock over a table while remembering some vague failure, or coldcock someone in a bar. Not the temperament needed for the doglegs, to lay up on an approach shot, say, instead of trying an impossible drive over a water hazard. All in all, he was perfect to hustle golf.

And that was what he did on occasion—not for the cash, simply for kicks. At first, he went to the municipal courses in Santa Cruz or Monterey wearing cutoffs and running shoes, carrying a pitiful Sunday half-bag. He'd walk up to a group and ask bashfully if he could make up the foursome, and hit duck hooks and shank two-irons and putt as if he had a croquet mallet between his hands until he was able to raise the stakes.

Very quickly, though, he switched tactics to what was more natural to his mien, assuming the role of the cocky punk who hadn't grown up, beaming teeth and confidence, always a tip of the baseball cap and a wink for the ladies. "Swoo-eet," he'd breathe after a pretty, young one passed by. He'd go into elaborate, lengthy motions to tee off, sprinkling grass to test the wind, sniffing the air, and rocking on his feet until they were positioned just so. Next he'd squint down the fairway, set his club, sniff, rock, and squint a few more times, and finally go into his backswing, eyes on the ball, hips twisting, legs shifting, ready to really rip one, and . . . he'd stop, just stop, and step away. "I don't know, maybe you fellas want to cover your ears," he'd say, " 'cause when I hit this thing, it's going to snap 'em back, it's going to pop your drums like a howitzer blast." He had a rowdy charm, something the suburban duffers couldn't resist trying to squash. He'd tell his sons about each game's unfolding with absolute glee, how he had suckered those butterballs and come through in the clutch with a dream of a shot.

Still, it was a sad outcome for a golfer who had had such promise. As a teenager in Tempe, Arizona, he had been known for the tremendous torque generated by his swing, which would almost yank his shirttails out of his pants. Even in high school, he was all intensity and concentration, and people said he was another Jack Nicklaus, destined for greatness. He was given a full golf scholarship to the University of Arizona, but after only two All-American seasons, he impulsively dropped out to enlist in the Marines, succumbing to a lingering case of wanderlust and setting a precedent for a fundamental character flaw—the inability to carry through with anything. He ended up serving two tours at Subic Bay, and then returned to Tempe with a Filipina wife, Lita Bautista. After some pro-ams and local tournaments, Davis went pro, and he did fairly well, enough to make a living, at least. He started off with mini-tours like the Space Coast, then progressed to the old Ben Hogan minor-league tour, where he had two wins, but it took him four trips to Q School, the annual three-stage qualifying tournament, before he was able to get his P.G.A. card. Even with his card, though, the P.G.A. Tour proved brutal: he would miss cuts and not finish in the money, leaving him with nothing to cover his expenses. He did better each year, collecting a handful of top-ten finishes, and he had phenomenal success overseas on the Asian and South American tours, three wins and several seconds in Korea, Malaysia, Singapore, Japan, and Argentina. But Davis wasn't satisfied. He had expected to be a star, not a journeyman. He wanted a P.G.A. victory.

The closest he got was at the Western Open in Chicago one year, when Patrick was nine. Because of rain delays, the field was forced to play thirty-six holes on the final day—a lucky convergence of events, as it happened, since Davis fell into a groove. He started the fourth round one shot behind the lead, was grouped with Freddie Couples and Tom Watson, and ripped through the front nine. At the turn, the leaderboard had him three ahead. Sitting at home in Tempe, Lita and Patrick watched

Davis on national television. They knew what a victory would mean: a two-year exemption from qualifying, appearance fees, big bucks for clinics and endorsements. But it began to rain on the course again, and on the fourteenth, Davis sliced his drive into a fairway bunker, the ball rolling into a tiny puddle of casual water. He was allowed to take a drop, but he tanked his second shot anyway and was lucky to bogey the hole. After that, he unraveled. He had a natural draw to his swing, right to left, but suddenly everything was going on a fade, slicing to the right. So he did the worst thing a golfer, any athlete, could do: he started thinking. He began adjusting his stance, his hands, trying to *change* what had taken years to get steady and automatic. He finished five strokes behind Tom Watson, came in fourth in the tournament. The following year, he lost his P.G.A. card, and then regularly had to attend Q School again because he wouldn't be among the top 125 money winners at the end of the season. Soon, he was relegated once more to the minor leagues.

Lita was lonely. Davis would be on the road for thirty-five consecutive weeks, and even if she had the opportunity, she never went to tournaments with him anymore. She had Patrick and Brian, and she felt snubbed by the other Tour wives, with their blond hair and cheerleader smiles. Patrick would come home from school and see her lying in a chaise longue chair in their backyard, sunbathing in the dry heat. She had no friends, nothing to occupy her. For a while, she pretended—for Patrick's sake—to share his passion for air shows, and they chased across the Southwest to attend acrobatic flying performances, especially by the Blue Angels and the Thunderbirds, but the driving quickly wore on her, and she fell back into a listless gloom.

When her mother became ill, Lita returned to the Philippines. She kept extending her trip, saying it'd only be another week. Finally, Patrick talked to her on the telephone and asked, "When are you coming back?"

"I don't think I come back, Patrick," she said. "There I have no life."

"What about me and Brian?"

"Maybe soon," she said, sobbing, "I visit?"

Davis took a job as the club pro at the Del Monte Golf Course in

San Vicente and bought the house in Rosarita Bay, and he thought he could raise his boys while still competing in one tournament a month, dropping them off with sundry baby-sitters so he could play on the Nike Tour or the Powerbilt Tour or the Hooters Tour. He brought back gifts, souvenirs: cowboy hats, clothing with the insignia of practically every baseball and football team, model planes, a kitten, a sheepskin toilet seat cover, an inflatable pool, and, incredibly one month, the seaplane—a hulking, ghostly piece of junk, stripped of everything salvageable.

The boys, who were so young then, began fighting over the souvenirs. During one of their arguments, Brian took the aluminum bat Davis had just given to them and smashed Patrick's favorite model Corsair. Thereafter, Davis gave them identical pairs of everything, but the situation did not improve, exacerbated by a succession of taffy-brained young girlfriends who needed more mothering than the boys. Brian was doing badly in school, and Patrick nagged his father about money, about responsibility. Davis finally acceded to the inevitable. He retired from competitive golf, stuck to his job as the club pro, teaching hackers, and made a faithful, pathetic attempt at fatherhood.

Julie Fulcher filed a petition for Brian to become a dependent of the court, under Section 300 of the California Welfare and Institution Code.

Without being asked, Brian dressed up for the hearing, changing into a white oxford shirt, gray slacks, and black shoes—his band recital outfit. As they waited for Becklund to give them a ride to the courthouse in San Vicente, Brian inspected Patrick's face. "Did you shave?" he asked.

"Yeah."

"It doesn't look like you shaved."

"Trust me. I did."

Brian continued to stare at him. "You always look tired," he said.

At the hearing in Juvenile Court, after some preliminaries, Fulcher presented a report. "Brian is experiencing intense feelings of rejection and abandonment from his father's absence and his brother's impending departure, compounded by his mother's prior relocation to the Philippines. While there are no findings of physical, sexual, or substance abuse in the home, Brian is clearly suffering severe emotional damage in the form of depression and withdrawal. He has developed self-destructive tendencies and is now a danger to himself, indicated by the self-inflicted wound to his head.

"His father, who left his children without adequate provisions for their support or supervision, cannot be reached. He has demonstrated a history of neglect and irresponsibility, and he is currently insolvent. Brian's brother, Patrick, has been the psychological parent in the family. He is exceptionally bright, but the lack of stable adult role models in his life has made him angry and oppositional. He is contemptuous with regard to authority figures and was uncooperative during the investigative phase. There is also some question about the veracity of his statements, as to the circumstances under which his father left and his current whereabouts."

The judge, who had been wearily paging through the case file, abruptly stood up. She was forty or so, and she had a weird, wide streak of gray in her hair, which was bunned. Underneath her robe, Patrick now saw, she wore jeans. She reached over to the bailiff and asked for a box of Kleenex, blew her nose, then sat down again. "What about this, Patrick?" she said in a faint Texan accent. "Are you telling the whole truth? Is your father coming home any day now, or should we file a missing persons report?"

Nonplussed, Patrick didn't respond. Beckland had warned him on the ride to San Vicente that this judge was unconventional, that she didn't talk like other judges. She had a nickname—"the cowgirl judge."

"Gene, any clue?" the judge asked.

"No," Becklund said. "I've called every golf tour in the country, and nothing. I can't even figure out how he's traveling. He left his car behind, but he hasn't charged anything like rentals or airline tickets or motels on his credit cards."

"Should I finish reading the petition?" Fulcher asked.

"Patrick," the judge said, ignoring Fulcher, "do you know where your father is? Is he really playing golf somewhere, or did he just take off on you?"

Patrick flushed, feeling all eyes on him.

"I know that your instinct is to protect your brother and your father both," the judge said, "but the position of this court is that it's always best, whenever possible, to preserve the family. What that means is we're not going to chuck Brian into some group home or youth authority, and we're not going to toss your father—if he ever comes back—in jail, no matter how much of a bum he's been. We're going to give him all the help he needs so he and Brian can stay together. We'll give him child care, housekeeping assistance, parent education classes, financial aid—"

"We're not poor," Patrick said. "We're middle-class."

"Ah, he speaks," the judge said. "So this is the deal, young man: if your father's on some extended postadolescent junket and eventually he comes to his senses and waddles back contrite, we'll reunite him with Brian, which is what we all want—the happy ending. But if he straight out abandoned you, and he had every reason to, with his debts and with you, his trusty, reliable slave, going off to the Naval Academy, we have to think about something more permanent. It's hard enough placing an eleven-year-old boy in foster care. Long-term is even more difficult. I know you don't want to hear this, Brian, but the best thing for you then would be something like Fost-Adopt, a fast track to adoption. The last thing we want is for you to be bounced from home to home, year after year."

Patrick turned to Brian, whose face was slick with tears. "Where's Dad?" Brian whispered to his brother. "Do you know?"

"He's not in the United States," Patrick finally admitted. "He said he was going to Malaysia to join the Asian Tour, and he'd be back in October."

"Has he called you since he left?" the judge asked.

"No."

"Do you believe he'll be back in October?"

"I don't know," Patrick said.

"What did he think would happen to Brian in the meantime?"

"I don't know," Patrick lied.

It was in February. Patrick had been doing the bills and couldn't find the calculator. He opened a drawer in his father's bureau and discovered a stack of papers: eligibility requirements for P.G.A. and Nike events, information about the Australian, South American, Asian, and European tours, an application for the upcoming Q School.

Patrick confronted his father, who was outside, washing his vintage Corvette in the driveway. "Are you thinking about playing full-time again?" he asked Davis. "Is that what you've been doing on these trips? Playing in tournaments?"

"I didn't want to tell you until I was sure."

"You can't."

"I've got someone who's willing to bankroll me for a year."

"You can't. You can't do it."

"Stop saying that. Something's different about my swing. It's liquid, it just flows. I heard someone call it true gravity once. You take back your club, and you just *know* where it's going to fall. You don't even have to try. It's almost embarrassing, how easy it is. Have you ever had that feeling?"

"Dad, I'm leaving for the academy in June."

"Just a year," Davis said. "Give me a year. I'll go overseas and fine-tune, and then I'll get my card back in October."

"What're you talking about, overseas?"

"I'm never going to make it here nonexempt. It's bullshit trying to enter these pissant tournaments by Monday qualifying. I'm playing hot, but I don't get practice rounds, I don't know the courses, there's just no way I'll get tournament-ready like this. But with my wins and career earnings, I get a free pass into any event on the Asian Tour."

"What will Brian do? He can't live here by himself."

"You could defer going to Annapolis. Couldn't you do that?" His father put both hands on Patrick's shoulders. "Listen, this is it for me. I don't want to regret not trying. I might as well be dead if I don't try."

"What about me?" Patrick said. He thought of his youth, the bur-
dens of domestic duties and part-time jobs, every minute taken up car-
ing for Brian or working, the flying lessons and girlfriends he'd never
had. How many times had he pictured the runway at Pensacola, shimmering in the Florida heat as he sped down it in an F-18? "You can't
keep doing this," he told his father. "What if by some miracle you get
your card back? Then what? Will you ask for another year? You have to
stop this. You have to grow up."

Davis pushed Patrick, who tripped and fell to the ground. "Don't
give me that shit," Davis said. "I raised you and Brian myself all these
years. You think that didn't take sacrifice? I gave up my P.G.A. career
for you, and now I'm asking you for one lousy fucking year. You've got
nothing but time, but you can't wait to bail out of here. You're the one
who wants to abandon this family, not me."

How was it, Patrick wondered, that they had no relatives? How was it
that not just one, but both of their parents had deserted them?

The judge deemed Brian a dependent child of the court. He would
be allowed to stay with Patrick until the end of the month, while Julie
Fulcher tried to find a suitable foster home for him. In six months, if
Davis did not return, his parental rights would be severed, and Brian
would be placed permanently in long-term foster care or guardianship
or adoption.

Over the next week, Fulcher took Brian and Patrick to visit two possible foster families. The first was "race-specific," a Filipino couple with
a squalling baby girl. They barely spoke English. The second couple—
white—had two teenage foster children and two kids of their own—
also white. The woman kept asking if there would be any special
dispensations if they decided to take Brian. Did he have a learning dis-
ability? Attention deficit disorder? "Well," she said, "we'll still get extra
because he's a boy, am I right?"

Throughout these visits and later at home, Brian was stonily stoic.
Patrick had quit his job at Clothilde's Bistro to spend all his remaining
time with him, but his brother hardly spoke to him. One afternoon,

Patrick suggested they go fishing, and Brian obligingly loaded the boat with him, making spitting sounds through pressed lips. But when Patrick couldn't get the Evinrude motor to turn over, Brian took off his life preserver, stowed it underneath the bench, and walked off without a word, Patrick calling after him, "Wait, I'll fix it. Hey, just give me a minute."

Over dinner that night, Patrick asked, "Do you want to talk?" and Brian said, "What's there to talk about?" and finished his meal.

At the end of the week, Ms. Fulcher drove up to the house, bringing Evelyn Yung with her. "Brian's at Billy Kim's," Patrick said, confused by Miss Yung's presence.

"That's okay," Fulcher told him. "Can we sit?"

In the living room, the two women sat together on the sofa, Patrick opposite them in an armchair. "There's something the judge didn't discuss, another possibility for Brian," Fulcher said.

"What?"

"There's a program called kinship care. If you really want to stay in Rosarita Bay, with Brian, you could. With court supervision and A.F.D.C., you could be his custodian."

"I'm not eighteen yet."

"You're close enough. We could get a special disposition."

"The judge would agree to that?"

"I think she would," Fulcher said. "I'll be honest with you, Patrick. I don't think it's such a hot idea, but I thought you should at least have the option. It's not your problem with authority, anything like that, I'm worried about. It's that if you stayed, you'd never get over all the things you could've done—the Academy, being a pilot, all your dreams. It's too much to give up, and you'd never forgive yourself, and then you'd blame your brother. What kind of life could you and Brian have, anyway?"

"Is this something you want to think about?" asked Miss Yung. "Do you want to stay with Brian?"

Patrick felt himself constricting—his throat, his lungs. Was this what Davis and Lita had felt, internal organs choking with guilt because

they had wanted, more than anything, to escape? Could Brian sense that
what Patrick had feared most was being forced to stay with him, and did
he hate him for it, hate him so much he had pounded his head into a
desk, disgusted that Patrick was no different than their mother and father? "Don't make me decide this," Patrick said. "I can't decide this."

"Then would you let Brian stay with me?" Miss Yung asked. "As his
guardian?"

"You'd be willing to do that?"

"I'd like to," she said. "I'd like to very much. It's not an entirely self-
less gesture. I have no one, Patrick. I don't know how it happened, but
somehow I've ended up alone, and I've begun to accept that maybe I'll
always be alone. It'd be nice, for a change, to think about someone other
than myself."

"Did you have an affair with Becklund?"

"Patrick," Fulcher said.

"You broke up his family. Did you think about them? His three
kids?"

"I did," Miss Yung said. "They're all I could think about. They're
why I ended it. They're why I told him to go back to his wife."

Patrick was silent for a long minute. Miss Yung was wearing a skirt,
and he stared at a scar on her knee. It looked like an old injury, from
childhood, but he had never noticed it before, although he thought he
had, over the years, memorized every bit of her. "Will you buy him a
trumpet?"

"Excuse me?"

"He's always worried he'll lose his embouchure because he doesn't
have his own trumpet and he can't practice enough. It doesn't have to be
new. A used one would be okay."

Miss Yung nodded. "I think I could manage that."

Usually on Saturdays, Patrick didn't get home until past one, but there
had been a power outage at the restaurant that night—a tree knocking
down a line—and if it had not been for this random intervention of nature, he wouldn't have caught his father in the act of abandoning them.

Patrick had been dismissed early, and as he drove up to the house, he saw a new Lexus Coupe beside it, the engine running. He peered at the person sitting in the driver's seat of the car—an outline of a face, a pretty Asian woman—and for a second, he had thought that it was his mother. Davis emerged from the house then, struggling with a suitcase and two golf bags. They had stared at each other, Davis's breath hurried, clouding in the cold. There had been no mistake about his intent: Brian was sleeping over at Billy Kim's, and Patrick hadn't been due home for hours. "I'll be back in October," Davis had said. "I'll come back to the States for Q School in October."

"You bastard."

"I left five thousand dollars for you. I'll try to wire more from Kuala Lumpur. If you need to, sell the Corvette."

Patrick had thought of his mother then, buying a ticket with an open return date, promising to be on the first plane home as soon as her mother was well. "You're not coming back, are you?"

"I will. I swear to you, I will."

"Goddamn you!" Patrick had screamed. He had grabbed Davis and shoved him against the side of the house. "You're dead to me. You don't exist. You're dead," he had whispered, and then he had let him go.

On their last full day together, Patrick and Brian went to the aquarium in Monterey.

Brian had taken the news about Miss Yung's offer with little comment at first, merely allowing that he wouldn't mind living with her, but he didn't have to say much to communicate his relief.

After the aquarium, the boys drove to the beach at Rummy Creek and piled logs of driftwood into a fortress, letting them bake in the sun, protected from the wind. They watched the windsurfers for an hour, then both needed to pee. They stole away behind the rocks and pissed side by side. Brian glanced at Patrick, then at himself. "When am I going to get some pubes on my pecker?" he asked.

At home, they packed his things. Patrick wasn't leaving for the Academy for another few days, but Julie Fulcher had recommended

Brian move to Miss Yung's early. He could get used to sleeping in his new bed while Patrick was still in town, while they could still see each other evenings. It'd be less traumatic for him, particularly since the bank was repossessing the house and Patrick had to clear it out.

Patrick made his brother's favorite meal—corned beef and boiled potatoes and cabbage, of all things. After washing the dishes, Brian held out a pair of scissors to Patrick. "You want to cut my hair now?"

Patrick wrapped a sheet around his brother's neck and began trimming hanks of hair. "Miss Yung said I could bring Lucy," Brian told him. "You want her? She's good company."

"No, you should take her. She's your cat." He pushed down Brian's ear so he could cut around it.

"He might come back, you know," Brian said.

Combing his hair, Patrick said, "You shouldn't count on it."

"I know."

Patrick moved in front of Brian to clip his bangs. He carefully snipped the hair over his eyes. "I'll come visit," Patrick said.

"I know you will."

Crying, the brothers hugged each other.

Patrick held a yard sale and sold the furniture. Afterward, he roamed through the house, collecting whatever was usable and making a stack in the corner for Goodwill to pick up. The rest he would drive to the dump. He would keep the boat and the Corvette at Miss Yung's place, but he didn't know what to do about the seaplane. He couldn't convince any scrap companies to pick it up. Nor could he decide about his father's things—the trophies and plaques, the discards of clothing and equipment—whether to store them or throw them away. He stood in his father's bedroom, looking at a couple of stray golf balls on the floor. Abstractly, Patrick remembered the hot, sweaty afternoons at the airstrip, the time he went airborne, snagged the Titleist in the webbing of his mitt.

He sat down on the carpet. He might return in October, Patrick let himself think for an instant. Bring home another pair of identical gifts.

But just as quickly, Patrick knew he wouldn't. What was it that made people so weak?

He gathered all of Davis's belongings and put them in the seaplane. He dismantled the outboard motor on the Boston Whaler, cleaned out the carburetor, changed the sparks and oil, and blew clear the fuel tubes. Rigging two pulleys to the transom, he fashioned a split towline out of rope, then tied it to the seaplane. Inside the cabin, he twisted rags and stuffed them into the mouths of four gasoline cans. He stepped into the boat and started the motor, idling until the line was pulled taut, then slowly, he opened up the throttle and towed the seaplane down the canal.

He would take it out to sea, far off the coast. He would remove the drain plugs from the pontoons, pour gasoline over the cabin, and throw in a lit book of matches. Then he would run the boat some distance away and drift with the swell, watch the fire accumulate, the gas cans erupt. He would wait until the seaplane began to crumple into the water, and then he would move the boat a little closer, and watch it sink.

GLOSSARY

paludal (23): marshy.

Titleist (23): brand of golf ball.

picayune (30): of little value; petty; a trifle.

howitzer (32): type of cannon characterized by a short barrel that propels projectiles at trajectories with a steep angle of descent.

wanderlust (32): from German, meaning a strong desire to travel.

pissant (37): not important or significant.

embouchure (40): from the French (*bouche*: mouth), meaning the use of the facial muscles and shaping of the lips to the mouthpiece of a wind instrument.

SHADES

by William Henry Lewis

Lewis's story explodes the notion of "cool," literally and metaphorically. It is an oppressively hot August day in a small Tennessee town. The fourteen-year-old narrator remembers that on just such a day, when he was about ten, he first learned that his father had raped and abandoned his mother. Though his mother tells of this incident "as if it were the story of someone else," she assures through its telling that her son will grow up fast and understand how fragile personal relationships are. Four years later, at a yearly blues festival that the boy attends with his mother, she not only points out his father but physically points her son in his father's direction. The narrator's inflated romantic fantasies about his father conflict with the more banal reality of who his father is: a man who travels with other tricksters like himself, hiding himself behind them and their itinerant life. Does he recognize his son? Does he regret the life he might have had? With his father's casual gift of his sunglasses tucked in his pocket, the narrator may neither treasure nor renounce this silent legacy of distance, his father's brand of coolness.

The uncertainty that underlies this story contrasts with the dependability of blues music and the pleasure of giving oneself over to its comforting sadness. The narrator notices that only at the yearly blues festival does his mother unwind and become herself, as if the music calls that self forth and gives her permission to revel in a universally acknowledged articulation of unhappiness. Though Lewis makes his narrator too young and inexperienced to be more than an observer of both mother and father, he does make him an astute assessor, someone who does not judge the participants—yet.

A prize-winning author of a previous short story collection, In the Arms of Our Elders, *William Henry Lewis has published fiction in several top American literary journals and in several anthologies. The collection from which this story comes,* I Got Somebody in Staunton, *was a finalist for the 2006 PEN/Faulkner Award for Fiction and received a Black Caucus of the American Library Association Literary Award. He currently teaches at Colgate University.*

"Shades" can best be compared to Adiele's "Fire: An Origin Tale" for the impact that family secrets have on young narrators— the sense that all is not over or even wholly revealed—and also to Louise Erdrich's "The Shawl," also about a family with a secret that begs to be reexamined.

I was fourteen that summer. August brought heat I had never known, and during the dreamlike drought of those days I saw my father for the first time in my life. The tulip poplars faded to yellow before September came. There had been no rain for weeks, and the people's faces along Eleventh Street wore a longing for something cool and wet, something distant, like the promise of a balmy October. Talk of weather was of the heat and the dry taste in their mouths. And they were frustrated, having to notice something other than the weather in their daily pleasantries. Sometimes, in the haven of afternoon porch shade or in the still and cooler places of late night, they drank and laughed, content because they had managed to make it through the day.

What I noticed was the way the skin of my neighbors glistened as they toiled in their backyards, trying to save their gardens or working a few more miles into their cars. My own skin surprised me each morning in the mirror, becoming darker and darker, my hair lightening, dispelling my assumption that it had always been a curly black—the whole of me a new and stranger blend of browns from day after day of basketball on asphalt courts or racing the other boys down the street after the Icee truck each afternoon.

I came to believe that it was the heat that made things happen. It was a summer of empty sidewalks, people I knew drifting through the alleyways where trees gave more shade, the dirt there cooler to walk on than any paved surface. Strangers would walk through the neighborhood seemingly lost, the dust and sun's glare making the place look like somewhere else they were trying to go. Sitting on our porch, I watched people I'd never seen before walk by and melt into those rippling pools of heat glistening above the asphalt as if something must be happening just beyond where that warmth quivered down the street. At night I'd look out from the porch of our house, a few blocks off Eleventh, and scan the neighborhood, wanting some change, something besides the nearby rumble of freight trains and the monotony of heat, something refreshing and new. In heat like that, everyone sat on their porches looking out into the night and hoping for something better to come up with the sun.

It was during such a summer, my mother told me, that my father got home from the third shift at the bottling plant, waked her with his naked body already on top of her, entered her before she was able to say no, sweated on her through moments of whiskey breath and indolent thrusting, came without saying a word, and walked back out of our house forever. He never uttered a word, she said, for it was not his way to speak much when it was hot. My mother was a wise woman and spoke almost as beautifully as she sang. She told me he left with the rumble of the trains. She told me this with a smooth, distant voice as if it were the story of someone else, and it was strange to me that she might have wanted to cry at something like that but didn't, as if there were no need anymore.

She said she lay still after he left, certain only of his sweat and the workshirt he left behind. She lay still for at least an hour, aware of two things: feeling the semen her body wouldn't hold slowly dripping onto the sheets, and knowing that some part of what her body did hold would fight and form itself into what became me, nine months later.

I was ten years old when she told me this. After she sat me down and said this is how you came to me, I knew that I would never feel like I was ten for the rest of that year. She told me what it was to love someone, what it was to make love to someone, and what it took to make someone. Sometimes, she told me, all three don't happen at once. I didn't quite know what that meant, but I felt her need to tell me. She seemed determined not to hold it from me. It seemed as if somehow she was pushing me ahead of my growing. And I felt uncomfortable with it, the way secondhand shoes are at first comfortless. I grew to know the discomfort as a way of living.

After that she filled my home life with lessons, stories, and observations that had a tone of insistence in them, each one told in a way that dared me to let it drift from my mind. By the time I turned eleven, I learned of her sister Alva, who cut off two of her husband's fingers, one for each of his mistresses. At twelve, I had no misunderstanding of why, someday soon, for nothing more than a few dollars, I might be stabbed by one of the same boys I played basketball with at the rec center. At thirteen, I came to know that my cousin Dexter hadn't become sick and been hospitalized in St. Louis, but had got a young white girl pregnant and was rumored to be someone's yardman in Hyde Park. And when I was fourteen, through the tree-withering heat of August, during the Watertown Blues Festival, in throngs of sweaty, wide-smiling people, my mother pointed out to me my father.

For the annual festival they closed off Eleventh Street from the downtown square all the way up to where the freight railway cuts through the city, where our neighborhood ends and the land rises up to the surrounding hills, dotted with houses the wealthy built to avoid flooding and neighbors with low incomes. Amidst the summer heat was the sizzle of barbecue at every corner, Blues bands on stages erected in the many empty lots up and down the street, and, of course, scores of people, crammed together, wearing the lightest clothing they could without looking too loose. By early evening the street would be completely filled with people, moving to the Blues.

The sad, slow Blues songs my mother loved the most. The Watertown Festival was her favorite social event of the year. She had a tight-skinned sort of pride through most days of the year, countered by the softer, bare-shouldered self of the Blues Festival, where she wore yellow or orange red outfits and deep, brownish red lipstick against the chestnut shine of her cheeks. More men took notice of her, and every year it was a different man; the summer suitors from past years learned quickly that although she wore that lipstick and although an orange red skirt never looked better on another pair of hips, no man would ever leave another workshirt hanging on her bedpost. With that kind of poise, she swayed through the crowds of people, smiling at many, hugging some, and stopping at times to dance with no one in particular.

When I was younger than fourteen, I had no choice but to go. Early in the afternoon, she'd make me shower and put on a fresh cotton shirt. *You need to hear the Blues, boy, a body needs something to tell itself what's good and what's not.* At fourteen, my mother approached me differently. She simply came out to the yard where I was watering her garden and said, "You going?" and waited for me to turn to her, and say yes. I didn't know if I liked the Blues or not.

We started at the top of Eleventh Street and worked our way downtown over the few hours of the festival. We passed neighbors and friends from church, my mother's boss from Belk's Dry Goods, and Reverend Riggins, who was drinking beer from a paper cup instead of a can. Midway down Eleventh, in front of Macky's Mellow Tone Lounge, I bumped into my cousin, Wilbert, who had sneaked a tallboy of Miller Hi-Life from a cooler somewhere up the street. A Zydeco band was warming up for Etta James. We stood as still as we could in the intense heat and shared sips of that beer while we watched my mother, with her own beer, swaying with a man twice her age to the zip and smack of the washboard.

Etta James had already captured the crowd when Wilbert brought back a large plate of ribs and another beer. My mother came over to share our ribs, and Wilbert was silent after deftly dropping the can of beer behind his back. I stood there listening, taking in the heat, the music, the hint of beer on my mother's breath. The crowd had a pulse to it, still moving up and down the street but stopping to hear the growl of Etta James's voice. The sense of closeness was almost too much. My mother was swaying back and forth on her heels, giving a little dip to her pelvis every so often and mouthing the words to the songs. At any given moment, one or two men would be looking at her, seemingly oblivious and lost in the music.

But she, too, must have felt the closeness of the people. She was looking away from the stage, focusing on a commotion of laughter in front of Macky's, where voices were hooting above the music. She took hold of my shoulders and turned me toward the front of Macky's. In a circle of loud men, all holding beer, all howling in laughter—some shirtless and others in work clothes—stood a large man in a worn gray suit tugging his tie jokingly like a noose, pushing the men into new waves of laughter each moment. His hair was nappy like he had just risen from bed. But he smiled as if that was never his main concern and he held a presence in that circle of people that made me think he had worn that suit for just such an appearance. My mother held my shoulders tightly for a moment, not tense or angry or anxious, just firm, and then let go.

"There's your father," she said and turned away, drifting back into the music and dancing people. Watching her glide toward the stage, I felt obligated not to follow her. When I could see her no longer, I looked back to the circle of men and the man that my mother had pointed out. From the way he was laughing, he looked like a man who didn't care who he might have bothered with his noise. Certainly his friends didn't seem to mind. Their group commanded a large space of sidewalk in front of the bar. People made looping detours into the crowd instead of walking straight through that wide-open circle of drunken activity. The men stamped their feet, hit each other in the arms and howled as if the afternoon were their own party. I turned to tell Wilbert, but he had gone. I watched the man who was my father slapping his friends' hands, bent over in laughter, sweat soaking his shirt under that suit.

He was a very passionate-looking man, full in his voice, expressively confident in his gestures, and as I watched him, I was thinking of that night fourteen years ago and the lazy thrust of his, that my mother told me had no passion in it at all. I wondered where he must have been all those years and realized how shocked I was to see the real man to fill the image my mother had made. She had made him up for me, but never whole, never fully able to be grasped. I was thinking of his silence, the voice I'd never heard. And wanting nothing else at that moment but to be closer, I walked toward that circle of men. I walked as if I were headed into Macky's Mellow Tone, and they stopped laughing as I split their gathering. The smell of liquor, cheap cologne, and musky sweat hit my nostrils, and I was immediately aware not only that I had no reason for going or chance of getting into Macky's, but that I was also passing through of a circle of strange people. I stopped a few feet from the entrance and focused on the quilted fake leather covering the door's surface. It was faded red fabric, and I looked at that for what seemed a long time because I was afraid to turn back into the men's laughter. The men had started talking again, slowly working themselves back into their own good time. But they weren't laughing at me. I turned to face them, and they seemed to have forgotten that I was there.

I looked up at my father, who was turned slightly away from me. His mouth was open and primed to laugh, but no sound was coming out. His teeth were large, and I could see where sometime before he had lost two of them. Watching him from the street, I had only seen his mouth move and had to imagine what he was saying. Now, so close to him, close enough to smell him, to touch him, I could hear nothing. But I could feel the closeness of the crowd, those unfamiliar men, my father. Then he looked down at me. His mouth closed and suddenly he wasn't grinning. He reached out his hand, and I straightened up as my mother might have told me to do. I arced my hand out to slide across his palm, but he pulled his hand back, smiling—a trickster, like he was too slick for my eagerness.

He reached in his suit jacket and pulled out a pair of sunglasses. Watertown is a small town, and when he put those glasses on he looked like he had come from somewhere else. I know I hadn't seen him before that day. I wondered when in the past few days he must have drifted into town. On what wave of early-morning heat had he arrived?

I looked at myself in the reflection of the mirrored lenses and thought, *So this is me.*

"Them's slick basketball sneakers you got," he said. "I bet you the baddest brother on the court."

I could see only the edge of one eye behind those glasses, but I decided that he was interested.

"Yeah, I am! I'm gonna be like George Gervin, you just watch." And I was sure that after that we'd go inside Macky's and talk. We'd talk about basketball in its entirety and then he'd ask me if I was doing well in school and I'd say not too hot and he'd get on me about that, as if he'd always been keeping tabs on me. Then we would toast to something big, something we could share in the loving of it, like Bill Russell's finger-roll lay-up or the pulled pork sandwich at Ray's Round Belly Ribs or the fact that I had grown two inches that year even though he wouldn't have known that. We might pause for a moment, both of us quiet, both of us knowing what the silence was about, and he'd look real serious and anxious at the same time, a man like him having too hard a face to explain anything that had happened or hadn't happened. But he'd be trying. He'd say, *hey, brother, cut me the slack, you know how it goes*, and I might say, *it's cool*, or I might say nothing at all but know that sometime, later on, we would spend hours shooting hoops together up at the rec center, and when I'd beaten him two out of three at twenty-one, he'd hug me like he'd always known what it was like to love me.

My father took off his sunglasses and looked down at me for a long, silent moment. He was a large man with a square jaw and a wide, shiny forehead, but his skin looked soft—a gentle, light brown. My mother must have believed in his eyes. They were gray—blue, calm, and yet fierce, like the eyes of kinfolk down in Baton Rouge. His mouth was slightly open; he was going to speak and I noticed when I saw him face to face that his teeth were yellow. He wouldn't stop smiling. A thought struck me right then that he might not know who I was.

One of his friends grabbed at his jacket. "Let's roll, brother. Tyree's leavin'!"

He jerked free and threw that man a look that made me stiffen.

The man read his face and then laughed nervously, "Be cool, nigger. Break bad someplace else. We got ladies waitin'."

"I'm cool, brother. I'm cool . . ." My father looked back at me. In the mix of the music and the crowd, which I'd almost forgotten about, I could barely hear him. "I'm cold solid." He crouched down, wiped his sunglasses on a shirttail, and put them in my pocket. His crouch was close. Close enough for me to smell the liquor on his breath. Enough for him to hug me. Close enough for me to know that he wouldn't. But I didn't turn away. I told myself that I didn't care that he was not perfect.

He rose without saying anything else, turned from me, and walked to the corner of Eleventh Street and to the alleyway, where his friends were waiting. They were insistent on him hurrying, and once they were sure that he was going to join them, they turned down the alley. I didn't cry, although I wouldn't have been embarrassed if I had. I watched them leave and the only thing I felt was a wish that my father had never known those men. He started to follow them, but before he left, he stopped to look over the scene there on Eleventh Street. He looked way up the street, to where the crowd thinned out and then beyond that, maybe to where the city was split by the train tracks, running on a loose curve around our neighborhood and to the river, or maybe not as far as that, just a few blocks before the tracks and two streets off Eleventh, where, sometime earlier than fourteen years ago, he might have heard the train's early-morning rumble when he stepped from our back porch.

GLOSSARY

Zydeco band (48): Zydeco is a form of call-and-response American folk music of black and multiracial French-speaking Creoles from the South and southwest Louisiana area. Bands include instruments such as the zydeco rubboard, and often the accordion, guitar, bass guitar, drums, fiddle, horns, and keyboard.

Etta James (48): born Jamesetta Hawkins, James is an American blues, soul, R&B, and jazz singer and songwriter.

George Gervin (51): known as "The Iceman" for his cool demeanor on the court, Gervin was a highly successful shooting guard whose trademark was his finger-roll shot, by which he rolled the basketball along his fingertips just before shooting it.

Bill Russell (51): center for the Boston Celtics, Russell was a five-time winner of the Most Valuable Player Award and was widely considered one of the best defensive players in National Basketball Association history.

MRS. TURNER'S LAWN JOCKEYS

by Emily Raboteau

While his family silently wallows in its unhappiness, twelve-year-old Bernie imagines that two lawn jockey statuettes from the yard that he mows across the street ask for his help. Bernie creates such a convincing lawn jockey scenario, right down to attributing different personality types for the pair, that we never stop to wonder about his grasp of reality; it seems that he understands more than he realizes or is willing to admit about what Raboteau calls the "bondage" of looking different (Bernie is of mixed African American and white descent).

The history of lawn jockeys—with their exaggerated features, such as bulging eyes, large red lips, and flat noses—is both interesting and contradictory. These statuettes are often considered to be offensive. Some say that the lawn jockey had its roots in the tale of Jocko Graves, a twelve-year-old African American groomsman who served with the slave-owning George Washington when he crossed the Delaware to carry out his surprise attack on the British forces at Trenton, New Jersey. Washington thought Graves too young to take along on the attack, so he left him on the Pennsylvania side to tend the horses and keep a light going to aid the army on their return. Faithful to Washington's orders, Graves froze to death on the riverbank during the night, the lantern still in his hand. Washington then commissioned a statue, "The Faithful Groomsman," for his estate at

Mount Vernon to commemorate Graves. Lawn jockeys also served as beacons for runaway slaves along Underground Railroad routes. If a lantern or an American flag appeared in the lawn jockey's forward-reaching hand, then the house was a safe stopping place; if a house were compromised, then the absence of the lantern or flag indicated that the runaway should move on.

Raboteau's story contains the usual, even predictable "message" represented by lawn jockey statuettes: that well-meaning white neighbors and friends may not even notice the offensiveness of these commonplace cultural artifacts, holdovers from a more overtly racist time; that the lawn jockeys themselves are, as Bernie explains to his younger sister, "stuck inside the way everyone looks at them," just as Bernie, his sister, and their black father are. Yet Bernie's promise to the lawn jockeys comes at the cost of his conscience, presided over by the ghostly figure of Martin Luther King Jr. conjured by his father. And his father, a ghostly figure himself, sitting alone in the kitchen in the middle of the night with his head in his hands, has secrets of his own, which the lawn jockeys cannot help observing from their immovable place across from Bernie's house.

Two things are remarkable about this story. Raboteau displays a keen understanding of the nature of secrets—that we all have them and that some of them are not even really secrets, but we treat them as such by refusing or being unable to talk about them. She also expresses an idea about freedom: the lawn jockeys no longer have voices—they are no longer alive—once Bernie has fulfilled their request; their new "white" identity allows them an invisibility that seems to shut them down. They are now free to be as ineffectual and silent as Bernie's well-meaning white neighbors and friends.

Emily Raboteau is an assistant professor of creative writing at the City College of New York. The story was inspired by a walk that she took with a white friend during a residency at the Virginia Center for Creative Arts. The two spotted a pair of lawn jockey statuettes. Her friend did not understand Raboteau's desire to slap white paint on them.

This story can be read in conjunction with two fine poems not included in this anthology. The first is "In Salem" by Lucille Clifton, also about taking a walk with a white friend in a town notorious for cruelty and bias; the second is "Those Winter Sundays" by Robert Hayden, about a boy's experience of his father's frustration and anger recalled by his later perception of that same father's loyalty and love. In this anthology, "Mrs. Turner's Lawn Jockeys" can be compared to Rodriguez's "The Boy Without a Flag," another story about a boy's attempt to assuage his father's unhappiness; to Tucker's "How I Learned to Fly," about a boy whose imagination helps to compensate for his fears about his absent father; and to Erdrich's "The Shawl," about a father learning from his son about his own past.

I'm mowing Mrs. Turner's front yard after school when one of her lawn jockeys tells me to help him. Mrs. Turner has two lawn jockeys that look exactly the same. They have the same white pants and black boots and red jacket and the same lantern in their hand and the same black face with the same dumb little cap on top. It's the one on the left side of her front steps that opens his mouth first. I think I hear someone call my name but the motor is running real loud on the mower and I'm not sure. Then I hear it again.

"Bernie!"

I look around and don't see anybody but those lawn jockeys. I cut the motor anyway and wipe my face with my towel. The one on the left is staring at me with his bubble eyes.

"Hello, Bernie," he says.

I wonder how he knows my name. I started mowing Mrs. Turner's lawn when I was ten. That was two years ago and neither one of them ever talked to me until now. He tells me to come over, so I go over and sit next to him on the steps. He's about three feet tall. The water at the shallow end of a swimming pool would cover his head.

"What do you want?" I ask him. I'm not sure yet if I should trust these guys, 'cause my dad hates them. "I hate those damn lawn jockeys," he always says. He says when Mrs. Turner got us as her neighbors she should have stuck them in the garage or something.

"We need your help," the lawn jockey tells me. The other one is looking at me through the side of his eyes and I feel nervous right away, like they're gonna ask me to do something bad. I just pick at the scab on my knee.

Then the first one starts talking about how awful things are for them and I start to feel kind of bad about what he's saying. The main point is how they're stuck there, "in bondage," he says, and how nothing ever changes. I look out over Mrs. Turner's yard and I think I know what he means. All you can see past the yard is a piece of the street and then our brick house across it. He says they've been there a long time, in the same place, since way before I was born. By the time the lawn jockey gets done talking I really like him. He's very polite and has a way with words.

"What can I do for you?" I ask.

"Come closer," he says, so I lean my ear down to his mouth and he whispers what he wants me to do.

"That doesn't make any sense!" I say. "Wouldn't you rather just have me take you somewhere with a better view?" I'm thinking I could strap them to my skateboard with dad's whipping belt and pull them down to Carnegie Lake. If I put them there by the water they could watch the Canada geese and the Princeton crew races and the ice skaters when the lake freezes over in the wintertime.

He says I'm missing the point, which is that even if they were in a different place, people would still look at them in the same way and that would spoil it. He has thought about it a lot and this is what he really wants.

"Him too?" I ask about the other one who hasn't said anything.

"Him too."

"I'm not sure," I tell them. I'm thinking about how I just got done getting grounded for my report card. "It seems kinda risky."

The quiet one on the right sighs. "We didn't want to have to resort to this, but . . ."

"But we've got a lot of dirt on you, buddy," the one on the left cuts in. He stomps his little black boot. He's got a real nasty look on his face all of a sudden.

"What do you mean?"

"That pack of Kools you smoked? We saw you do it."

The quiet one is shaking his head, like he is disappointed.

"So?"

"That time you tried on your mother's lipstick and jerked off on your parents' bed? We saw that too. *Disgusting.*"

"Please don't think we enjoy spying," the quiet one explains.

But I'm getting a creepy feeling, the same one I get about Dr. Martin Luther King Jr. My dad always tells me to pretend like Martin Luther King is standing behind me, watching whatever I'm doing. I'm supposed to try to honor his legacy. That way I won't do anything bad.

"We know you like to wipe your boogers on the bathroom wall."

"It's just that there's nothing else for us to watch."

I turn around and see how all the front windows of our house are like little TV screens.

"We also saw you—"

"All right, Lawn Jockey," I say to the loudmouth, "I'll do it."

I excuse myself because I have to finish up Mrs. Turner's front yard. Once I get done cutting the grass I push the lawn mower into her garage and go back dragging the hose to water the rosebushes. She has five different color roses growing in front: white, pink, peach, yellow, and red. Once she got a prize for how pretty they looked. I can tell the roses are thirsty so I give them a lot of water. Then I dig out the dandelions. I put them in my pocket to make my mom a dandelion crown. The lawn jockeys are watching me and I'm wondering how I'm going to do what they asked me without getting in trouble.

I look over Mrs. Turner's yard and I think it looks pretty good. Not like the backyard. Mrs. Turner won't let me mow the backyard. Mr. Turner used to keep bees back there before he died. He used to wear a white space suit so the bees couldn't sting him, and they used to buzz all around and sit on his arms and head. After he died all the bees flew off to find him. Pretty soon the weeds back there grew as tall as my knees and the neighborhood cats started going back there to crap in the broken beehives. The fact is, Mrs. Turner's front yard and backyard don't seem like they go with the same house.

Once, after Mr. Turner died, Mrs. Turner slipped in the bathtub and broke her hip and I asked her what does it feel like to be almost dead. She told me to button my lip. That wasn't fair. I never told her to button her lip when she asked me what it feels like to be half black. "It feels like I'm half white," I told her. But she wouldn't talk about being almost dead. Some things you're just not supposed to talk about even though they're not exactly a secret. Like her backyard; I'm just supposed to pretend it's not there and focus on making the front yard pretty. That just shows how there's two worlds—the one we talk about and the one we don't.

I coil up the garden hose on the side of the house and start back up to Mrs. Turner's front door so I can get my five dollars. The one on the right is crying. He looks a little different from the loudmouth because one of his ears is cracked off and there's bird shit on his cap.

"What's the matter?" I ask him.

"He's fine," snaps the one on the left, even though I wasn't talking to him.

"Don't you ever talk?" I ask the quiet one.

"If you must know, I'm crying because I'm happy," he says.

I go in and find Mrs. Turner in the dining room reading a big mystery book with a magnifying glass and I tell her I'm done with her yard. She says marvelous and will I take some refreshments. I can't say no 'cause she already has a place mat set up across the table from her with a glass of milk and a plate of potato chips. So I sit down and put a chip in my mouth. It's soggy. I make a point to tell her that her hair looks pretty. The fact is her hair is blue and it looks like a helmet, but it's OK to lie if it makes somebody happy. Mrs. Turner blushes and touches her hair. Then she stands up with her walker and hobbles over to the sideboard. That's where she keeps her checkbook.

I drink the milk and look up at her chandelier. I like Mrs. Turner's chandelier 'cause it makes little rainbows all over the wallpaper. I'm pretty sure the rainbows are alive. They're tiny like the size of bees.

Once she paid me five dollars extra to climb up on the table in my socks and take down all the pieces of crystal on that chandelier and dip them in a bucket of soapy water. I sneaked one of them in my sweatpants and gave it to my sister for her birthday. I felt kind of bad thinking Dr. Martin Luther King Jr. knew I stole Mrs. Turner's crystal, but the fact is she couldn't tell it was missing anyway. She's almost blind.

I wipe off my milk mustache and start wondering about Mr. Turner and the bees. If he knew how to talk to them.

"Remind me how to spell your last name, won't you?" Mrs. Turner says. She forgets a lot of stuff. I say the letters in my last name and she says, "That doesn't sound accurate," and she's right 'cause when I try to spell out loud I remember all the letters but I forget which one comes first. I tell her I'll write it myself.

My first name looks just like a little bird hopped around on the check how she wrote it 'cause her handwriting's so shaky. I write my last name next to it: B-O-U-D-R-E-A-U-X. I don't know if the B is pointing the right way or not, and the middle letters are falling down under the line. I know the X is in the right place at the end of our name, just like how at the end of a treasure hunt X marks the spot.

She fills out the rest of the check and says, "There you are, young man." Mrs. Turner gives out teeny tubes of toothpaste at Halloween and says the same thing: "There you are, young man. There you are, young lady. Don't forget to brush." Toothpaste as a treat is even worse than raisins and that's how come she gets eggs in her mailbox.

On my way down her front steps I look at the lawn jockeys again. The one on the left who is now on the right winks at me and says, "Remember your promise," and the other one with the missing ear says, "We're ready when you are, Bernie."

"I'll be ready tonight," I say. My dad always says there's no time like the present. "There's no time like the present," I say. The lawn jockeys smile like they're proud of me.

My mom is helping me with my homework later in the living room and I keep looking out the window across the street. The lawn jockeys are watching so I wave and they both wave back with the same hand, the one they usually keep on their hips.

"Earth to Bernie," my mom says. She wants to know what I'm looking at.

"Mrs. Turner's lawn jockeys," I tell her. She pulls the string to close the drapes and tells me to concentrate on my book, but the whole time I'm planning out how I'm going to help them.

"Earth to Bernie. Earth to Bernie," my mom keeps saying, like I'm on another planet. I put the dandelion crown on her head. The yellow flowers look pretty in her brown hair. I'm not lying this time, they really do. I tell her that and she smiles a little and shakes her head. She points at the book, but the letters are smashing into each other like bumper cars.

The same thing happens at dinner. I'm looking at the lawn jockeys through the dining room window and my dad puts down his fork and says, "Pay attention to your plate, son. You're setting a bad example for your sister." Emma isn't really eating her salmon loaf either, but that's 'cause she's so picky she has to pick out all the little bones, not 'cause I'm setting a bad example. She eats like a bird.

I see the lawn jockey on the right put his lantern on the ground and rub his shoulder. I'm thinking how those two lawn jockeys can see right into all the front windows of our house like five TV shows and how they probably know a whole lot about us.

"Why can't you focus?" my dad says. "What's the matter with you?" He always says that. I shrug my shoulders.

"Dad?" says Emma, but he's not listening to her. He wants to know if I did my homework.

"He finished it before dinner," my mom tells him. "Does anyone want another baked potato?"

"Let's see it," he says, "right now." He's mad at me; I can tell from his voice.

"I learned a new word in Spanish today," Emma says.

"Let him finish eating first, Bernard," my mom tells him.

"No. *Now.*"

I bring him my geography workbook and show him the page where I copied down the state capitals how my mom showed me.

"What does this say?" he asks. He's pointing at one of the square states in the middle of the country. There's four of them. My teacher told us if you stand in the middle where they touch corners, then you can be in all four states at once. But I can't remember which one it is my dad has his finger on, and I can't remember the name of the capital.

"Does anyone want to hear my new word?" Emma asks. "It's a noun." She's chewing on the end of her braid.

"Read it," my dad tells me.

Everybody's waiting. Even the lawn jockeys. The dining room is too hot. The grandfather clock in the hallway gets louder and that's the only noise. Tick tock. Tick tock. I scratch the scab on my knee. The fact is, I can't read what I wrote. I look away from my book to my seat. I'm hoping Dr. Martin Luther King Jr. will be sitting there in his robes, and he'll tell me the answer. But he's not. My chair is empty.

"Traje de baño," says Emma, "Guess what it means?" but nobody guesses. Instead, my dad tells me to go upstairs and get the belt.

Later, when they're getting ready to go to bed, I can hear him fighting with my mom. He's saying he moved us here for the school system so we could have a good education. He's not saying he hates it here, but I know that's what he means. The fact is, sometimes I hate it here too. Everybody looks at us like we did something wrong.

He's telling my mom I'm not pulling my weight. He wants me to be like the other boys. "I just want him to fit in," he says.

"Why? Why in the world would you want that?" my mom says.

"Trust me. It's better that way."

"Can't you see how special he is, Bernard?"

"*Trust me*," says my dad.

"I don't understand."

"No. You wouldn't." I hear something slam. Maybe the drawer he keeps his handkerchiefs in with the BB in the corner.

In the middle of the night when I'm getting ready, my sister comes down to the kitchen in her nightgown and her retainer. She asks me what I'm putting on my face.

"What are you doing up, Pocahontas?" I say. I call her that sometimes when she's wearing braids 'cause she looks like a little Indian girl.
"You should be in bed."

"Yeah, but what are you putting on your face?" she wants to know.

"Shoe polish," I say. A ski mask would be better, but I don't have
one of those.

Emma also wants to know where I'm going, and when I won't tell
her she says she's coming with me. I think about it and decide it might
be good to have a lookout so I say fine with me on one condition: she
has to get dressed all in black like I am and keep her mouth closed about
the whole thing.

"That's two conditions," she says, and she goes upstairs to change.
When she comes down again she's wearing her black tights and her
black ballet slippers and my blue Mets jersey. She says she doesn't have
anything black to go on top. I tell her that's no good; the point is that
we have to be invisible and she better go put on dad's overcoat. She does
that and I black up her face with the shoe polish and then we take the
flashlight out to the garage to get the things I'm gonna need.

Everything looks different since this is the middle of the night. I notice some things, like how all the houses up and down the street are
sleeping but how most of the trees are awake. Also, the air is softer than
in the day. Like velvet almost. We cross the street and a raccoon mama
crosses the other way with her raccoon baby in her mouth. She slinks
real slow without looking at us. Then I can see the grass in Mrs.
Turner's front yard growing back already, but slow, like the raccoon.

"Who's she?" says the lawn jockey on the left.

"That's the sister," says the one on the right.

"She's keeping a lookout," I tell them. Emma is standing by the sidewalk and she's supposed to whistle if she sees a person coming or a car.

I get the lid off the paint can with the screwdriver I brought and ask
which one of them wants to go first.

"Me," they both say at the same time, so I flip my lucky penny and
the one on the right calls heads and wins 'cause there's Abraham Lin-
coln, looking at the rosebushes. I dip the paintbrush and I'm about to
get started when Emma tugs on the back of my sweatshirt and scares

the shit out of me. She's so quiet I didn't even know she snuck up behind me. Dad's overcoat is hanging down off her hands and dragging in the grass.

"Who are you talking to, Bernie?" she asks.

"The lawn jockeys."

"Oh. You're going to paint them white?"

I nod my head.

"Why?"

" 'Cause they're stuck inside their bodies. See?" I point at them with the paintbrush. The one on the right and the one on the left. She looks at them and blinks. Her eyes look real bright and pretty with her face all black like that.

"I don't get it," she says.

"They're stuck inside the way everybody looks at them, and they want me to change it. Now go back over there and do your job." She goes back over to the edge of the sidewalk and I get started. The smell of the paint goes over the smell of the roses. I start under the lawn jockey's cap and brush going down from his forehead, over his cheeks and under his chin to his neck, and I stop at his collar. I'm careful not to drip on his red jacket. I paint his little fists white too. The paint job looks pretty good, but then I think about Dr. Martin Luther King Jr. watching and decide to do another coat so it's perfect.

"How do I look?" the quiet one whispers when I'm finished.

"Different," I say.

"It's remarkable," says the one on the left. I paint him too. I'm putting the lid back on the can when Emma starts to whistle so I run over.

"What'd you see?" I ask 'cause I don't see anybody coming.

"Look," she whispers and she points up at our attic window. "It's Dad." The light is on and we can see him sitting in the broken highchair eating out of the ice-cream carton. After a while he stops that and puts his head in his hands.

"What's he doing now?" Emma wants to know.

"He's thinking," I tell her. "He had a bad dream." Our dad is in four places at once, and it's giving him a headache, but I don't tell Emma that. She's too little to understand.

He's thinking about who he used to be, who he is, who people think
he is, and who he wants me to become.

"Can he see us?"

"No," I say. "We're invisible."

We wait a long time for him to get up and turn out the light, and
then we wait some more before we cross the street to go back home. I
ask Emma about her new word. "It means bathing suit," she tells me. I
tug on one of her braids and tell her I'll teach her the butterfly stroke
when the swimming pool opens up for summer. We wipe off the shoe
polish in the garage with socks dipped in turpentine, which it turns out
later is a bad idea 'cause we both wake up with an itchy rash.

In the night I dream about the bees. I'm following my dad down some
train tracks going over the map of America. A dizzy bee comes and
stings him on the neck, but he doesn't notice. Then another one comes
and another and soon it's a whole swarm of bees stinging him. He
doesn't stop walking. He's walking fast in a shell of bees. I can't catch
him. I'm pulling a boxcar full of rocks behind me and I can hardly
move. He goes away from me fast as a train, down into Mississippi,
where he was born.

I wake myself up early in the morning so I can watch him. I scratch
my face. I think there's something crawling under there, trying to dig
out of my skin.

I look out my window to check on the white lawn jockeys. I wave
but they don't wave back. I can tell they're free at last and aren't alive
anymore, just plaster.

Then I hear our screen door slam and I watch him go down the path
in his pajamas. I hold my breath. He bends down to pick up the newspaper with his hand on his back like maybe it's hurting him. When he
stands up he sees them. He drops the newspaper. The lawn jockeys are
holding out their lanterns to him like they're giving him a New Year's
toast. I can tell by the way my dad's shoulders go up and down, up and
down, that he's laughing.

KNUCKLES

by Mary F. Chen-Johnson

Children of recent immigrants struggle with the very real difficulty of leading a double life—the completely assimilated identity they strive to adopt in public, and the traditional expectations they face at home—whether they want to or not. Add to this struggle a child's perspective of racial characteristics or personal preferences sanctioned by her culture of choice, and you have Mary F. Chen-Johnson's "Knuckles," at once hilarious and painful.

In a sense, this story concerns an eating disorder—not the kind inspired by the usual body image problems, however. This eating disorder derives from the narrator Grace's acute sense of otherness. She does not want to be associated with her Taiwanese parents— represented by the various body parts of animals cooked by her mother—and instead fantasizes that she has blue eyes and blond braids and ties with her "friend" Cecilia for most popular girl in the second grade. In reality, the narrator, despite her attempts to eat only American sweets in foil wrappers, can only gaze longingly at the blond Cecilia and her "crowd" during school lunch, eating lunch-box food cut in "geometric shapes." Saving her lunch money to buy forbidden sweets later, Grace must rely on the school's disgusting "free lunch" and on her black friend Misty's ingenuity at disposing of it without getting caught.

Not only does Grace incur her mother's frustration and

disapproval when she is discovered throwing her home-cooked food out the window, her dentist also betrays her. All of her teeth, victims to Grace's obsession with sweetening her life exclusively through American junk food, must be removed. Most of the story oscillates between two narratives: Grace's drug-induced dreams of mostly funny but occasionally frightening experiences involving the consumption of sweets, and her mother's rambling story of former youthful affluence in Taiwan and more recent hardship, sacrifice, and finally success in America. Neither Grace's nor her mother's vision of the world seems slated to win out over the other, and although both visions are predictable in the values they espouse, both are also painful: the "sweets" of the new culture can rot your teeth, and while the attendant dental work can be assuaged by soothing Chinese tea, that tea tastes bitter.

Mary F. Chen-Johnson is a Taiwanese American fiction writer who studied at Cornell University and the University of Montana. Taiwan, an island formerly known as Formosa located off the coast of mainland China, looms as a not-so-distant ghost over this story and over much of Chen-Johnson's work. The mother in this story cannot let go of her former life there. Taiwan's "illegitimate Kuomintang government" history, quite different from its Mainland Communist counterpart, suggests that since the 1960s—aided by an earlier exodus from Mainland China of the military, intellectual, and business elite with considerable gold and foreign currency reserves—its prosperity had much to offer many who lived there. Yet the allure of safety, independence, and prosperity in America, like Grace's attraction to blond hair and blue eyes, promises more than it can provide, leaving regret and a wave of perpetual nausea.

You can compare this story, with its narrator's desperate attempt to assimilate into a different, prevalent culture, to the ex-cerpt from Wild Meat and the Bully Burgers, *by Lois-Ann Yamanaka, and to the excerpt from* Burnt Bread and Chutney: Growing Up Between Cultures—A Memoir of an Indian Jewish Girl, *by Carmit Delman. It can also be read in conjunction*

*with Lan Samantha Chang's "The Eve of the Spirit Festival," an-
other story about assimilation and its relationship to loss.*

A dog would have saved my life. Under the table, gulping down
greasy chunks of squid or duck. A bone-crunching dog. Still, I had
my sister, Jane. She ate steadily, her droopy baby cheeks flapping in and
out with each bite. After dinner, my parents would go into the living
room to watch the news. Minutes later, Jane finished eating and ran
clumsily up our long hallway after them. I could hear the bells on her
shoes as she raced the whiteness of the walls. I switched our two bowls.

"Finished, Ma!" I smiled at Jane and flopped down in front of my
father's chair. "But Jane didn't."

A sigh and my mother bustled up the hall to check. Jane was mildly
confused, but accepting, and she ate. A few days later the routine made
my mother suspicious. She began staying in the kitchen with me until I
finished. I stared at bulging fish eyes and clutching chicken feet on the
plates, mouthing my apologies to the dead things. Did it hurt, I wondered, when they ripped the hook out of your mouth? Did you do a
funny legless dance?

One day Mama tired of my lamenting over sectioned eel and
hopped up and down furiously. "Stop it! Stop it! Why are you talking to
the eel?" She held the plate up to my nose. "Eat!"

On television earlier that day, the animal people had slipped into
black rubber suits and sunk into the ocean. Eels waved lazily back and
forth between giant rocks while the men prodded them with long poles.
Suddenly one of the eels flashed out at a diver and the man grabbed his
arm. They had to return to the boat.

"I don't like eel!"

"Stupid. They're a delicacy. You should be grateful. Eat!"

I held my breath.

Cecilia Grottenmyer and the other second-grade girls would laugh
when they found out I had been electrocuted by an eel. All that would
be left of me: ashes. My parents would keep me in a jar on the top shelf

of the pantry next to the cocoa tin. On a dry, winter day, the jar would tilt during an unguarded nudge, then crash as Mama reached for the cocoa. In her confusion, Mama would drop the tin. Dust fumes, me and cocoa, everywhere until an efficient swoop of the vacuum left the floor slick again.

I gasped for breath and sucked in eel, the smell tumbling me out of my chair and back against the wall.

"No!"

She shoved a spoonful of the meat past my pressed lips, quickly jerked out the spoon, and squeezed my lips shut. She stepped back and folded her arms. I smiled sadly at her and threw up.

After that, she left me alone in the kitchen. I became creative. I sifted through garbage until my dinner was safely at the bottom of the bag. I threw food out of our kitchen window and watched it pop like a balloon two floors down. When I felt hungry, I took the honey from the top of the refrigerator and dipped spoonfuls of fish or pork in it, careful not to let any food fall into the jar.

They must all come out.

I clenched my teeth. What if I promise to brush after every meal? Eat stuff that doesn't come in foil? The dentist smiled. He tucked in my bib and flicked on the light, sucking my thoughts into the glare.

My mother shook her head at the dentist. Nonono. I do not let my children eat candy. Her bad friends must have given her candy. I cook only things that are good for her.

I leaned away from the glaring light, but dancing green spots veiled my eyes. The spots looked like tiny floating faces, laughing and scolding. They taunted and followed my vision until I hid myself again in the yellow of the light.

"We ate rice noodles and almost nothing else for months when I arrived. All of Baba's savings paid to bring me to America." Mama was knitting in the dark, speaking to me softly as I cried. "Your grandmother always made sure that our dinner table had plenty of red-braised meats, vegetables in spicy sauces. Two kinds of soup. But I wouldn't let myself think about that then or I would have hated your baba for being poor every time I cooked noodles."

I couldn't see Mama. Her voice seemed to come from the darkness itself. I wanted to call out and tell her to turn on the light, but my mouth was still numb and clogged with blood and tears. My gums throbbed. The *click-click* of the knitting needles made the softness in her voice less scary.

Cecilia slipped in and out of my dreams. Over lunches of finger foods, we sat laughing together. We were tied for prettiest girl in class. Now we were in her ruffled pink bedroom, exchanging confidential tips on how to braid our long, golden hair. We traded clothes. Mama barged in, wearing her familiar printed housecoat and handed me shimmering, high-collared gowns of jeweled reds and purples. I touched the silk, slowly fingering the embroidered buttons. Mama was a girl again, with happy slaps of pink in her cheeks and dangling ornaments twirled into her glossy hair. She motioned for me to try on the gowns, but my arms were full of Cecilia's jeans and sweaters. Mama was floating away. Cecilia was floating away. I wanted to yell for them to wait but I had forgotten the words to say.

Mama wiped away my tears with a cool cloth and slid back into the darkness. "After a while, we were able to buy chicken once a week and I began learning to cook. In Taiwan, the servants prepared the meals."

At school I stood in line to get free lunch tickets. The white envelope marked "Grace Lin Lunch Money" remained hidden inside my jacket where my mother pinned it each Monday morning. In the lunchroom I handed my green ticket to the cashier and carried my tray to the first-grade table.

"Hey, Gracie! It's my turn to dump." Misty nudged in next to me. Her thin, black fingers scooped up the gray lumps from my plate and plopped them into paper napkins. She sauntered to the water fountain. Bending over for a drink, she quickly dropped the bundle in the trash. She glanced around before skipping back toward me.

I laughed, putting an arm around her.

"We've only got fifteen minutes left, we'd better hurry." Misty grabbed her emptied tray and headed for the Mean Lady. I followed, but a third-grader cut in front of me.

"Hold it." A huge brown hand snatched the third-grader's shoulder and pushed him into an empty seat. "That's not enough. Eat some more." The boy peered up at the black-walnut face and frantically stuffed forkfuls of mush into his mouth.

I gripped my tray and stared at Misty waving at me from the other end of the line. I shrunk under the stare of the Mean Lady and walked quickly to the dirty-forks bin.

On our way outside we passed the table where Cecilia and her friends sat. The girls pulled thermoses and neat squares of sandwiches out of bright lunch boxes. The ends of their long blond hair brushed back and forth over their food as each turned from side to side, laughing and talking. Cecilia always sat at the middle of the table. She ate foods in geometric shapes.

We followed the thick rope of children streaming past the Texaco station to Mr. Henry's. I stopped in front of the fat Italian ice man for a limie. He stared sadly into the distance as he poured the green liquid, his mustache pointing dejectedly, accusingly down at me. Grabbing the cone, I dropped a dime into his open palm. I was careful to avoid looking at the dark, glazed eyes.

Inside Mr. Henry's, we jostled and screamed along and paid for chips and twirled wands of licorice with coins carefully counted out from white envelopes. Misty leafed through comic books and slipped Hershey bars into her coat pocket. I bought peppermint, chocolate malt balls, Pixie Sticks.

I stashed leftover purchases under the love seat in the living room. For hours I would lie in the space between the furniture and the wall, slowly and slowly chewing potato chips. I listened to Jane yelling for me as chocolate melted in my mouth. My mother minced garlic while I twirled gum slowly around my fingers, stretching the orange wads into wisps.

The dentist held up a poster of a magnified set of teeth. He handed me a giant toothbrush. Show me how you brush dear show me. I swirled the toothbrush over the glossy teeth but he frowned. No dear it's up and down do it for me dear can you show me how to brush your teeth dear? I swirled the brush faster but he shook his head. No no can you do it right dear show me the way it's supposed to be. But I could only hang on to the toothbrush as it swirled in frantic circles. The dentist clucked at me and, with a black magic marker, X'ed out each tooth.

"I was very careful to buy the best food for the least amount of money. Anything that didn't have to be cold, I put in milk crates. Long strips of sticky tape around the boxes kept the cockroaches from our things."
Click-click.
I could feel my mother nodding and smiling.
"Every morning, cockroaches of all sizes were stuck on the tape. Some dead, some still moving. I threw them into the garbage and put on new tape."

The nurse finished cleaning my teeth and patted my head. Okay doctor everything is ready I'm sorry Mrs. Lin you'll have to wait outside okay. I jammed my feet against the footrest and sunk back into the green cushion, but the fat hand brought the white mask closer and closer. I shook my head and whipped my hair until the nurse grabbed my ears. The dentist slipped the mask over my nose and mouth. Thank you Nurse she'll be out soon boy she's a wild one.
I thought about Misty's black fingers and Italian ices and not letting

anyone take my teeth. The hissing of the gas sounded like shaken-up Coke bottles opened just a little.

I used to ask what we were having for dinner. "Shaun chiao tu tzu and hai dai hua sheng pai ku tang." Was it a special occasion? My stomach snarled in approval until I realized we were having pork stomach and kelp-and-peanut soup. I wondered vaguely if Mama was trying to trick me. How could something that sounded as good as "Chao ku feng dan" be chicken liver?

There was never new food. The same dishes reappeared week after week. The amount, the smell, the seasonings, the colors, never changing. Mama must have dug underground vats while I was at school, filling them with day-long-made pots of stuff. Filling and filling until there would always be more to spoon out year after year. Filling until the brown and gold and green sauces hiding animal parts spilled out over the edges of the vats and flowed out into the basement. Shredded pork with sweet bean paste and stuffed glutinous duck with brown sauce spread across the floor. Crispy chicken legs crept up the walls. Sharks' fin soup seeped into the living room and into our bedrooms, into our clothes and noses. Nagging at our brains day and night. At school everyone knew what I ate because my clothes smelled and had turned into the familiar browns and golds and greens.

Even the ceiling was discolored. My mother stood for hours in front of the sink and stove, chopping and frying and not throwing anything away. She made dinners from one animal: ribs floating in soup and tongues cleverly sliced and sauced to look like steak. Great balls of steam leaped from popping vegetables and hovered over her head like angry genies until, with a wave of her apron, they vanished. Years of wrestling smelly fish and hot oil had left a huge brown splotch on the ceiling above the stove. During the winter's darkness I crept up the hall to watch Mama cooking under a single dull light. The brown stain looked black in the dimness and the hot vapors flew up and into their depths. I shivered at the thought of severed chicken and pig souls trying to find their way to heaven to piece themselves together again.

I was relieved when we moved. I raced through our new house, happy to see and touch the unblemished walls. I rolled on the new carpeting, letting the dust go up my nose and cling to my hair. I shut myself in the closet to sit with the stillness and trapped air.

Pushing the furniture away from the walls, I crawled into the space. Flicking up the back skirt of the love seat, I reached up and unpinned bags of chocolate. I ripped the bags open and smelled the drowsy sweetness. One by one, the chunks melted in my mouth and oozed down my throat.

My mother went straight to work cleaning, slicing, and cooking. Under the new fluorescent light, she raised her spatula and wooden chopsticks, plunging them down to stir and turn the crackling food. Oil snapped out at her, but again and again, her hands forged into the pans. The screaming of the frying foods was tamer on the new electric stove, but my mother tricked the meats and vegetables into the familiar flavors. Within minutes, the smell had found us.

Somebody turned on a light in the hallway and a little brightness pushed in under the crack of my door. I could see the silhouette of my mother's feet, and I tried to imagine the dried, callused toes snug in sapphire slippers trimmed in pearl. The girlhood slippers Mama stored, wrapped in plastic, in her drawer.

My mother shifted in her chair and continued knitting. The clicking was becoming steadier as her hands learned to see in the dark.

"When you were born, I was already a good cook. Your baba was getting fat and friends came to visit. I never bought baby food. You ate what Baba and I ate. I chewed a mouthful of food until it was soft and smooth, then fed it to you. You were always so happy to eat. By the time you were two, you could use chopsticks and eat by yourself." Her sigh filled the room.

One Monday night my parents promised us dinner at Lenny's Pizza & Subs on the corner. Jane and I boasted about who was hungrier and how much could we eat and worried about do we have enough money. It was our first dinner out.

"Can we help you order?"

My father carefully picked us off his arm and pushed us toward the tables. "Go sit down, I will order."

Jane ran to a corner booth, but I dragged her toward a center table. A group of older girls from school sat a few seats away. I yawned loudly and looked bored, but watched the girls' reflection carefully in the window.

"Here we are. I hope you're hungry."

My father proudly passed out small cartons of milk and one straw each. He tucked a napkin under his chin and waited expectantly. My mother opened her bag, taking out chopsticks and round, metal tins. She grinned broadly and pulled the lids off the containers, releasing swirls of steam. I felt the other girls' eyes staring at our colorful dinner and knew that I would never be asked to sit at their table.

"I hope you children are hungry. This is a special occasion so I made a lot." My mother chewed happily and passed me a napkin.

I watched the food churning in her mouth; her blunt fingers reached in to loosen chunks of food stuck between her teeth. Mama brought out a small bag from under the table. "A special surprise for this special occasion." She pulled out neat rectangles of cherry pie wrapped in shiny cardboard. "The sign says these are very good. Here." She placed one in front of each of us.

I put mine over the metal tin and peered at the girls' reflection through my bangs. They were sharing milkshakes and pulling pepperoni off their pizza. My mother was eating cherry pie with her chopsticks. She spoke loudly in Taiwanese, proclaiming the blandness of American food and the cleanliness of some public rest rooms.

Why are you doing this to me, I grumbled in my cheeks. Everyone's going to know now.

"Huh? What did you say?" Mama peered suspiciously at me. "Speak louder."

I want to go home. Everybody's looking at us. I raised my voice but kept it in my throat. I want pepperoni, too.

"Huh?"

I bit into my cherry pie and screamed, "This isn't eating out! What do you mean this is eating out? This is worse than eating at home! If we have to eat this stuff, do we have to do it where everyone can see?" I pinched Jane until she screamed. "See, Jane wants to go, too!"

The girls at the other table had stopped eating to stare at me. I sat down. My father sighed and popped the last of his pie into his mouth. Mama slapped some pennies in front of me and continued eating. "Want everything? Want peeza? Here. You get it."

The girls were leaving. I ran to the bathroom and threw the coins into the toilet.

My mother was standing by the dentist again. She frowned at the black X's on the chart and asked if she could use some of the sleeping gas. She pulled a huge wok out of her bag and made a stove out of the dentist's equipment. She put my teeth into the pan and started stirring. But the dentist said he wasn't hungry. My mother told him he had to eat anyway.

Breakfasts were soothing after anxious dinners. I liked the baldness of toast and the sogginess of cereal. I knew where to find the butter and the stainless-steel knives. One morning a fat cockroach the size of my nose fell from the ceiling into my father's coffee. It didn't die. Fluttering and fluttering, its blackness made it invisible except for the dimples of its feet.

The soreness in my neck made me realize that I was straining to hear my mother. She dropped her words softly as if knitting them into a sweater to keep herself warm. I was leaning out toward the clicking of her needles.

"I don't understand why you stopped liking my food." Mama stopped knitting.

The silence loosened the tethers of time. I could feel the dull ache in my mouth but couldn't be sure whether my imagination was still dancing with white masks. Slowly the clicking began again.

"Later, when Jane was born, I fed her the same way I fed you and she became happy. Fat. The other mothers were jealous at the way she could eat." Mama laughed. "She ate more than other children twice her age."

My head snapped back and forth as the Mean Lady shook me. Not enough not enough. I wanted to tell her to stop, but I couldn't find her face beneath the brown creases and thick glasses. I can't eat anymore, I couldn't tell her. All my teeth are gone. Quiet quiet, a fat man said. Girls with no teeth cannot have special ice.

Far away, someone chanted, "Wakeupwakeupwakeup."

"Not you. No. Not my firstborn. So picky now. Everything is 'Yucky' and you're always 'Not hungry.' To me, everything is delicious after I work many hours making dinner. When I sit down, the food tastes good. I eat until I am full."

My body was absorbing the numbness of my mouth and pushing the pain outward. I could feel the cavities eating away teeth that weren't there anymore. The throbbing of my gums pulsed in time with the *click-click* of my mother's needles.

"Just look at your baba. He eats and eats and is happy. He's quiet because he likes his life. It's a good life with family, job, house, food, and clothes."

I pictured the man who sat like a boulder to eat with us once a week. Fourteen hours a day, six days a week, in a Chinatown rice shop he worked. The man who only wanted to sleep and be left alone.

I carefully picked out tendons and gooey things, but my mother told me that only Indians eat with their fingers and to just swallow the whole thing.

"Just because you like it doesn't mean I do." I winced at the rubbery pig knuckles.

"You children just don't know what's good." She placed another helping in my bowl. "When I was young, my mother made pig knuckles and porridge to warm us up in the winter. We had to walk seven kilometers to school. Nothing was better for keeping us warm."

"How come Jane got a smaller piece than me?" I held my knuckles against hers.

"Stupid. In Taiwan, everyone would be fighting for the biggest pieces, and you're complaining because I gave you a big piece? You don't know." She tapped my bowl with her chopsticks, motioning for me to eat.

"Be quiet!" my father said. "Dinnertime is supposed to be peaceful."

I stared at the rice dangling from his ragged mustache.

"Hurry up." My mother tapped my bowl.

I buried the knuckles under the rice and stabbed them, making my chopsticks stand straight up.

"I can't eat my rice. I'm full."

Mama's hand swept over my ear, cheek, nose. "Don't do that!" She jerked my chopsticks up, pork knuckles and all, with rice flying in a snowy arch, and placed the utensils on the table.

"Do what?" I rubbed my cheek and picked up the scattered rice on the table, squishing the ones on the floor with my toes.

She pulled off a huge strip of meat and chewed in gulping breaths. "Don't stick your chopsticks up like that!"

"That's why you hit me?" I silently pounded the table. "What's wrong with that anyway? I was resting my chopsticks." I considered putting them back up.

"Chopsticks up in food are offerings for dead people." She pried the knuckles off my sticks and placed the utensils across my bowl. "Keep them like this when you're not eating. Who taught you to put them up? My mother would have said, 'You want to give your food to the dead, then we will give it to the dead!' and I would go hungry. How come you do things like that? You children think you're so great."

I lifted my tongue but all I could feel was soggy gauze. Somehow I thought I was a hero. I had undergone something terrible, something that hurt. I had blood on my clothes.

Mama pulled out the soaked wads of gauze and stuffed fresh rolls in. I wanted her to look at my blood and see me sweating with pain. I wanted her to hear how I didn't cry.

"Eat."

I pulled the knuckles off my chopsticks and plopped them into my bowl. I ate my rice one by one, chewing and swallowing each grain before continuing. Soon everyone wandered into the living room and I was alone. Taking careful aim, I speared the knuckles with my chopsticks, but the huge blocks, with no rice packed around them, kept tipping over. I pushed up the window screen and tossed the knuckles out.

"I should make you go outside and pick that up." My mother stood in the doorway, pulling back a strand of hair and pushing it behind her ear. "I spend hours cooking for you and you throw food out the window?"

I put my bowl in the sink. Once, she made me stand in a corner for six hours because I forgot to practice playing the piano. "Sorry. I'll go get it."

She picked up her stained apron and snapped it loudly in the air. "No. What's the use? Will you eat it? Of course not. You don't care how much time I spend preparing the food. You'll flush it down the toilet. You'll throw it in the closet. You're a very mean girl."

As Mama gestured wildly, I noticed the numerous nicks and spots of oil burns on her hands.

"You never appreciate anything." She began pacing, tossing her head like a gored bull. "I work so hard to make dinner. If we lived in Taiwan, we would have maids and cooks and I could sit in the garden fanning myself all day and not getting my clothes dirty. I could wear my beautiful gowns again. Every color. All silk." She walked faster. "No more cooking. Like when I was a girl. My father rang a bell and the servants put the food on the table. He rang another bell and everyone came to eat. A feast every night. We finished everything. Even during poor harvests, our family always had a lot. We ate and ate."

I picked a grain of rice off the floor.

She stopped walking and glared at me. Her eyes shone. "All you do is complain! I didn't come to this country to be a servant to my own children! I should have stayed in Taiwan!"

Mama led me from the dentist's office and stretched me out across the backseat of our car. Baba sat quietly behind the steering wheel, turning to smile. My face was an overstuffed sack of cotton and blood. One hand clutched a small cloth doll. It was ugly with orange yarn hair and limp arms, but it had been enough to lure me into the dentist's chair. I wasn't a hero. I was hungry and humiliated. Spots of color had followed me out of the dental office.

We drove thousands of miles to get home. The whistle of wind from a cracked window blew me back to fight the charm of white masks in a sterile room. The light was an orange cinnamon fireball. The white paper cups were filled with strawberry syrup. A seat belt kept me strapped to the padded chair, bound my hands. The mask stilled my shrieks. In the seats next to me, Cecilia was having her teeth polished and Misty was feeding pig knuckles to the Mean Lady. Chinese sauces came up a tube, into the mask and down my throat. The light went out and everything was gone except the tightening mask. I was choking. My stomach felt like the blown-out throat of a bullfrog, but the sauces kept pouring into me. Choking me in spiciness. Sesame oil thickening my throat. Ginger roots burning my tongue. The distant tastes mingling with the blood from my gums.

A hand brought sudden air and the tightness lifted. A cool cloth smoothed away sweat and tears, I could open my eyes. The bitter, soothing taste of tea trickled down my throat, forcing the passage open and washing down the thickness. My mother tilted the cup again and waited for me to swallow.

THE SHAWL

by Louise Erdrich

This story starts off with a tale that uses the past as if it were part of a body of Native American myth. It tells of generational despair, starting with a husband and his moody wife Aanakwad, their son and daughter, and a new baby, the passion child of Aanakwad and her lover. Despite the husband's willingness to accept this child as his own, Aanakwad's marriage cannot survive. She becomes obsessed with the infant and her absent lover— expressed through frightening bouts of bad temper toward her husband. Since this is a culture in which such realities are treated practically and respectfully, what happens next speaks to its habit of tallying loss within the tragedy of sacrifice.

The narrator turns out to be Aanakwad's thirteen-year-old grandson. His father is the haunted son, his manhood destroyed when he is left behind by Aanakwad, who departs with her daughter and her newborn. Unable to keep his life clear of the marauding wolves that shadow him and have already violated his family, the narrator's father holds his rage close to his heart, but he passes his despair down to the narrator as if it were a precious raiment like the torn and shredded plaid shawl last seen wrapped around his sister.

The narrator's own struggles to survive, grow strong, and protect his siblings from his father's terrifying and violent alcoholic outbursts mirror that tenderness in the older story which exists alongside sacrifice and loss. Erdrich understands that rage and despair can be mitigated by a terrible joy in the power that the narrator finally manages to exert over his father. She creates an author who can look back on his father's story with interpretive powers that mimic her own by offering his father an altogether different reading of his bitter tale.

Erdrich's story, which first appeared in the March 5, 2001 issue of the New Yorker *magazine, later became, in a slightly edited version, an interpolated, cautionary tale in her 2005 novel* The Painted Drum *about the importance of letting go of the memories of lost children. She is the author of many novels, several children's books, three volumes of poetry, and two nonfiction books; she has won the National Book Circle Award and been a finalist for the National Book Award. She lives in Minnesota with her daughters.*

"The Shawl" can be compared with Adiele's "Fire: An Origin Tale" and Alma Luz Villanueva's "La Llorona/Weeping Woman" for its mythic elements. You might also want to compare it with Senna's "Triad," which provides three different versions of the same story about a girl's reading of her family in the wake of her mother's death. Another interesting comparison occurs in the excerpt from Burnt Bread and Chutney *by Carmit Delman; that story also provides a different perspective from the narrator's that requires a reassessment.*

Among the Anishinaabeg on the road where I live, it is told how a woman loved a man other than her husband and went off into the bush and bore his child. Her name was Aanakwad, which means cloud, and like a cloud she was changeable. She was moody and sullen one moment, her lower lip jutting and her eyes flashing, filled with storms. The next, she would shake her hair over her face and blow it straight out in front of her to make her children scream with laughter. For she also had two children by her husband, one a yearning boy of five years and the other a capable daughter of nine.

When Aanakwad brought the new baby out of the trees that autumn, the older girl was like a second mother, even waking in the night
to clean the baby and nudge it to her mother's breast. Aanakwad slept
through its cries, hardly woke. It wasn't that she didn't love her baby;
no, it was the opposite—she loved it too much, the way she loved its father, and not her husband. This passion ate away at her, and her feelings
were unbearable. If she could have thrown off that wronghearted love,
she would have, but the thought of the other man, who lived across the
lake, was with her always. She became a gray sky, stared monotonously
at the walls, sometimes wept into her hands for hours at a time. Soon,
she couldn't rise to cook or keep the cabin neat, and it was too much for
the girl, who curled up each night exhausted in her red-and-brown plaid
shawl and slept and slept, until the husband had to wake her to awaken
her mother, for he was afraid of his wife's bad temper, and it was he who
roused Aanakwad into anger by the sheer fact that he was himself and
not the other.

At last, even though he loved Aanakwad, the husband had to admit
that their life together was no good anymore. And it was he who sent for
the other man's uncle. In those days, our people lived widely scattered,
along the shores and in the islands, even out on the plains. There were
no roads then, just trails, though we had horses and wagons and, for the
winter, sleds. When the uncle came around to fetch Aanakwad, in his
wagon fitted out with sled runners, it was very hard, for she and her husband had argued right up to the last about the children, argued fiercely
until the husband had finally given in. He turned his face to the wall,
and did not move to see the daughter, whom he treasured, sit down beside her mother, wrapped in her plaid robe in the wagon bed. They left
right away, with their bundles and sacks, not bothering to heat up the
stones to warm their feet. The father had stopped his ears, so he did not
hear his son cry out when he suddenly understood that he would be left
behind.

As the uncle slapped the reins and the horse lurched forward, the
boy tried to jump into the wagon, but his mother pried his hands off the
boards, crying, *Gego, gego,* and he fell down hard. But there was something in him that would not let her leave. He jumped up and, although

he was wearing only light clothing, he ran behind the wagon over the packed drifts. The horses picked up speed. His chest was scorched with pain, and yet he pushed himself on. He'd never run so fast, so hard and furiously, but he was determined, and he refused to believe that the increasing distance between him and the wagon was real. He kept going until his throat closed, he saw red, and in the ice of the air his lungs shut. Then, as he fell onto the board-hard snow, he raised his head. He watched the back of the wagon and the tiny figures of his mother and sister disappear, and something failed in him. Something broke. At that moment he truly did not care if he was alive or dead. So when he saw the gray shapes, the shadows, bounding lightly from the trees to either side of the trail, far ahead, he was not afraid.

The next the boy knew, his father had him wrapped in a blanket and was carrying him home. His father's chest was broad and, although he already spat the tubercular blood that would write the end of his story, he was still a strong man. It would take him many years to die. In those years, the father would tell the boy, who had forgotten this part entirely, that at first when he talked about the shadows the father thought he'd been visited by *manidoog*. But then, as the boy described the shapes, his father had understood that they were not spirits. Uneasy, he had decided to take his gun back along the trail. He had built up the fire in the cabin, and settled his boy near it, and gone back out into the snow. Perhaps the story spread through our settlements because the father had to tell what he saw, again and again, in order to get rid of it. Perhaps as with all frightful dreams, *amaniso*, he had to talk about it to destroy its power—though in this case nothing could stop the dream from being real.

The shadows' tracks were the tracks of wolves, and in those days, when our guns had taken all their food for furs and hides to sell, the wolves were bold and had abandoned the old agreement between them and the first humans. For a time, until we understood and let the game increase, the wolves hunted us. The father bounded forward when he saw the tracks. He could see where the pack, desperate, had tried to slash the tendons of the horses' legs. Next, where they'd leaped for the back of the wagon. He hurried on to where the trail gave out at the broad empty ice of the lake. There, he saw what he saw, scattered, and the ravens, attending to the bitter small leavings of the wolves.

For a time, the boy had no understanding of what had happened. His father kept what he knew to himself, at least that first year, and when his son asked about his sister's torn plaid shawl, and why it was kept in the house, his father said nothing. But he wept when the boy asked if his sister was cold. It was only after his father had been weakened by the disease that he began to tell the story, far too often and always the same way: he told how when the wolves closed in Aanakwad had thrown her daughter to them.

When his father said those words, the boy went still. What had his sister felt? What had thrust through her heart? Had something broken inside her, too, as it had in him? Even then, he knew that this broken place inside him would not be mended, except by some terrible means. For he kept seeing his mother put the baby down and grip his sister around the waist. He saw Aanakwad swing the girl lightly out over the side of the wagon. He saw the brown shawl with its red lines flying open. He saw the shadows, the wolves, rush together, quick and avid, as the wagon with sled runners disappeared into the distance—forever, for neither he nor his father saw Aanakwad again.

When I was little, my own father terrified us with his drinking. This was after we lost our mother, because before that the only time I was aware that he touched the *ishkode waaboo* was on an occasional weekend when they got home late, or sometimes during berry-picking gatherings when we went out to the bush and camped with others. Not until she died did he start the heavy sort of drinking, the continuous drinking, where we were left alone in the house for days. The kind where, when he came home, we'd jump out the window and hide in the woods while he barged around, shouting for us. We'd go back only after he had fallen dead asleep.

There were three of us: me, the oldest at ten, and my little sister and brother, twins, and only six years old. I was surprisingly good at taking

care of them, I think, and because we learned to survive together during
those drinking years we have always been close. Their names are Doris
and Raymond, and they married a brother and sister. When we get together, which is often, for we live on the same road, there come times in
the talking and card-playing, and maybe even in the light beer now and
then, when we will bring up those days. Most people understand how it
was. Our story isn't uncommon. But for us it helps to compare our
points of view.

How else would I know, for instance, that Raymond saw me the first
time I hid my father's belt? I pulled it from around his waist while he
was passed out, and then I buried it in the woods. I kept doing it after
that. Our father couldn't understand why his belt was always stolen
when he went to town drinking. He even accused his *shkwebii* buddies
of the theft. But I had good reasons. Not only was he embarrassed, afterward, to go out with his pants held up by rope, but he couldn't snake
his belt out in anger and snap the hooked buckle end in the air. He
couldn't hit us with it. Of course, being resourceful, he used other
things. There was a board. A willow wand. And there was himself—his
hands and fists and boots—and things he could throw. But eventually it
became easy to evade him, and after a while we rarely suffered a bruise
or a scratch. We had our own place in the woods, even a little campfire
for the cold nights. And we'd take money from him every chance we
got, slip it from his shoe, where he thought it well hidden. He became,
for us, a thing to be avoided, outsmarted, and exploited. We survived
off him as if he were a capricious and dangerous line of work. I suppose
we stopped thinking of him as a human being, certainly as a father.

I got my growth earlier than some boys, and one night when I was
thirteen and Doris and Raymond and I were sitting around wishing for
something besides the oatmeal and commodity canned milk I'd stashed
so he couldn't sell them, I heard him coming down the road. He was
shouting and making noise all the way to the house, and Doris and Raymond looked at me and headed for the back window. When they saw
that I wasn't coming, they stopped. C'mon, *ondaas*, get with it—they
tried to pull me along. I shook them off and told them to get out
quickly—I was staying. I think I can take him now is what I said.

He was big; he hadn't yet wasted away from the alcohol. His nose had been pushed to one side in a fight, then slammed back to the other side, so now it was straight. His teeth were half gone, and he smelled the way he had to smell, being five days drunk. When he came in the door, he paused for a moment, his eyes red and swollen, tiny slits. Then he saw that I was waiting for him, and he smiled in a bad way. My first punch surprised him. I had been practicing on a hay-stuffed bag, then on a padded board, toughening my fists, and I'd got so quick I flickered like fire. I still wasn't as strong as he was, and he had a good twenty pounds on me. Yet I'd do some damage, I was sure of it. I'd teach him not to mess with me. What I didn't foresee was how the fight itself would get right into me.

There is something terrible about fighting your father. It came on suddenly, with the second blow—a frightful kind of joy. A power surged up from the center of me, and I danced at him, light and giddy, full of a heady rightness. Here is the thing: I wanted to waste him, waste him good. I wanted to smack the living shit out of him. Kill him, if I must. A punch for Doris, a kick for Raymond. And all the while I was silent, then screaming, then silent again, in this rage of happiness that filled me with a simultaneous despair so that, I guess you could say, I stood apart from myself.

He came at me, crashed over a chair that was already broken, then threw the pieces. I grabbed one of the legs and whacked him on the ear so that his head spun and turned back to me, bloody. I watched myself striking him again and again. I knew what I was doing, but not really, not in the ordinary sense. It was as if I were standing calm, against the wall with my arms folded, pitying us both. I saw the boy, the chair leg, the man fold and fall, his hands held up in begging fashion. Then I also saw that, for a while now, the bigger man had not even bothered to fight back.

Suddenly, he was my father again. And when I knelt down next to him, I was his son. I reached for the closest rag, and picked up this piece of blanket that my father always kept with him for some reason. And as I picked it up and wiped the blood off his face, I said to him, Your nose is crooked again. He looked at me, steady and quizzical, as though he had never had a drink in his life, and I wiped his face again with that frayed piece of blanket. Well, it was a shawl, really, a kind of old-fashioned woman's blanket-shawl. Once, maybe, it had been plaid. You could still see lines, some red, the background a faded brown. He watched intently as my hand brought the rag to his face. I was pretty sure, then, that I'd clocked him too hard, that he'd really lost it now. Gently, though, he clasped one hand around my wrist. With the other hand he took the shawl. He crumpled it and held it to the middle of his forehead. It was as if he were praying, as if he were having thoughts he wanted to collect in that piece of cloth. For a while he lay like that, and I, crouched over, let him be, hardly breathing. Something told me to sit there, still. And then at last he said to me, in the sober new voice I would hear from then on, *Did you know I had a sister once?*

There was a time when the government moved everybody off the farthest reaches of the reservation, onto roads, into towns, into housing. It looked good at first, and then it all went sour. Shortly afterward, it seemed that anyone who was someone was either drunk, killed, near suicide, or had just dusted himself. None of the old sort were left, it seemed—the old kind of people, the Gete-anishinaabeg, who are kind beyond kindness and would do anything for others. It was during that time that my mother died and my father hurt us, as I have said.

Now, gradually, that term of despair has lifted somewhat and yielded up its survivors. But we still have sorrows that are passed to us from early generations, sorrows to handle in addition to our own, and cruelties lodged where we cannot forget them. We have the need to forget. We are always walking on oblivion's edge.

Some get away, like my brother and sister, married now and living quietly down the road. And me, to some degree, though I prefer to live alone. And even my father, who recently found a woman. Once, when he brought up the old days, and we went over the story again, I told him at last the two things I had been thinking.

First, I told him that keeping his sister's shawl was wrong, because we never keep the clothing of the dead. Now's the time to burn it, I said. Send it off to cloak her spirit. And he agreed.

The other thing I said to him was in the form of a question. Have you ever considered, I asked him, given how tenderhearted your sister was, and how brave, that she looked at the whole situation? She saw that the wolves were only hungry. She knew that their need was only need. She knew that you were back there, alone in the snow. She understood that the baby she loved would not live without a mother, and that only the uncle knew the way. She saw clearly that one person on the wagon had to be offered up, or they all would die. And in that moment of knowledge, don't you think, being who she was, of the old sort of Anishinaabeg, who thinks of the good of the people first, she jumped, my father, *n'dede*, brother to that little girl? Don't you think she lifted her shawl and flew?

GLOSSARY

Anishinaabeg (81): people belonging to the Odawa, Ojibwe, and Algonkin Native Americans of North America.

Between School
and Home

School and home provide adolescents with the two main—and sometimes contradictory—resources for learning. A school's curriculum, rife with positive and negative experiences, takes place in and out of the classroom; life at home can bring comfort, despair, confusion, and nostalgia for a time when home represented a real or imagined sanctuary rather than a place where you feel most acutely that nobody knows you. In these stories, the relationship between school and home influences is assessed, and only the resilience of adolescence comes out the winner.

THE BOY WITHOUT A FLAG

by Abraham Rodriguez Jr.

This memory piece narrated by young Abraham attempts to demystify his father and his father's rage and disappointment at being a Puerto Rican in America. It focuses on Abraham's life in his school, where he experiences the classic crush on an attractive teacher, contempt for her unworthy fellow-teacher suitor, and terror of the reptilian, Godzilla-like assistant principal with her clacking heels. Abraham decides that his father's approval requires him to refuse to pledge allegiance to the American flag, an action that incurs frustration, confusion, but also the sympathy of his peers, teachers, and administrators. His defiance, costly though it may be with its unpleasant confrontations, will bring him, he is certain, his father's coveted admiration and respect.

Abraham's action is not impulsive, but rather the outcome of careful study. His subjects are found in his precocious reading and in observing his father and his crushed dreams. Puerto Rico, a United States protectorate since 1898, was "allowed" to have its own constitution in 1952, subject to United States laws. The government suppressed Nationalist leaders like Pedro Albizu Campos, one of Abraham's father's heroes, and as a result, the influence of the Nationalist Party waned. While Abraham's prolific reading takes him to a history of the rise and fall of the Nazis (his own choice), his father pushes other topics, like the CIA's association

*with Chile and its efforts to destroy the socialist regime of Salvador
Allende, and autobiographies of Dominican and Puerto Rican
revolutionaries.*

   *Why does what Abraham learns at home conflict with obeying
school rules? At what age will Abraham be old enough to have
convictions of his own, and how will he accept the contradictions
suggested by saluting the American flag, and the challenge of being a Puerto Rican American with his father's "enemy" already
within him? Rodriguez wisely leaves us with those questions, only
assuring us that his imperfect father is "someone I would love forever."*

   *This piece can be compared with Adiele's "Fire: An Origin
Tale" for its discovery of a deeper, more complicated truth, a truth
that promises to keep on revealing itself as both the young Adiele
and Rodriguez mature. It can also be compared with Raboteau's
"Mrs. Turner's Lawn Jockeys," Erdrich's "The Shawl," and Sharma's
"Surrounded by Sleep" for the protagonists' evolving relationships
with their fathers.*

To Ms. Linda Falcón, wherever she is

Swirls of dust danced in the beams of sunlight that came through the
tall windows, the buzz of voices resounding in the stuffy auditorium. Mr. Rios stood by our Miss Colon, hovering as if waiting to catch
her if she fell. His pale mouse features looked solemnly dutiful. He was
a versatile man, doubling as English teacher and gym coach. He was
only there because of Miss Colon's legs. She was wearing her neon pink
nylons. Our favorite.

   We tossed suspicious looks at the two of them. Miss Colon would
smirk at Edwin and me, saying, "Hey, face front," but Mr. Rios would
glare. I think he knew that we knew what he was after. We knew, because on Fridays, during our free period when we'd get to play records
and eat stale pretzel sticks, we would see her way in the back by the tall

windows, sitting up on a radiator like a schoolgirl. There would be a strange pinkness on her high cheekbones, and there was Mr. Rios, sitting beside her, playing with her hand. Her face, so thin and girlish, would blush. From then on, her eyes, very close together like a cartoon rendition of a beaver's, would avoid us.

Miss Colon was hardly discreet about her affairs. Edwin had first tipped me off about her love life after one of his lunchtime jaunts through the empty hallways. He would chase girls and toss wet bathroom napkins into classrooms where kids in the lower grades sat, trapped. He claimed to have seen Miss Colon slip into a steward's closet with Mr. Rios and to have heard all manner of sounds through the thick wooden door, which was locked (he tried it). He had told half the class before the day was out, the boys sniggering behind grimy hands, the girls shocked because Miss Colon was married, so married that she even brought the poor unfortunate in one morning as a kind of show-and-tell guest. He was an untidy dark-skinned Puerto Rican type in a colorful dashiki. He carried a paper bag that smelled like glue. His eyes seemed sleepy, his Afro an uncombed Brillo pad. He talked about protest marches, the sixties, the importance of an education. Then he embarrassed Miss Colon greatly by disappearing into the coat closet and falling asleep there. The girls, remembering him, softened their attitude toward her indiscretions, defending her violently. "Face it," one of them blurted out when Edwin began a new series of Miss Colon tales, "she married a bum and needs to find true love."

"She's a slut, and I'm gonna draw a comic book about her," Edwin said, hushing when she walked in through the door. That afternoon, he showed me the first sketches of what would later become a very popular comic book entitled "Slut at the Head of the Class." Edwin could draw really well, but his stories were terrible, so I volunteered to do the writing. In no time at all, we had three issues circulating under desks and hidden in notebooks all over the school. Edwin secretly ran off close to a hundred copies on a copy machine in the main office after school. It always amazed me how copies of our comic kept popping up in the unlikeliest places. I saw them on radiators in the auditorium, on benches in the gym, tacked up on bulletin boards. There were even some in the teachers' lounge, which I spotted one day while running an errand for

Miss Colon. Seeing it, however, in the hands of Miss Marti, the pig-faced assistant principal, nearly made me puke up my lunch. Good thing our names weren't on it.

It was a miracle no one snitched on us during the ensuing investigation, since only a blind fool couldn't see our involvement in the thing. No bloody purge followed, but there was enough fear in both of us to kill the desire to continue our publishing venture. Miss Marti, a woman with a battlefield face and constant odor of Chiclets, made a forceful threat about finding the culprits while holding up the second issue, the one with the hand-colored cover. No one moved. The auditorium grew silent. We meditated on the sound of a small plane flying by, its engines rattling the windows. I think we wished we were on it.

It was in the auditorium that the trouble first began. We had all settled into our seats, fidgeting like tiny burrowing animals, when there was a general call for quiet. Miss Marti, up on stage, had a stare that could make any squirming fool sweat. She was a gruff, nasty woman who never smiled without seeming sadistic.

Mr. Rios was at his spot beside Miss Colon, his hands clasped behind his back as if he needed to restrain them. He seemed to whisper to her. Soft, mushy things. Edwin would watch them from his seat beside me, giving me the details, his shiny face looking worried. He always seemed sweaty, his fingers kind of damp.

"I toldju, I saw um holdin hands," he said. "An now lookit him, he's whispering sweet shits inta huh ear."

He quieted down when he noticed Miss Marti's evil eye sweeping over us like a prison-camp searchlight. There was silence. In her best military bark, Miss Marti ordered everyone to stand. Two lone, pathetic kids, dragooned by some unseen force, slowly came down the center aisle, each bearing a huge flag on a thick wooden pole. All I could make out was that great star-spangled unfurling, twitching thing that looked like it would fall as it approached over all those bored young heads. The Puerto Rican flag walked beside it, looking smaller and less confident. It clung to its pole.

"The Pledge," Miss Marti roared, putting her hand over the spot where her heart was rumored to be.

That's when I heard my father talking.

He was sitting on his bed, yelling about Chile, about what the CIA had done there. I was standing opposite him in my dingy Pro Keds. I knew about politics. I was eleven when I read William Shirer's book on Hitler. I was ready.

"All this country does is abuse Hispanic nations," my father said, turning a page of his *Post*, "tie them down, make them dependent. It says democracy with one hand while it protects and feeds fascist dictatorships with the other." His eyes blazed with a strange fire. I sat on the bed, on part of his *Post*, transfixed by his oratorical mastery. He had mentioned political things before, but not like this, not with such fiery conviction. I thought maybe it had to do with my reading Shirer. Maybe he had seen me reading that fat book and figured I was ready for real politics.

Using the knowledge I gained from the book, I defended the Americans. What fascism was he talking about, anyway? I knew we had stopped Hitler. That was a big deal, something to be proud of.

"Come out of fairy-tale land," he said scornfully. "Do you know what imperialism is?"

I didn't really, no.

"Well, why don't you read about that? Why don't you read about Juan Bosch and Allende, men who died fighting imperialism? They stood up against American big business. You should read about that instead of this crap about Hitler."

"But I like reading about Hitler," I said, feeling a little spurned. I didn't even mention that my fascination with Adolf led to my writing a biography of him, a book report one hundred and fifty pages long. It got an A-plus. Miss Colon stapled it to the bulletin board right outside the classroom, where it was promptly stolen.

"So, what makes you want to be a writer?" Miss Colon asked me quietly one day, when Edwin and I, always the helpful ones, volunteered to assist her in getting the classroom spiffed up for a Halloween party.

"I don't know. I guess my father," I replied, fiddling with plastic pumpkins self-consciously while images of my father began parading through my mind.

When I think back to my earliest image of my father, it is one of him sitting behind a huge rented typewriter, his fingers clacking away. He was a frustrated poet, radio announcer, and even stage actor. He had sent for diplomas from fly-by-night companies. He took acting lessons, went into broadcasting, even ended up on the ground floor of what is now Spanish radio, but his family talked him out of all of it. "You should find yourself real work, something substantial," they said, so he did. He dropped all those dreams that were never encouraged by anyone else and got a job at a Nedick's on Third Avenue. My pop the counterman.

Despite that, he kept writing. He recited his poetry into a huge reel-to-reel tape deck that he had, then he'd play it back and sit like a critic, brow furrowed, fingers stroking his lips. He would record strange sounds and play them back to me at outrageous speeds, until I believed that there were tiny people living inside the machine. I used to stand by him and watch him type, his black pompadour spilling over his forehead. There was energy pulsating all around him, and I wanted a part of it.

I was five years old when I first sat in his chair at the kitchen table and began pushing down keys, watching the letters magically appear on the page. I was entranced. My fascination with the typewriter began at that point. By the time I was ten, I was writing war stories, tales of pain and pathos culled from the piles of comic books I devoured. I wrote unreadable novels. With illustrations. My father wasn't impressed. I guess he was hard to impress. My terrific grades did not faze him, nor the fact that I was reading books as fat as milk crates. My unreadable novels piled up. I brought them to him at night to see if he would read them, but after a week of waiting I found them thrown in the bedroom closet, unread. I felt hurt and rejected, despite my mother's kind words. "He's just too busy to read them," she said to me one night when I mentioned it to her. He never brought them up, even when I quietly took them out of the closet one day or when he'd see me furiously hammering on one of his rented machines. I would tell him I wanted to be a writer, and he would smile sadly and pat my head, without a word.

"You have to find something serious to do with your life," he told me one night, after I had shown him my first play, eighty pages long. What was it I had read that got me into writing a play? Was it Arthur Miller?

Oscar Wilde? I don't remember, but I recall my determination to write a truly marvelous play about combat because there didn't seem to be any around.

"This is fun as a hobby," my father said, "but you can't get serious about this." His demeanor spoke volumes, but I couldn't stop writing. Novels, I called them, starting a new one every three days. The world was a blank page waiting for my words to recreate it, while the real world remained cold and lonely. My schoolmates didn't understand any of it, and because of the fat books I carried around, I was held in some fear. After all, what kid in his right mind would read a book if it wasn't assigned? I was sick of kids coming up to me and saying, "Gaw, lookit tha fat book. Ya teacha make ya read tha?" (No, I'm just reading it.) The kids would look at me as if I had just crawled out of a sewer. "Ya crazy, man." My father seemed to share that opinion. Only my teachers understood and encouraged my reading, but my father seemed to want something else from me.

Now, he treated me like an idiot for not knowing what imperialism was. He berated my books and one night handed me a copy of a book about Albizu Campos, the Puerto Rican revolutionary. I read it through in two sittings.

"Some of it seems true," I said.

"Some of it?" my father asked incredulously. "After what they did to him, you can sit there and act like a Yankee flag-waver?"

I watched the Yankee flag making its way up to the stage over indifferent heads, my father's scowling face haunting me, his words resounding in my head.

"Let me tell you something," my father sneered. "In school, all they do is talk about George Washington, right? The first president? The father of democracy? Well, he had slaves. We had our own Washington, and ours had real teeth."

As Old Glory reached the stage, a general clatter ensued.

"We had our own revolution," my father said, "and the United States crushed it with the flick of a pinkie."

Miss Marti barked her royal command. Everyone rose up to salute the flag.

Except me. I didn't get up. I sat in my creaking seat, hands on my knees. A girl behind me tapped me on the back. "Come on, stupid, get up." There was a trace of concern in her voice. I didn't move.

Miss Colon appeared. She leaned over, shaking me gently. "Are you sick? Are you okay?" Her soft hair fell over my neck like a blanket.

"No," I replied.

"What's wrong?" she asked, her face growing stern. I was beginning to feel claustrophobic, what with everyone standing all around me, bodies like walls. My friend Edwin, hand on his heart, watched from the corner of his eye. He almost looked envious, as if he wished he had thought of it. Murmuring voices around me began reciting the Pledge while Mr. Rios appeared, commandingly grabbing me by the shoulder and pulling me out of my seat into the aisle. Miss Colon was beside him, looking a little apprehensive.

"What is wrong with you?" he asked angrily. "You know you're supposed to stand up for the Pledge! Are you religious?"

"No," I said.

"Then what?"

"I'm not saluting that flag," I said.

"What?"

"I said, I'm not saluting that flag."

"Why the . . . ?" He calmed himself; a look of concern flashed over Miss Colon's face. "Why not?"

"Because I'm Puerto Rican. I ain't no American. And I'm not no Yankee flag-waver."

"You're supposed to salute the flag," he said angrily, shoving one of his fat fingers in my face. "You're not supposed to make up your own mind about it. You're supposed to do as you are told."

"I thought I was free," I said, looking at him and at Miss Colon.

"You are," Miss Colon said feebly. "That's why you should salute the flag."

"But shouldn't I do what I feel is right?"

"You should do what you are told!" Mr. Rios yelled into my face.

"I'm not playing no games with you, mister. You hear that music? That's the anthem. Now you go stand over there and put your hand over your heart." He made as if to grab my hand, but I pulled away.

"No!" I said sharply. "I'm not saluting that crummy flag! And you can't make me, either. There's nothing you can do about it."

"Oh yeah?" Mr. Rios roared. "We'll see about that!"

"Have you gone crazy?" Miss Colon asked as he led me away by the arm, down the hallway, where I could still hear the strains of the anthem. He walked me briskly into the principal's office and stuck me in a corner.

"You stand there for the rest of the day and see how you feel about it," he said viciously. "Don't you even think of moving from that spot!"

I stood there for close to two hours or so. The principal came and went, not even saying hi or hey or anything, as if finding kids in the corners of his office was a common occurrence. I could hear him talking on the phone, scribbling on pads, talking to his secretary. At one point I heard Mr. Rios outside in the main office.

"Some smart-ass. I stuck him in the corner. Thinks he can pull that shit. The kid's got no respect, man. I should get the chance to teach him some."

"Children today have no respect," I heard Miss Marti's reptile voice say as she approached, heels clacking like gunshots. "It has to be forced upon them."

She was in the room. She didn't say a word to the principal, who was on the phone. She walked right over to me. I could hear my heart beating in my ears as her shadow fell over me. Godzilla over Tokyo.

"Well, have you learned your lesson yet?" she asked, turning me from the wall with a finger on my shoulder. I stared at her without replying. My face burned, red hot. I hated it.

"You think you're pretty important, don't you? Well, let me tell you, you're nothing. You're not worth a damn. You're just a snotty-nosed little kid with a lot of stupid ideas." Her eyes bored holes through me, searing my flesh. I felt as if I were going to cry. I fought the urge. Tears rolled down my face anyway. They made her smile, her chapped lips twisting upwards like the mouth of a lizard.

"See? You're a little baby. You don't know anything, but you'd better learn your place." She pointed a finger in my face. "You do as you're told if you don't want big trouble. Now go back to class."

Her eyes continued to stab at me. I looked past her and saw Edwin waiting by the office door for me. I walked past her, wiping at my face. I could feel her eyes on me still, even as we walked up the stairs to the classroom. It was close to three already, and the skies outside the grated windows were cloudy.

"Man," Edwin said to me as we reached our floor, "I think you're crazy."

The classroom was abuzz with activity when I got there. Kids were chattering, getting their windbreakers from the closet, slamming their chairs up on their desks, filled with the euphoria of soon-home. I walked quietly over to my desk and took out my books. The other kids looked at me as if I were a ghost.

I went through the motions like a robot. When we got downstairs to the door, Miss Colon, dismissing the class, pulled me aside, her face compassionate and warm. She squeezed my hand.

"Are you okay?"

I nodded.

"That was a really crazy stunt there. Where did you get such an idea?"

I stared at her black flats. She was wearing tan panty hose and a black miniskirt. I saw Mr. Rios approaching with his class.

"I have to go," I said, and split, running into the frigid breezes and the silver sunshine.

At home, I lay on the floor of our living room, tapping my open notebook with the tip of my pen while the Beatles blared from my father's stereo. I felt humiliated and alone. Miss Marti's reptile face kept appearing in my notebook, her voice intoning, "Let me tell you, you're nothing." Yeah, right. Just what horrible hole did she crawl out of? Were those people really Puerto Ricans? Why should a Puerto Rican salute an American flag?

I put the question to my father, strolling into his bedroom, a tiny M-1 rifle that belonged to my G.I. Joe strapped to my thumb.

"Why?" he asked, loosening the reading glasses that were perched on

his nose, his newspaper sprawled open on the bed before him, his cigarette streaming blue smoke. "Because we are owned, like cattle. And because nobody has any pride in their culture to stand up for it."

I pondered those words, feeling as if I were being encouraged, but I
didn't dare tell him. I wanted to believe what I had done was a brave
and noble thing, but somehow I feared his reaction. I never could impress him with my grades, or my writing. This flag thing would probably upset him. Maybe he, too, would think I was crazy, disrespectful, a
"smart-ass" who didn't know his place. I feared that, feared my father
saying to me, in a reptile voice, "Let me tell you, you're nothing."

I suited up my G.I. Joe for combat, slipping on his helmet, strapping
on his field pack. I fixed the bayonet to his rifle, sticking it in his clutching hands so he seemed ready to fire. "A man's gotta do what a man's
gotta do." Was that John Wayne? I don't know who it was, but I did
what I had to do, still not telling my father. The following week, in the
auditorium, I did it again. This time, everyone noticed. The whole place
fell into a weird hush as Mr. Rios screamed at me.

I ended up in my corner again, this time getting a prolonged, pen-
sive stare from the principal before I was made to stare at the wall for
two more hours. My mind zoomed past my surroundings. In one
strange vision, I saw my crony Edwin climbing up Miss Colon's curvy
legs, giving me every detail of what he saw.

"Why?" Miss Colon asked frantically. "This time you don't leave until you tell me why." She was holding me by the arm, masses of kids flying by, happy blurs that faded into the sunlight outside the door.

"Because I'm Puerto Rican, not American," I blurted out in a weary
torrent. "That makes sense, don't it?"

"So am I," she said, "but we're in America!" She smiled. "Don't you
think you could make some kind of compromise?" She tilted her head
to one side and said, "Aw, c'mon," in a little-girl whisper.

"What about standing up for what you believe in? Doesn't that matter? You used to talk to us about Kent State and protesting. You said
those kids died because they believed in freedom, right? Well, I feel like
them now. I wanna make a stand."

She sighed with evident aggravation. She caressed my hair. For a moment, I thought she was going to kiss me. She was going to say something, but just as her pretty lips parted, I caught Mr. Rios approaching.

"I don't wanna see him," I said, pulling away.

"No, wait," she said gently.

"He's gonna deck me," I said to her.

"No, he's not," Miss Colon said, as if challenging him, her eyes taking him in as he stood beside her.

"No, I'm not," he said. "Listen here. Miss Colon was talking to me about you, and I agree with her." He looked like a nervous little boy in front of the class, making his report. "You have a lot of guts. Still, there are rules here. I'm willing to make a deal with you. You go home and think about this. Tomorrow I'll come see you." I looked at him skeptically, and he added, "to talk."

"I'm not changing my mind," I said. Miss Colon exhaled painfully.

"If you don't, it's out of my hands." He frowned and looked at her. She shook her head, as if she were upset with him.

I reread the book about Albizu. I didn't sleep a wink that night. I didn't tell my father a word, even though I almost burst from the effort. At night, alone in my bed, images attacked me. I saw Miss Marti and Mr. Rios debating Albizu Campos. I saw him in a wheelchair with a flag draped over his body like a holy robe. They would not do that to me. They were bound to break me the way Albizu was broken, not by young smiling American troops bearing chocolate bars, but by conniving, double-dealing, self-serving Puerto Rican landowners and their ilk, who dared say they were the future. They spoke of dignity and democracy while teaching Puerto Ricans how to cling to the great coat of that powerful northern neighbor. Puerto Rico, the shining star, the great lapdog of the Caribbean. I saw my father, the Nationalist hero, screaming from his podium, his great oration stirring everyone around him to acts of bravery. There was a shining arrogance in his eyes as he stared out over the sea of faces mouthing his name, a sparkling audacity that invited and incited. There didn't seem to be fear anywhere in him, only the urge to rush to the attack, with his armband and revolutionary tunic. I stared up at him, transfixed. I stood by the podium, his personal adjutant, while his voice rang through the stadium. "We are not, nor will we ever be, Yankee flag-wavers!" The roar that followed drowned out the whole world.

The following day, I sat in my seat, ignoring Miss Colon as she neatly drew triangles on the board with the help of plastic stencils. She was using colored chalk, her favorite. Edwin, sitting beside me, was beaning girls with spitballs that he fired through his hollowed-out Bic pen. They didn't cry out. They simply enlisted the help of a girl named Gloria who sat a few desks behind him. She very skillfully nailed him with a thick wad of gum. It stayed in his hair until Edwin finally went running to Miss Colon. She used her huge teacher's scissors. I couldn't stand it. They all seemed trapped in a world of trivial things, while I swam in a mire of oppression. I walked through lunch as if in a trance, a prisoner on death row waiting for the heavy steps of his executioners. I watched Edwin lick at his regulation cafeteria ice cream, sandwiched between two sheets of paper. I was once like him, laughing and joking, lining up for a stickball game in the yard without a care. Now it all seemed lost to me, as if my youth had been burned out of me by a book.

Shortly after lunch, Mr. Rios appeared. He talked to Miss Colon for a while by the door as the room filled with a bubbling murmur. Then, he motioned for me. I walked through the sudden silence as if in slow motion.

"Well," he said to me as I stood in the cool hallway, "have you thought about this?"

"Yeah," I said, once again seeing my father on the podium, his voice thundering.

"And?"

"I'm not saluting that flag."

Miss Colon fell against the doorjamb as if exhausted. Exasperation passed over Mr. Rios' rodent features.

"I thought you said you'd think about it," he thundered.

"I did. I decided I was right."

"*You* were right?" Mr. Rios was losing his patience. I stood calmly by the wall.

"I told you," Miss Colon whispered to him.

"Listen," he said, ignoring her, "have you heard of the story of the man who had no country?"

I stared at him.

"Well? Have you?"

"No," I answered sharply; his mouse eyes almost crossed with anger at my insolence. "Some stupid fairy tale ain't gonna change my mind anyway. You're treating me like I'm stupid, and I'm not."

"Stop acting like you're some mature adult! You're not. You're just a puny kid."

"Well, this puny kid still ain't gonna salute that flag."

"You were born here," Miss Colon interjected patiently, trying to calm us both down. "Don't you think you at least owe this country some respect? At least?"

"I had no choice about where I was born. And I was born poor."

"So what?" Mr. Rios screamed. "There are plenty of poor people who respect the flag. Look around you, dammit! You see any rich people here? I'm not rich either!" He tugged on my arm. "This country takes care of Puerto Rico, don't you see that? Don't you know anything about politics?"

"Do you know what imperialism is?"

The two of them stared at each other.

"I don't believe you," Mr. Rios murmured.

"Puerto Rico is a colony," I said, a direct quote of Albizu's. "Why I gotta respect that?"

Miss Colon stared at me with her black saucer eyes, a slight trace of a grin on her features. It encouraged me. In that one moment, I felt strong, suddenly aware of my territory and my knowledge of it. I no longer felt like a boy but some kind of soldier, my bayonet stained with the blood of my enemy. There was no doubt about it. Mr. Rios was the enemy, and I was beating him. The more he tried to treat me like a child, the more defiant I became, his arguments falling like twisted armor. He shut his eyes and pressed the bridge of his nose.

"You're out of my hands," he said.

Miss Colon gave me a sympathetic look before she vanished into the classroom again. Mr. Rios led me downstairs without another word. His face was completely red. I expected to be put in my corner again, but this time Mr. Rios sat me down in the leather chair facing the principal's desk. He stepped outside, and I could hear the familiar clack-clack that could only belong to Miss Marti's reptile legs. They were talking in whispers. I expected her to come in at any moment, but the principal walked in instead. He came in quietly, holding a folder in his hand. His soft brown eyes and beard made him look compassionate, rounded cheeks making him seem friendly. His desk plate solemnly stated: Mr. Sepulveda, PRINCIPAL. He fell into his seat rather unceremoniously, opened the folder, and crossed his hands over it.

"Well, well, well," he said softly, with a tight-lipped grin. "You've created quite a stir, young man." It sounded to me like movie dialogue.

"First of all, let me say I know about you. I have your record right here, and everything in it is very impressive. Good grades, good attitude, your teachers all have adored you. But I wonder if maybe this hasn't gone to your head? Because everything is going for you here, and you're throwing it all away."

He leaned back in his chair. "We have rules, all of us. There are rules even I must live by. People who don't obey them get disciplined. This will all go on your record, and a pretty good one you've had so far. Why ruin it? This'll follow you for life. You don't want to end up losing a good job opportunity in government or in the armed forces because as a child you indulged your imagination and refused to salute the flag? I know you can't see how childish it all is now, but you must see it, and because you're smarter than most, I'll put it to you in terms you can understand.

"To me, this is a simple case of rules and regulations. Someday, when you're older," he paused here, obviously amused by the sound of his own voice, "you can go to rallies and protest marches and express your rebellious tendencies. But right now, you are a minor, under this school's jurisdiction. That means you follow the rules, no matter what you think of them. You can join the Young Lords later."

I stared at him, overwhelmed by his huge desk, his pompous mannerisms, and status. I would agree with everything, I felt, and then, the following week, I would refuse once again. I would fight him then, even though he hadn't tried to humiliate me or insult my intelligence. I would continue to fight, until I . . .

"I spoke with your father," he said.

I started. "My father?" Vague images and hopes flared through my mind briefly.

"Yes. I talked to him at length. He agrees with me that you've gotten a little out of hand."

My blood reversed direction in my veins. I felt as if I were going to collapse. I gripped the armrests of my chair. There was no way this could be true, no way at all! My father was supposed to ride in like the cavalry, not abandon me to the enemy! I pressed my wet eyes with my fingers. It must be a lie.

"He blames himself for your behavior," the principal said. "He's already here," Mr. Rios said from the door, motioning my father inside. Seeing him wearing his black weather-beaten trench coat almost asphyxiated me. His eyes, red with concern, pulled at me painfully. He came over to me first while the principal rose slightly, as if greeting a head of state. There was a look of dread on my father's face as he looked at me. He seemed utterly lost.

"Mr. Sepulveda," he said, "I never thought a thing like this could happen. My wife and I try to bring him up right. We encourage him to read and write and everything. But you know, this is a shock."

"It's not that terrible, Mr. Rodriguez. You've done very well with him, he's an intelligent boy. He just needs to learn how important obedience is."

"Yes," my father said, turning to me, "yes, you have to obey the rules. You can't do this. It's wrong." He looked at me grimly, as if working on a math problem. One of his hands caressed my head.

There were more words, in Spanish now, but I didn't hear them. I felt like I was falling down a hole. My father, my creator, renouncing his creation, repentant. Not an ounce of him seemed prepared to stand up for me, to shield me from attack. My tears made all the faces around me melt.

"So you see," the principal said to me as I rose, my father clutching me to him, "if you ever do this again, you will be hurting your father as well as yourself."

I hated myself. I wiped at my face desperately, trying not to make a spectacle of myself. I was just a kid, a tiny kid. Who in the hell did I think I was? I'd have to wait until I was older, like my father, in order to have "convictions."

"I don't want to see you in here again, okay?" the principal said sternly. I nodded dumbly, my father's arm around me as he escorted me through the front office to the door that led to the hallway, where a multitude of children's voices echoed up and down its length like tolling bells.

"Are you crazy?" my father half whispered to me in Spanish as we stood there. "Do you know how embarrassing this all is? I didn't think you were this stupid. Don't you know anything about dignity, about respect? How could you make a spectacle of yourself? Now you make us all look stupid."

He quieted down as Mr. Rios came over to take me back to class. My father gave me a squeeze and told me he'd see me at home. Then, I walked with a somber Mr. Rios, who oddly wrapped an arm around me all the way back to the classroom.

"Here you go," he said softly as I entered the classroom, and everything fell quiet. I stepped in and walked to my seat without looking at anyone. My cheeks were still damp, my eyes red. I looked like I had been tortured. Edwin stared at me, then he pressed my hand under the table.

"I thought you were dead," he whispered.

Miss Colon threw me worried glances all through the remainder of the class. I wasn't paying attention. I took out my notebook, but my strength ebbed away. I just put my head on the desk and shut my eyes, reliving my father's betrayal. If what I did was so bad, why did I feel more ashamed of him than I did of myself? His words, once so rich and vibrant, now fell to the floor, leaves from a dead tree.

At the end of the class, Miss Colon ordered me to stay after school. She got Mr. Rios to take the class down along with his, and she stayed with me in the darkened room. She shut the door on all the exuberant hallway noise and sat down on Edwin's desk, beside me, her black pumps on his seat.

"Are you okay?" she asked softly, grasping my arm. I told her every-thing, especially about my father's betrayal. I thought he would be the cavalry, but he was just a coward.

"Tss. Don't be so hard on your father," she said. "He's only trying to do what's best for you."

"And how's this the best for me?" I asked, my voice growing hoarse with hurt.

"I know it's hard for you to understand, but he really was trying to take care of you."

I stared at the blackboard.

"He doesn't understand me," I said, wiping my eyes.

"You'll forget," she whispered.

"No, I won't. I'll remember every time I see that flag. I'll see it and think, 'My father doesn't understand me.'"

Miss Colon sighed deeply. Her fingers were warm on my head, stroking my hair. She gave me a kiss on the cheek. She walked me down-stairs, pausing by the doorway. Scores of screaming, laughing kids brushed past us.

"If it's any consolation, I'm on your side," she said, squeezing my arm. I smiled at her, warmth spreading through me. "Go home and lis-ten to the Beatles," she added with a grin.

I stepped out into the sunshine, came down the white stone steps, and stood on the sidewalk. I stared at the towering school building, white and perfect in the sun, indomitable. Across the street, the dingy row of tattered uneven tenements where I lived. I thought of my father. Her words made me feel sorry for him, but I felt sorrier for myself. I couldn't understand back then about a father's love and what a father might give to insure his son safe transit. He had already navigated treacherous waters and now couldn't have me rock the boat. I still had to learn that he had made peace with The Enemy, that The Enemy was already in us. Like the flag I must salute, we were inseparable, yet his compromise made me feel ashamed and defeated. Then I knew I had to find my own peace, away from the bondage of obedience. I had to ac-cept that flag, and my father, someone I would love forever, even if at times to my young, feeble mind he seemed a little imperfect.

GLOSSARY

Chile and the CIA (95): In 1970, the CIA, unsuccessful at preventing the election of socialist candidate Salvador Allende as president, continually tried to undermine support for Allende by creating a "coup climate" with sponsored acts of sabotage and terror, demonstrations and strikes. The Chilean military, with its respect for the democratic process of Allende's election, gradually lost faith in him, believing in the rumor and innuendo of alleged Marxist atrocities and fearing that a Soviet base would be established. A coup finally came in September 1973. Allende was said to have committed suicide (though some believe that he was murdered by the CIA), and many Chileans, from lists provided by the CIA, were tortured and killed as "radicals." Under the military committee headed by General Augusto Pinochet, torture of dissidents became routine and drew Nazi ex-patriots from all over South America to continue the work that they had begun in the Nazi death camps.

William Shirer's book on Hitler (95): *The Rise and Fall of the Third Reich*, at 1,264 pages, is the most complete single-volume account of the history of Nazi Germany ever written by war correspondent and journalist William L. Shirer.

Juan Bosch (95): A historian, short-story writer, and educator, Bosch, founder of the Dominican Revolutionary Party in 1939, became the first democratically elected president of the Dominican Republic after the assassination of Raphael Trujillo in 1961.

Albizu Campos (97): A leader and president of the Puerto Rican Nationalist Party and advocate of Puerto Rican independence from the United States by whatever means necessary.

Godzilla over Tokyo (99): reference to a 1954 film about a giant lizard that all but destroys Tokyo.

Young Lords (105): a 1960s Puerto Rican nationalist group located in several American cities, notably Chicago and New York; they focused most of their activity around self-determination for Puerto Rico and on local community issues such as gentrification, health, and police abuse.

THE ALUMNI INTERVIEW

by David Levithan

The forbidden pleasures of a secret love take a novel turn in this story about two high school senior boys who are lovers. It takes place while the boys are also engaged in the arduous and competitive rat race of applying to college. Ian, the narrator, is open about his sexual identity and is a top student, slated for one of "those" schools, while his boyfriend, Thom, shorter, more reticent about himself but no less passionate, does not appear to be as ambitious. Ian, by a twist of fate, is scheduled for an alumni interview with Thom's father for his top-choice university. During this interview, he discovers more about Thom from his father than Thom's father learns about him.

This is a story about coming out, but it's also about what you can know about someone from a transcript (which Ian aptly calls "a bloodless, calendar version of my life"). Already well acquainted with his favorite university, Ian does not need to ask any more questions about it; instead, he feels the urge to go beyond the calendar version of Thom's life to try to discover why Thom's father chooses to remain ignorant of who his son is, despite Thom's attempts to signal him. The actual interview—and Ian's hilarious attempt to cover for Thom's sake what he would never cover for himself (the GSA, Gay/Straight Alliance, becomes "God Smiles Always"; the Pride March becomes a school-spirit mascot parade,

*with students marching dressed as lions)—ends in an unexpected
confrontation and revelation.*

*Interesting here is the change in perspective. We see through
Levithan's willingness to take us behind the scenes that Thom may
not be the expendable person that his father takes him for, nor the
more passive individual that we read him as. Much of what the
narrator tells Thom's father about himself beyond his transcript
(and that Thom's father admires) is scripted from Thom and the
metaphysical conversations that he and Ian have had together. We
can appreciate Thom even more having endured his father, a man
without faith in his son. By the story's end, Thom comes into his
own, and we wonder whether in fact both boys are equally quali-
fied for this prestigious university—or whether such a place de-
serves either one of them.*

*David Levithan is a children's book editor in New York. He is
the author of several novels, such as* Boy Meets Girl, Wide
Awake, *and* Are We There Yet? *He is also the author of a volume
of poetry,* The Realm of Possibility. *He started writing stories as
valentine presents for his friends. At sixteen, he was on the fencing
team, Quiz Bowl, and took AP physics. He views the story, with its
sixteen-year-old narrator, as representing the first nervous step toward the future (college), intersected with love and identity.*

*This story's psychologically abusive father can be compared to
the father in Rodriguez's "The Boy Without a Flag," who, while
not abusive, seems equally clueless about his sensitive and talented
son. As a coming out story, it can be compared to ZZ Packer's
"Drinking Coffee Elsewhere," in which Dina, the narrator, undergoes a self-awakening.*

I t is never easy to have a college interview with your closeted boyfriend's
father. Would I have applied to this university if I had known that of
all the alumni in the greater metropolitan area, it would choose Mr.
Wright to find me worthy or unworthy? Maybe. But maybe not.

Thom took it worse than I did. We had been making out in the boys' room, with him standing on the toilet so no one would know we were in the stall together. Even though I was younger, he was a little shorter and had much better balance than I did. Dating him, I'd learned to kiss quietly, and from different inclinations.

He found the letter as he searched through my bag for a Certs.

"You heard from them?" he asked.

I nodded.

"An interview?"

"Yeah," I answered casually. "With your dad."

"Yeah, right."

The bell had rung. The bathroom sounded empty. I looked under the stall door to see if anyone's feet were around, then opened it.

"No, really," I said.

His face turned urinal-white.

"You can't."

"I have to. I can't exactly refuse an alumni interview."

He thought about it for a second and then concluded, succinctly, "Shit."

I had almost met Mr. Wright before. He had come home early one day when his office's air-conditioning had broken down. Luckily, Thom's room is right over the garage, so the garage door heralded his arrival with an appropriately earthquakian noise. Thom was tugging on my shirt at the time, and as a result, I lost at least two buttons. At first, I figured it was just his mom. But the footsteps beat out a different tune. I did the mature, responsible thing, which was to hide under the bed for the next three hours. Happily, Thom hid with me. We found ways to occupy ourselves. Then, once the family was safely wrapped up in dinner, I climbed out the window. I could've gone out the window earlier, but I'd been having a pretty good time.

The trick was getting Thom to enjoy it, too. I wasn't his first boyfriend, but I was the first he could admit to himself. We'd reached the stage where he felt comfortable liberating his affections when we were alone together, or even within our closest circle of friends. But outside that circle, he got nervous. He became paralyzed at the very thought of his parents discovering his—*our*—secret.

We'd been going out without going out for three months.

I'd picked my first choice for college before Thom and I had gotten together, long before I'd known his father had gone to the same school. Thom couldn't believe I wanted to go to a place that had helped spawn the person his father had become.

"Your dad wasn't in the drama program," I pointed out. "And I think he was there before Vietnam."

It helped that my first-choice college was in the same city as Thom's. We'd vowed that we wouldn't think or talk about such things. But of course we did. All the time.

We were trapped in the limbo between where we were and where we wanted to be. The limbo of our age.

The day of the alumni interview, we were both as nervous as a tightrope walker with vertigo. We spun through the day at school, the clock hands spiraling us to certain doom. We found every possible excuse to touch each other—hand on shoulder, fingers on back, stolen kisses, loving looks. Everything that would stop the moment his father walked into the room.

Thom gave me a ride home, then drove back to his house. I counted to a hundred, then walked over.

He answered the door. We'd agreed on this beforehand. I didn't want to be in his house without seeing him. I wanted to know he was there.

"I've got it!" he yelled to the study as he opened the door.

"Here we go," I said.

He leaned into me and whispered, "I love you."

And I whispered, "I love you, too."

We didn't have time for any more than that. So we said all that needed to be said.

I'd never been in Mr. Wright's study before. The man fit in well with the furniture. Sturdy. Wooden. Upright.

It is a strange thing to meet your boyfriend's father when the father doesn't know you're his son's boyfriend—or even that his son *has* a

boyfriend. It puts you at an advantage—you know more than he does—
and also puts you at a disadvantage. The things you know aren't things
you can let him know.

I was not ordinarily known for my discretion. But I was trying to
make an exception in this case. It seemed like an exceptional situation.

Thom stood in the doorway, hovering.

"Dad, this is Ian."

"Have a seat, Ian," the man said, no handshake. "Thank you, Thom."

Thom stayed one beat too long, the last beat of linger that we'd
grown accustomed to, the sign of an unwanted good-bye. But then the
situation hit him again, and he left the room without a farewell glance.

I turned to Mr. Wright as the door closed behind him.

I can do this, I thought. Then: *And even if I can't, I have to.*

Mr. Wright had clearly done the alumni interview thing a hundred
times before. As if reciting a message beamed in from central campus,
he talked about how this interview was not supposed to be a formal one;
it was all about getting to know me, and me getting to know the college
where he had spent some of the best years of his life. He had a few questions to ask, and he was sure that I had many questions to ask as well.

In truth, I had already visited the campus twice and knew people
who went there. I didn't have a single question to ask. Or, more accu-
rately, the questions I wanted to ask didn't have anything to do with the
university in question.

Thom says you've never in all his life hugged him. Why is that?

*What can I do to make you see how wonderful he is? If I told you the
way I still smile after he kisses me—the way my head feels like helium and
my heart feels like a song, not because it's a sexy kiss, but because it's a kind
kiss—is there any possible way you'd understand what he means to me?*

*Don't you know how wrong it is when you wave a twenty-dollar bill in
front of your son and tell him that when he gets a girlfriend, you'll be happy
to pay for the first date?*

And then I'd add:

My father isn't like you at all. So don't tell me it's normal parent behavior.

I am not by nature an angry person. But as this man kept saying he
wanted to get to know me, I wanted to throw that phrase right back at

him. How could he possibly get to know me when he didn't want to know his son?

Taking out a legal pad and consulting a folder with my transcript in it, he asked me about school and classes. As I prattled on about AP Biology and my English awards, I kept thinking about the word *transcript*. What exactly did it transcribe? My life. No, not that. It was a bloodless, calendar version of my life. It transcribed nothing but the things I was doing in order to get into a good college. It was the biography of my paper self. Getting to know it wasn't getting to know me at all.

Sitting in that room, talking to Mr. Wright, I knew I had to get all of my identities in order. I realized how many identities I had, at a time when I really should have been focusing on having one.

"Have you taken economics?" Mr. Wright asked.

"No," I answered. It had never occurred to me to take economics.

"Why not?" he harrumphed.

I explained that our school offered only one economics class, and I had a conflict. A complete lie, but how would he know?

"I see."

He wrote something down, then told me how important economics was to an education, and how he would have never gotten through college—not to mention life—without a firm foundation in economics.

I nodded. I agreed. I succumbed to the lecture, because I really didn't have any choice. Judgmental. I considered the word *judgmental*. The mental state of always judging. His tone. I knew he wasn't singling me out. I knew this was probably the way he always was.

There were times I had gotten mad at Thom. Argument mad. Cutting-comment mad. Because his inability to be open made me a little closed. I didn't want to be a conditional boyfriend. I didn't want to be anybody's secret. As much as I said I understood, I never entirely understood.

Can't you just tell them? I'd ask. After they became the excuse for why we couldn't go out on Saturday. After they became the reason he pulled his hand away from mine as we were walking through town—*what if they drove by?* But then I'd feel bad, feel wrong. Because I knew this was not the way he wanted it to be. That even though we were sixteen, we

were still that one leap away from independence. We were still caught on
the dependence side, staring over the divide.

Now, bearing the brunt of his father's disapproval, I understood.
Not all of it. But a little more.

". . . too many of you students ignore economics. You dillydally. You
spend your time on such expendable things. Like Thom. You know
Thom, right? No focus. He has no focus. He wouldn't be right for this
university. You show more promise. But I have to say, you need to make
sure you don't spend time on expendable things. . . ."

And suddenly I was sick of it.

I looked to the door and saw something. A shadow in the keyhole.
And I knew. Thom had never left. He was on the outside of the door,
holding his breath for me. Trying to keep quiet. Stay quiet, because his
father was around.

I was sick of it.

The economics lecture was over. Mr. Wright didn't alter his tone
when he asked, "What are your interests?"

"Your son in my room," I said.

"Excuse me?"

"The sun and the moon," I said. "Astronomy."

Mr. Wright looked pleased. "I didn't know kids liked astronomy
anymore. When I was a child, we all had telescopes. Now you just have
telephones and televisions instead."

"You couldn't be more right, sir." I nodded emphatically, as if I believed for a second that he hadn't watched television or spoken on the
telephone as a child. "A telescope is a fine instrument. And there's something about the stars. . . ." I paused dramatically.

"Yes?"

"Well, there's something about the stars that makes you realize both
the smallness and the enormity of everything, isn't there?"

Thom had first told me this as we lay on our backs on a golf course
outside of town, too late for the twilight, but early enough to catch the
rise of the moon, the pinprick arrival of the stars. His words were like a
grasping.

Now here was his father, agreeing with him, through me.

"Yes, yes, absolutely," Mr. Wright said.

I looked to the keyhole, to Thom's shadow there. Knowing he was near. Speaking to him in this code.

Saying to his father what I've said to him.

"Sometimes I wish we could open ourselves up to each other as much as we do to the sky. To the smallness and the enormity."

"I see," Mr. Wright said, looking back at his notes. "And do you have any other interests?

Must interests be interesting? That is, must they be interesting to someone other than yourself? This is why I hate these interviews, these applications. *List your interests.* I wanted to say, *Look, interests aren't things that can be listed. My interests are impulses, are moods, are never-ending. Sometimes it's as simple as Thom holding my hand. Sometimes it's as complicated as wanting to be able to hold his hand in front of his father. That want is an interest of mine.*

"I swim," I answered instead.

"Are you on the swim team?" Mr. Wright looked vaguely interested.

"No."

"Why is that?"

"I like to do it alone."

"I see."

He wrote something else down. *Not a team player,* no doubt.

"Thom is on the swim team," he added.

"I know," I said.

"Very competitive." As if that was the marker of a fine activity.

"So I've heard." I had grown so tired of competitions. Of sacrificing the nights of stargazing in order to make the paper self as impressive as possible.

"Do you know Thom well?"

"We're friends," I said. Not a lie, but not the whole truth.

"Well, do me a favor and make sure he stays on track."

"Oh, I will."

He picked up my transcript again, frowned, and asked, "What is the GSA?"

It had now gone from uncomfortable to downright fierce. I tried to imagine him coming to one of our Gay-Straight Alliance meetings. I tried to imagine that if I told him what it was, he would understand. I tried to think of a way to avoid his shiver of revulsion, his dismissive disdain.

Thom had tried to signal him once. I'd placed a pink triangle pin on his bag after a meeting, and he didn't take it off when he got home. Instead he put the bag in a spot where it could be seen. But it didn't work. Mr. Wright brushed past it. He didn't notice or didn't say. When all Thom wanted was for him to notice without being told.

"GSA stands for God Smiles Always, sir," I said with my most sincere expression.

"I didn't know the high school had one of those."

"It's pretty new, sir."

"How did it start?"

"Because of the school musical," I earnestly explained. "A lot of the kids in the musical wanted to start it."

"Really?"

"It was *Jesus Christ Superstar,* sir. I think we were all moved by how much of a superstar Jesus was. It made us want to work to make God smile."

"And the school is okay with this?" Mr. Wright asked, his eyebrow raising slightly, a vague irritation in his voice.

"Yes, sir. It's all about bringing people together."

"It says here you were on the dance committee for the GSA?"

I nodded, imagining Thom's reaction behind the door. "I was one of the coordinators," I elaborated. "We wanted to create a wholesome atmosphere for our fellow students. We only played Christian dance music. It's like Christian rock music, only the beat is a little faster. The lyrics are mostly the same."

"Did Thom go to that dance?"

"Yes, sir. I believe I saw him there." *In fact, he was my date. Afterwards, we had sex.*

"It also says you were involved in something called the Pride March?"

"Yes. We dress up as a pride of lions and we march. It's a school-spirit thing. Our mascot is a lion."

He did not look amused. "Do you march in costume?"

"Yes. But we don't wear the heads of costumes."

"Why not?"

"Because we're proud to be wearing them. We want people to know who we are."

He looked back down at my application.

"It says the Pride March is tied to Coming Out Day."

Damn. The transcript might as well have been written in lavender ink.

I faked a laugh. "Oh, that. It's another school-spirit thing. First day of the football season, someone dresses up as a lion and comes out from under the bleachers onto the field. If we see its shadow, we know the season will be a long one. If not, we know it's pretty much over before it's begun. The whole school gets really into it."

"I can't recall Thom mentioning that."

"He hasn't? Maybe he thought it was a secret."

"I know what's going on here."

Mr. Wright put down the transcript.

Now it was my turn to say, "Excuse me?"

"I know what's going on here," Mr. Wright said again, more pronounced. "And I don't like it one bit."

"I'm sorry, sir, but . . ."

He stood up from his chair. "I will *not* be ridiculed in my own house. That you should have the *presumption* to apply to my alma mater and then to sit there and *mock* me. I know what you are, and I will not stand for it here."

I wish I could say that I hurled a response right back at him. But mostly, I was stunned. To have such a blast directed at me. To be yelled at.

I couldn't move. I couldn't figure out what to say.

Then the door opened and Thom said, "Stop it. Stop it right now."

Suddenly Mr. Wright and I had something in common—disbelief. But I also had faith. In Thom.

"If you say one more word, I'm going to scream," he said to his father. "I don't give a shit what you say to me, but you leave Ian out of it, okay? You're being a total asshole, and that's not okay."

Mr. Wright started to yell. But it was empty yelling. Desperate yelling. And while he yelled, Thom came over to me and took my hand. I stood up and together we faced his father. And his father fell silent. And his father began to cry.

As if the world had ended.

I could feel Thom shaking, the tremors of that world exploding. As we stood there. As we watched. As we broke free from limbo.

And I wanted to say, *All you need to know about me is that I love your son. And if you get to know your son, you will know what that means.*

But the words were no longer mine to say.

Except here. I am writing this to let you know why it is likely that you received a very harsh alumni interview report about me. I'm hoping my campus interview will provide a contrast. (Thom and I will be heading your way next week.) I do not hold it against your university that a person like Mr. Wright should have received such a poor education. I understand those were different times then, and I am glad these are different times now.

It is never easy to have a college interview with your closeted boyfriend's father. It is never easy, I'm sure, to conduct a college interview with your closeted son's boyfriend. And, I am positive, it is least easy of all to be the boy in the hallway, listening.

But if I've learned one thing, it's this:

It's not the easy things that get you to know a person.

Know, and love.

OBITUARY

by Lois-Ann Yamanaka

In this excerpt from Yamanaka's novel Wild Meat and the Bully
Burgers, *the young narrator, Lovey, describes her school experience.
Through it, she expresses the shame that she feels about pidgin, the
language indicating that she and her classmates, according to her
English teacher, "sound uneducated" and will have no future.
Pidgin is in fact the unofficial language of Hawaii, originally
conceived so that immigrants—Japanese, Chinese, Portuguese, Filipino, as well as native Hawaiian and mainland American—could
do business together (ironically, after years of struggling to keep the
different ethnic groups who worked on the plantations from com-
municating with one another). But pidgin now represents Lovey's
shame about her Japanese Hawaiian family, the traditional dishes
they eat, the housing project where they live, their broken-down car,
their worn-out and dirty clothes, her "low-class" life. The question
becomes will Standard English help her toward a more fulfilling
life?*

*Lovey's sense of herself as hopelessly stupid is further confirmed
by her placement in the "dumb" math class and a particularly
hurtful bias—that "all Japs sappose for be smut." But since she
cannot reduce fractions, she's "Jap Crap. . . . Rice Eye, good-for-
nuttin' Pearl Harba bomba." Lovey's attempt to deflect attention
from her own deficiencies onto Pillis, the diminutive Filipina*

Hawaiian, offers no real respite. Creating a scapegoat when she has been and continues to be one herself only makes Lovey feel worse about the way that her language inevitably seems to identify her.

When Lovey and her classmates are asked to compose their own obituaries, she has an unusual opportunity to ponder death, religious beliefs, and her love for a grandmother who lives on the island of Moloka'i. By the time Lovey writes the final draft, we are not sure whether she intends to submit it or whether it simply provides proof positive that Standard English will not impede her eloquence, inevitably shaped by the pidgin that informs it.

Lois-Ann Yamanaka was born on the island of Moloka'i but grew up in Pahala on the Big Island of Hawaii. Many of her critically acclaimed works are written in Hawaiian Pidgin. In 1993, she received the Pushcart Prize for Poetry for Saturday Night at the Pahula Theatre. *That volume, along with her novel* Blu's Hanging, *sparked controversy in the Asian American literary community for their alleged stereotype promoting of Filipino men. Indeed, in this excerpt, Lovey recognizes that she has an easy target in Pillis, the Filipina Hawaiian whose social status appears to be below her own.*

This story can best be compared to Tucker's "How I Learned to Fly" and to Lowenthal's "Ordinary Pain" for their studies of how fantasy serves to replace realities that fail to compensate for a real or imagined loss. It can also be compared to Rodriguez's "The Boy Without a Flag" and Alexie's "Indian Education" for its depiction of how the impact of school can extend beyond the classroom.

E nglish class, we got Mr. Harvey. Jerome looks at me and puts his middle finger on the desk to our worst teacher, because Mr. Harvey says for the fiftieth time this year:

"No one will want to give you a job. You sound uneducated. You will be looked down upon. You're speaking a low-class form of good Standard English. Continue, and you'll go nowhere in life. Listen, students, I'm telling

you the truth like no one else will. Because they don't know how to say it to
you. I do. Speak Standard English. DO NOT speak pidgin. You will only be
hurting yourselves."

I tell Jerry, "No make f-you finger to Mr. Harvey. We gotta try talk
the way he say. No more dis and dat and wuz and cuz 'cause we only
hurting ourselfs."

I don't tell anyone, not even Jerry, how ashamed I am of pidgin English. Ashamed of my mother and father, the food we eat, chicken luau
with can spinach and tripe stew. The place we live, down the house lots
in the Hicks Homes that all look alike except for the angle of the house
from the street. The car we drive, my father's brown Land Rover without the back window. The clothes we wear, sometimes we have to wear
the same pants in the same week and the same shoes until it breaks.
Don't have no choice.

Ashamed of my aunties and uncles at baby luaus, yakudoshis, and
mochi pounding parties. "Eh, bradda Larry, bring me one nada Primo,
brah. One cold one fo' real kine. I rey-day, I rey-day, no woray, brah.
Uncap that sucka and come home to Uncle Stevie." I love my Uncle
Steven, though, and the Cracker Jacks he brings for me every time he
visits my mother. One for me and one for my sister, Calhoon. But I'm
so shame.

Ashame too of all my cousins, the way they talk and act dumb, like
how they like Kikaida Man and "Ho, brah, you seen Kikaida Man kick
Rainbow Man's ass in front Hon Sport at the Hilo Shopping Center?
Ho, brah, and I betchu Godzilla kick King Kong's ass too. Betchu ten
dollas, brah, two fur balls kicking ass in downtown Metropolis, nah,
downtown Hilo, brah."

And my grandma. Her whole house smells like mothballs, not just in
the closets but in every drawer too. And her pots look a million years old
with dents all over. Grandma must know every recipe with mustard
cabbage in it. She can quote from the Bible for everything you do in a
day. Walks everywhere she goes downtown Kaunakakai, sucks fish eyes
and eats the parsley from our plates at Midnight Inn.

And nobody looks or talks like a haole. Or eats like a haole. Nobody
says nothing the way Mr. Harvey tells us to practice talking in class.

Sometimes I secretly wish to be haole. That my name could be Betty Smith or Annie Anderson or Debbie Cole, wife of Dennis Cole who lives at 2222 Maple Street with a white station wagon with wood panel on the side, a dog named Spot, a cat named Kitty, and I wear white gloves. Dennis wears a hat to work. There's a coatrack as soon as you open the front door and we all wear our shoes inside the house.

"Now let's all practice our Standard English," Mr. Harvey says. *"You will all stand up and tell me your name, and what you would like to be when you grow up. Please use complete sentences."* Mr. Harvey taps Melvin Spencer on his shoulders. Melvin stands up slowly and pulls a Portagee torture of wedged pants and BVDs out of his ass.

"Ma name is Mal-vin Spenca." Melvin has a very Portagee accent. Before he begins his next sentence, he does nervous things like move his ankles side to side so that his heels slide out of his slippers. He looks at the ceiling and rolls his eyes. "I am, I mean, I wanna. I like. No, try wait. I going be. No, try wait. I will work on my Gramma Spenca's pig farm when I grow up cuz she said I can drive the slop truck. Tank you."

No one laughs at Melvin. Otherwise he'll catch you on the way home from school and shove your head in the slop drum. Melvin sits down. He blinks his eyes hard a couple of times, then rubs his face with two hands.

Jerry stands up very, very slowly and holds on to the edge of his desk. "My name is Jerome." His voice, weak and shivering, his fingers white. "I in. Okay, wait. I stay in. No, try wait. Okay, try wait. I stay. I stay real nervous." His face changes and he acts as if he has to use the bathroom. He looks out the window to the eucalyptus trees beyond the schoolyard.

Jerry continues, "I am going be one concert piano-ist when I get big. Tank you."

I'm next. Panic hits me like a rock dropped in a hollow oil drum.

Mr. Harvey walks up to my desk, his face red and puffy like a pink marshmallow or a bust-up boxer. He has red hair and always wears white double-knit pants with pastel-colored golf shirts. He walks like Walter Matthau. Mr. Harvey taps my desk with his red pen.

The muscles in my face start twitching and pulling uncontrollably. My eyes begin darting back and forth. And my lips, my lips—

"I'm waiting," Mr. Harvey says.

Jerry looks at me. He smiles weakly, his face twitching and pulling too. He looks at Mr. Harvey, then looks at me as if to say, "Just get it over with."

"*Cut the crap,*" Mr. Harvey spits. "*Stop playing these goddamn plantation games. Now c'mon. We've got our outlines to finish today.*" Mr. Harvey's ears get red, his whole face like fire with his red hair and red face.

"My name Lovey. When I grow up pretty soon, I going be what I like be and nobody better say nothing about it or I kill um."

"*OH REALLY,*" he says. "*Not the way you talk. You see, that was terrible. All of you were terrible and we will have to practice and practice our Standard English until we are perfect little Americans. And I'll tell you something, you can all keep your heads on your desks for the rest of the year for all I care. You see, you need me more than I need you. And do you know what the worst part is, class? We're not only going to have to work on your usage, but your pronunciations and inflections too. Jee-zus Christ! For the life of me, it'll take us a goddamn lifetime.*"

"See," Jerry whispers, "now you the one made Mr. Harvey all mad with us. We all going get it from him, stupid."

I want to tell Jerry about being a concert pianist. Yeah, right. Good luck. How will he ever do it? Might as well drive the slop truck if you cannot talk straight or sound good and all the haoles talk circles around you. Might as well blend in like all the locals do.

Mr. Harvey walks past my desk. "*C'mon, Lovey. Start your outline. You too, Jerome.*" Sometimes I think that Mr. Harvey doesn't mean to be mean to us. He really wants us to be Americans, like my kotonk cousins from Santa Ana, he'd probably think they talked real straight.

But I can't talk the way he wants me to. I cannot make it sound his way, unless I'm playing pretend-talk-haole. I can make my words straight, that's pretty easy if I concentrate real hard. But the sound, the sound from my mouth, if I let it rip right out the lips, my words will always come out like home.

In our homeroom is Pillis. But Pillis is not her name. Her name is Phyllis. She's the one who pronounces it Pillis. Pillis Pilmoca the Pilipina.

She doesn't look like the midgets I saw on *The Wizard of Oz*. To me, she looks like a regular-looking person except in small portions. Her legs dangle off her chair.

Sometimes I wonder what size clothes Pillis buys. She has this nice sweater with pearl buttons and a chain with hearts across the neckline. Pillis wears it like a cape. If I wear a girl's size 12, I figure she must be a girl's size 6. So small. Sometimes I wish I could have a sweater with a chain like hers.

I hate math, especially fractions. I cannot reduce them, and today I cannot reduce 8/14. And no one in the dumbest math class helps me.

Us dumb ones from Mr. Harvey's class go with Miss Mona Saiki for math. And we all like Miss Saiki, except that when math time comes, all the dum-dums have to stand up to leave, while all the smart ones stare and snicker.

If Jerry were in this class, he'd give me the answers real fast. Jerry or Melvin. But I'm in this class with other dum-dums and they laugh at me instead like I'm *very* stupid, stupider than them for not knowing how to reduce a stupid fraction.

"You real stoopid for one fricken Jap," says Thomas Lorenzo. "But you ack real smut when you stay wit' all the odda Japs, eh, girl?"

"Yeah," says Wilma Kahale. "I thought all Japs sappose for be smut. But you cannot even reduce one stupid fraction, eh, you, Jap Crap. Stupid, thass why, you Rice Eye, good-for-nuttin' Pearl Harba bomba."

I feel so small. I want to die. I want to die, it feels like a small little fist inside, twisting.

"What," says Wilma. "What you looking at, hah, Jap? Watch how you make them Jap eyes at me. Like me buss' yo face?"

"Yeah, Wilma. Beef um recess time," Thomas Lorenzo whispers to her.

Die before recess. I put my knees on my chair and draw my body into the desk. I put my head down. I see Pillis from the corner of my eye, thinking very hard.

She puts the eraser part of her pencil in her nose and twirls it around slowly as she thinks. She scratches her head with her short wrinkled finger and writes her answer quickly on her paper. Then she puts the eraser up her nostril again.

"Jap. Jap Crap. Rice Eye. Stupid shit. I catch you recess time, you wait."

They keep talking, so I yell very suddenly, "Ooooh, Pillis, digging your nose with your eraser. Ooooh, Pillis, eraser digger." Thomas, Wilma, and the whole class look at Pillis, so stunned that she leaves the pencil eraser stuck in her nose. Her eyes open wide and buglike.

"Midget digging for small nuggets?"

"Ho, Pillis, stretching your mina-chure nostrils?"

"Midget eraser digging for gold?"

I see Pillis get small, smaller than a girl's size 6, smaller and smaller until she looks like a white-sweatered ball. She shoulder-shakes at her desk and sniffles to Miss Saiki, "I hate them. They make me like die." All of Pillis' pencils and erasers fall to the ground.

Miss Saiki waits. No one helps Pillis. Everyone continues laughing and calling her Eraser Digger. Miss Saiki says, "You are all so appalling. You are dis-gusting." She comes over quickly to Pillis and places her hand on Pillis' back, rubs gently. "Don't say things like that, Phyllis. Everything's gonna be o-kay." Then Miss Mona Saiki tells the rest of us, "Back to work. Now."

Pillis doesn't look at me. She doesn't look at anyone. She smooths her wet binder paper with both tiny hands.

Jerry likes Pillis. So do I, actually. Her big gummy laugh and her short legs that try to kick us when we tease her. She waves to us when the school bus drops her off outside their cane field and her tiny body getting tinier and tinier up the dirt road. She walks eight-tenths of a mile to her house next to the sugar mill.

I don't know what to say. Jerry would know. But I don't tell him.

That night, I struggle with my math problems on the linoleum table. My mother asks if I need my father's help. I tell her no, I'm just reducing fractions. The light above the table slides across the binder paper.

I think about Pillis. I put my pencil eraser up my nose. What a wonderful feeling, especially when you twirl it and you have to think. I do this to the other nostril too.

My mother tells me to knock it off. To get a Kleenex instead. I wonder if Thomas Lorenzo and Wilma Kahale are at home trying Pillis' eraser digger too.

I don't know what I'll say to Pillis tomorrow. I don't know if she will ever wave at me from outside the school bus again. But I know now how she feels. It is something I have always known.

Here lies Jerry all cold and skinny. He was a good son. He tried very hard to learn how to swim.
C–.
Here lies Lovey dead as a doorknob. She hated math and shot a mongoose.
D–/F.
We had to do this twice already. Every time we study a newspaper unit, we end up making a newspaper in class. The smartest girl be the editor-in-chief, the most creative one be the features editor, the boy best in dodgeball be the sports editor. Lori Shigemura be the "Dear Lori" column so she can read all the problems, try solve them, and then tell the whole world who "I Honestly Love You, Junior Ah Chong" or "Stone in Love with Raymond" really is.

And this newspaper is not even typewritten. And the rest of us beat reporters write articles about "The New Turtle in Rm. 5." Or "Fifth Grade Dances to the Age of Aquarius."

Then you know it, we gotta write our own obituary. Like I even care. Dead is dead. Can't see or feel or care. I seen dead. Dead rabbits. Dead dogs. Dead goats. Dead sheep. Dead chickens. Dead fish. You name it, my father shown it to me.

I saw my Aunty Kawa dead. They made her wear peach lipstick and a nice satin peach dress. Like somebody should've told them she wore red lipstick every day and a plaid button-down shirt with denim knickers.

And all of her family, they kissed her dead face, even my mother—but when my mother lifted the veil for me, I couldn't do it. Her face looked like stone.

Jerry says it's fun to write our own obituary. Like witnessing our own funeral. He wants to see all the people he hates and who hate him attend his funeral to cry. Of course, he wants me to play songs like "Seasons in the Sun," "Wishing You Were Here," "You've Got a Friend," and "I Haven't Got Time for the Pain" so that the people cry more.

Me, I don't want to go deaf or blind before I die of old age, but if I had to choose, I'd rather be deaf and learn sign language than blind and have to buy a Seeing Eye dog.

Please God forbid that I go crazy before I die.

And God forbid that I die by drowning and have that frantic, leg-kicking feeling I had when Jerry's big brother, Larry, held my ankles down in Mizuno Pond or suffocate with a pillow or garbage bag over my face with my claustrophobia.

I think about dying every night. Sometimes I want to die at strange moments in the day. Sometimes every day. My mother says it's all those books I read about concentration camps. The arsenic in the heart that I tell her about and the gas chambers with fingernail markings on the walls and ceilings.

Once I thought about suicide. Maybe twice or three times. Once when Clayton Young, who had the longest bangs with side comb for a skinny second saxophone player, said I smelled like his sister's rags to the whole woodwinds section. Twice when Jamielyn Trevino, the butchie in ceramics, pulled the chair out from under me, then whipped a wad of clay across the room which splat flat to my forehead. Three times when I heard my uncle say to my aunty in the kitchen that "Cal and Lovey, yeah, maybe my sista Verva right when she brag that they cute and well behave, but they stupid, stupid, stupid." I was sitting in his garage. He thought I'd walked home. I wanted to dedicate my death to them with a suicide note that said, "Lovey, yeah, maybe cute, but stupid, stupid, stupid."

Grandma said to me a long time ago that the Bible says suicide is a sin. Those who do it burn in the eternal flames of hell forever and will never see Jesus' sweet face. Grandma says when I die of natural causes, I'll be with Jesus, and she tries to describe the warm light and eternal peace, but it sounds like a long, hot nap to me.

Sometimes when my grandma leaves for Moloka'i, I feel like a funeral. It's a big hollow ache inside of me. Even if we did have to eat fish-head soup for two nights, then mustard cabbage and pork soup the night before she left.

I lie very still at night and wonder when I'll see her again and why days go by so fast when she's here.

This year, Mr. Harvey says, *"What would you do if your parents died in a train crash?"*

Jerry says, "Ain't no trains in Hawai'i." But he puts his head down to think.

Mr. Harvey makes us close our eyes and tells us about the changing landscape, the awful crash, the blood, the body parts, the glass cuts, and the screaming, all while we see it in our minds.

This is what I *want* to write:

If my parents died in a train crash, God forbid, knock three times, I'll probably live with my grandma on Moloka'i, who makes me take Flintstones vitamins every morning and eat S&S saimin with chopped green onions, scrambled eggs, and sliced Spam for lunch.

At five o'clock Aunty Bing will drive the Malibu to the drugstore where Grandma works. Grandma will have a whole box of chocolate wafer candy in gold paper for me.

One weekend, we'll go to Vacation Bible School. I make miniature gospels with matchbooks and construction paper. We write a Bible newspaper based on the stories by the apostles like we were there to interview them and call it *The New Testament Tribune*. I write a headline called "Jesus Born in Bethlehem Manger."

I'll advertise in the classified ads. "Wanted: A New Bible. Not the King James Version." And maybe Grandma will put one on my bed for me. Then we'll carve Ivory soaps into crosses or Virgin Marys.

At night, Grandma will cut watermelons and Aunty Bing and me sit on the porch and eat watermelon and sunflower seeds and spit the seeds and shells on the driveway.

All of this I'll do over and over again until Pal, Grandma's poi dog, comes home from the gully after two heats with her new litters of puppies.

This is what I actually write:

If my parents die in a train crash. I dunno what I am going do.

D–/F.

Jerry writes:

If my parents die in a train crash. Then stops. I see him thinking. I know he's about to take this too seriously, and when he does, he might cry.

"I dunno what I might do if my parents dies. Who going buy all the food and bath soap and where I going eat at night?"

Mr. Harvey listens to our whispering and lets us go.

"What if I all by myself, Lovey," he says, "can I live with you?"

"You and me can live with my grandma on Moloka'i," I tell him, "and pick pineapples for Del Monte and go to church on Sundays with Grandma and clean the communion glasses and eat the leftover communion crackers. You and me," I tell him.

I don't want him to cry. He starts to write his obituary. All the things I told him we would do.

Here lies Lovey.

When she died, she didn't know how or why. She did not attend her own funeral like she planned. What do angels look like, so she'll know when she gets there? And Grandma, if you get there first, don't yell "Lovey, Lovey," because I might be deaf, or wave your arms, because I might be blind.

Lovey is dead. Come close when you take me home. I know you by the smell of a brand-new Bible and green onions on your fingers. I know you by the feel of gold paper.

GLOSSARY

luaus (123): Hawaiian feasts.

yakudoshis (123): critical years in a person's adult life (for Hawaiian men, the usual age is forty-two; for Hawaiian women, it is thirty-three) marking important physical, mental, and social changes. It is customary to visit shrines and receive the blessings of gods as well as celebrate at parties thrown by family and friends.

mochi pounding parties (123): also known as mochitsuki, a traditional ceremony in Japan where glutinous rice is soaked overnight, cooked, pounded, and usually shaped into spheres or cubes.

Hilo (123): a coastal city, the largest community on the Big Island of Hawaii.

Kaunakakai (123): main city of island of Moloka'i, only about three blocks in size.

haole (123): Hawaiian for Anglo; can be explanatory or insulting.

kotonk (125): word of questionable origins and meaning, probably referring to the Japanese Hawaiian notion of mainland—not necessarily a compliment.

Pearl Harba (126): harbor on the island of Oahu, much of which is the Navy base headquarters for the U.S. Pacific Fleet; the attack on Pearl Harbor by the Japanese on December 7, 1941, brought the United States into World War II.

Moloka'i (129): fifth largest Hawaiian island lying east of Oahu.

saimin (130): noodle soup unique to Hawaii, inspired by Japanese ramen, Chinese mein, and Filipino pancit; often garnished with green onion, bok choy, and sliced luncheon meat like Spam.

poi dog (130): said to be extinct, a "pariah" (wild or feral) dog used by communities as a protector of children despite its small size; by temperament, said to be slow and lazy, and unusually fat from its diet of poi, a pasty substance made of taro root. These dogs were often eaten before they could die a natural death.

INDIAN EDUCATION

by Sherman Alexie

*Sherman Alexie's collection of vignettes provides a painfully hu-
morous, largely autobiographical account of his school years. A
Spokane/Coeur d'Alene Indian, Alexie was born in 1966 and
grew up on the Spokane Indian reservation in Wellpinit, Washington, about fifty miles northwest of Spokane. He underwent a
brain operation at the age of six to correct a congenital hydro-
cephalic condition; he was not expected to survive, and when he
did, doctors predicted that he would be severely mentally retarded.
Alexie, however, trumped these predictions by learning to read by
the age of three and becoming an avid novel reader by age five—
activities which alienated him from his peers on the reservation,
where he was often the brunt of other kids' jokes. Both Alexie's pre-
cociousness and his vulnerability can be seen in his elementary-
school vignettes. After excelling in high school, he enrolled in
premed courses at Washington State University before fainting
spells during human anatomy classes and taking a poetry workshop
persuaded him to change his vocation.*

*Finding his mother's name written in the decades-old textbook
assigned to him at the Wellpinit Elementary School inspired Alexie
to attend a more rigorous high school off the reservation in Rear-
dan, Washington, about twenty miles south of Wellpinit; there, he
was the only Indian except for the school mascot (a hurtful*

reminder of loss in his eleventh-grade vignette) and the star player on the basketball team. In this collection of vignettes, his culture shock is best characterized by his eighth-grade entry, contrasting junior high school girls' anorexic and bulimic vomiting with his alcoholic father's chronic vomiting. Their privileged form of starving is juxtaposed with the scarce and nauseating government-issued food gratefully obtained after waiting in line for it on the reservation. Alexie's basketball success also becomes a factor in these vignettes, where, after a particularly enervating game, he faints during a school dance and is mistakenly thought to be drunk by a Chicano teacher. Basketball offers Alexie the opportunity to comment on the Indian stereotypes commonly accepted even by those who share dark skin.

At the end, Alexie reveals his awareness of how lucky he is. As the pseudonymous Victor, he sees his picture run side by side with that of his former classmates in the reservation newspaper; while they look back toward a tradition of loss, he looks ahead, victorious. One senses that the rest of Alexie's life—filled with successes, awards, honors, publications (he has published nineteen books to date)—is the payback.

The vignette style of this story can be compared with Diaz's "How to Date a Browngirl, Blackgirl, Whitegirl, or Halfie." The gradual blow-by-blow quality of each of Alexie's entries is similar in tone to Diaz's piece. Alexie's sense of alienation from his peers can also be compared with Lovey's in Yamanaka's excerpt from Wild Meat and the Bully Burgers.

First Grade

My hair was too short and my U.S. Government glasses were horn-rimmed, ugly, and all that first winter in school, the other Indian boys chased me from one corner of the playground to the other. They pushed me down, buried me in the snow until I couldn't breathe, thought I'd never breathe again.

They stole my glasses and threw them over my head, around my outstretched hands, just beyond my reach, until someone tripped me and sent me falling again, facedown in the snow.

I was always falling down; my Indian name was Junior Falls Down. Sometimes it was Bloody Nose or Steal-His-Lunch. Once, it was Cries-Like-a-White-Boy, even though none of us had seen a white boy cry.

Then it was a Friday morning recess and Frenchy SiJohn threw snowballs at me while the rest of the Indian boys tortured some other *top-yogh-yaught* kid, another weakling. But Frenchy was confident enough to torment me all by himself, and most days I would have let him.

But the little warrior in me roared to life that day and knocked Frenchy to the ground, held his head against the snow, and punched him so hard that my knuckles and the snow made symmetrical bruises on his face. He almost looked like he was wearing war paint.

But he wasn't the warrior. I was. And I chanted, *It's a good day to die, it's a good day to die,* all the way down to the principal's office.

Second Grade

Betty Towle, missionary teacher, redheaded and so ugly that no one ever had a puppy crush on her, made me stay in for recess fourteen days straight.

"Tell me you're sorry," she said.

"Sorry for what?" I asked.

"Everything," she said and made me stand straight for fifteen minutes, eagle-armed with books in each hand. One was a math book; the other was English. But all I learned was that gravity can be painful.

For Halloween I drew a picture of her riding a broom with a scrawny cat on the back. She said that her God would never forgive me for that.

Once, she gave the class a spelling test but set me aside and gave me a test designed for junior high students. When I spelled all the words right, she crumpled up the paper and made me eat it.

"You'll learn respect," she said.

She sent a letter home with me that told my parents to either cut my braids or keep me home from class. My parents came in the next day and dragged their braids across Betty Towle's desk.

"Indians, indians, indians." She said it without capitalization. She called me "indian, indian, indian."

And I said, *Yes, I am. I am Indian. Indian, I am.*

Third Grade

My traditional Native American art career began and ended with my very first portrait: *Stick Indian Taking a Piss in My Backyard.*

As I circulated the original print around the classroom, Mrs. Schluter intercepted and confiscated my art.

Censorship, I might cry now. *Freedom of expression,* I would write in editorials to the tribal newspaper.

In third grade, though, I stood alone in the corner, faced the wall, and waited for the punishment to end.

I'm still waiting.

Fourth Grade

"You should be a doctor when you grow up," Mr. Schluter told me, even though his wife, the third grade teacher, thought I was crazy beyond my years. My eyes always looked like I had just hit-and-run someone.

"Guilty," she said. "You always look guilty."

"Why should I be a doctor?" I asked Mr. Schluter.

"So you can come back and help the tribe. So you can heal people."

That was the year my father drank a gallon of vodka a day and the same year that my mother started two hundred different quilts but never finished any. They sat in separate, dark places in our HUD house and wept savagely.

I ran home after school, heard their Indian tears, and looked in the mirror. *Doctor Victor,* I called myself, invented an education, talked to my reflection. *Doctor Victor to the emergency room.*

Fifth Grade

I picked up a basketball for the first time and made my first shot. No. I missed my first shot, missed the basket completely, and the ball landed in the dirt and sawdust, sat there just like I had sat there only minutes before.

But it felt good, that ball in my hands, all those possibilities and angles. It was mathematics, geometry. It was beautiful.

At that same moment, my cousin Steven Ford sniffed rubber cement from a paper bag and leaned back on the merry-go-round. His ears rang, his mouth was dry, and everyone seemed so far away.

But it felt good, that buzz in his head, all those colors and noises. It was chemistry, biology. It was beautiful.

Oh, do you remember those sweet, almost innocent choices that the Indian boys were forced to make?

Sixth Grade

Randy, the new Indian kid from the white town of Springdale, got into a fight an hour after he first walked into the reservation school.

Stevie Flett called him out, called him a squawman, called him a pussy, and called him a punk.

Randy and Stevie, and the rest of the Indian boys, walked out into the playground.

"Throw the first punch," Stevie said as they squared off.

"No," Randy said.

"Throw the first punch," Stevie said again.

"No," Randy said again.

"Throw the first punch!" Stevie said for the third time, and Randy reared back and pitched a knuckle fastball that broke Stevie's nose.

We all stood there in silence, in awe.

That was Randy, my soon-to-be first and best friend, who taught me the most valuable lesson about living in the white world: *Always throw the first punch.*

Seventh Grade

I leaned through the basement window of the HUD house and kissed the white girl who would later be raped by her foster-parent father, who was also white. They both lived on the reservation, though, and when the headlines and stories filled the papers later, not one word was made of their color.

Just Indians being Indians, someone must have said somewhere and they were wrong.

But on the day I leaned through the basement window of the HUD house and kissed the white girl, I felt the good-byes I was saying to my entire tribe. I held my lips tight against her lips, a dry, clumsy, and ultimately stupid kiss.

But I was saying good-bye to my tribe, to all the Indian girls and women I might have loved, to all the Indian men who might have called me cousin, even brother.

I kissed that white girl and when I opened my eyes, she was gone from the reservation, and when I opened my eyes, I was gone from the reservation, living in a farm town where a beautiful white girl asked my name.

"Junior Polatkin," I said, and she laughed.

After that, no one spoke to me for another five hundred years.

Eighth Grade

At the farm town junior high, in the boys' bathroom, I could hear voices from the girls' bathroom, nervous whispers of anorexia and bulimia. I could hear the white girls' forced vomiting, a sound so familiar and natural to me after years of listening to my father's hangovers.

"Give me your lunch if you're just going to throw it up," I said to one of those girls once.

I sat back and watched them grow skinny from self-pity.

Back on the reservation, my mother stood in line to get us commodities. We carried them home, happy to have food, and opened the canned beef that even the dogs wouldn't eat.

But we ate it day after day and grew skinny from self-pity.

There is more than one way to starve.

Ninth Grade

At the farm town high school dance, after a basketball game in an overheated gym where I had scored twenty-seven points and pulled down thirteen rebounds, I passed out during a slow song.

As my white friends revived me and prepared to take me to the emergency room where doctors would later diagnose my diabetes, the Chicano teacher ran up to us.

"Hey," he said. "What's that boy been drinking? I know all about these Indian kids. They start drinking real young."

Sharing dark skin doesn't necessarily make two men brothers.

Tenth Grade

I passed the written test easily and nearly flunked the driving, but still received my Washington State driver's license on the same day that Wally Jim killed himself by driving his car into a pine tree.

No traces of alcohol in his blood, good job, wife and two kids.

"Why'd he do it?" asked a white Washington state trooper.

All the Indians shrugged their shoulders, looked down at the ground.

"Don't know," we all said, but when we look in the mirror, see the history of our tribe in our eyes, taste failure in the tap water, and shake with old tears, we understand completely.

Believe me, everything looks like a noose if you stare at it long enough.

Eleventh Grade

Last night I missed two free throws which would have won the game against the best team in the state. The farm town high school I play for is nicknamed the "Indians," and I'm probably the only actual Indian ever to play for a team with such a mascot.

This morning I pick up the sports page and read the headline: INDI-ANS LOSE AGAIN.

Go ahead and tell me none of this is supposed to hurt me very much.

Twelfth Grade

I walk down the aisle, valedictorian of this farm town high school, and my cap doesn't fit because I've grown my hair longer than it's ever been. Later, I stand as the school board chairman recites my awards, accomplishments, and scholarships.

I try to remain stoic for the photographers as I look toward the future.

Back home on the reservation, my former classmates graduate: a few can't read, one or two are just given attendance diplomas, most look forward to the parties. The bright students are shaken, frightened, because they don't know what comes next.

They smile for the photographer as they look back toward tradition.

The tribal newspaper runs my photograph and the photograph of my former classmates side by side.

Postscript: Class Reunion

Victor said, "Why should we organize a reservation high school re-union? My graduating class has a reunion every weekend at the Pow-wow Tavern."

HOW I LEARNED TO FLY

by George Tucker

Tucker, a science fiction writer who lives in Florida, relies on a technique resembling magical realism in this story about how a boy's fantasy life helps him negotiate his way at a new school. Norman, Oklahoma—a place where everything is "bent permanently toward the east"—seems far away from his newly estranged parents, and especially far from his father, a soldier in the Gulf War. Here, living with an uncle, the narrator struggles to cope with feeling that he has lost control over his life. Imagining himself able to fly to school, he experiences both danger and self-sufficiency. At the same time, he draws closer to the man he knows least and fantasizes about the most: his father.

Flying, according to the narrator, is something that only thin, vulnerable kids do, "the haunted ones"; older kids, high school juniors and seniors, are too burdened by reality, whereas younger ones can still soar above a world of awful classes, sadistic teachers, and harassment by cruel classmates. Once he's aloft, the narrator finds a perspective that is larger and more abstract. While watching the war in which his father fights unfold on CNN, the narrator comes to share his terror and helplessness with an attractive classmate whose father is a helicopter pilot in that same war. Though he finds a soul mate, he pays a price: now his days are darkened by the all-too-real, all-too-nightmarish nature of their shared reality, a reality that youthful fantasy and solitude have held at bay. Behind this story looms the magical dream world of flight and the terrifying reality of death. At one point, the narrator considers his future choices: to become an astrophysicist, a writer, a fighter pilot. Then he wonders about the relevance of any of these choices in the face of midnight Baghdad, the first televised war.

At the story's core is Operation Desert Shield, President George H. W. Bush's attempt to protect United States oil interests in the Middle East. In 1990, Iraqi leader Saddam Hussein tried to force a cut in Arab Gulf States oil production and an increase in oil prices by amassing troops and invading Kuwait. Bush, in retaliation, ordered warplanes and ground forces to Saudi Arabia with King Fahd's approval, and when Hussein threatened Saudi Arabian borders, Operation Desert Shield began—the largest American military deployment since Vietnam.

Tucker's narrator, with his keen sense of impending disaster and his helplessness in confronting it, can best be compared to the narrator-in-crisis of Perabo's "Some Say the World," but also to the more subtle discoveries of Junot Diaz's hapless Dominican American dating instructor. His desire to disassociate himself from a disturbing reality can be compared to Dina's similar desire in Packer's "Drinking Coffee Elsewhere."

The Oklahoma mornings are so cold and windy that, when you step outside your uncle's house, you can unbutton your jacket and fly to high school. The chilly blast of wind fills the loose bags of fabric under your arms and lifts you into the air. You fly clumsily, like a bear or a rhinoceros suddenly given wings. Other kids stream past you. They bank and turn with ease, calling to one another and diving like kingfishers. You feel alien among them.

The older kids, the juniors and seniors, are mostly too heavy to fly anymore, except on stormy days. They trudge on sidewalks in heavy leather jackets while the younger kids flap by in denim or plastic windbreakers. It's mostly the thin kids who fly. Mostly the kids with twig-thin arms and legs, the eyes of Medieval saints. The haunted ones.

Flying's fun, and you like it a lot, but Oklahoma's a new and not entirely wonderful place to you. You've only been here since your mother's nervous breakdown from trying to decide how to split up the property when your dad comes home from the Persian Gulf. You decided you were not property and called your Uncle Ted, who has brown teeth and bad breath, asking if you could stay with him. You've been here two weeks.

You've been doing your homework in study hall so you won't have to carry books home. A shifting backpack full of biology and algebra texts could kill you, drag you down if the wind slacked, maybe in front of an eighteen-wheeler full of construction equipment that wouldn't even have time to honk before you were crushed under the wheels.

To say you've made no friends would be an understatement. Not even your teachers have talked to you yet. No, wait, there was that group of older Indian boys that harassed you at Hardee's, then followed you halfway home, yelling. Your newness is like a huge birthmark on your forehead, like Gorbachev's, only worse. Your voice box is paralyzed with shyness.

You fly past the only tree in the whole neighborhood, a sad mulberry which has surrendered to the constant wind by bowing to the ground. Before Oklahoma, you thought of the word "prairie" as some quaint landscape, full of tall grasses bordered with stately trees, stitched with springs, filled with jackrabbits and deer. That's the impression you had from books and movies. The real place, real prairie, is more like the moon. Everything in Norman, Oklahoma, is bent permanently toward the east—you imagine that even the natives' legs are longer on one side than the other. Any buildings over three stories (of which there are five in the town) have a distinctive eastward list. The weeds that grow in ditches touch their heads to the ground facing the morning sun. You think you remember something about Hopi kivas in the Southwest all facing east, too—worshipping the sun, or for spiritual-religious reasons. Here most doors face east so, when you open them in the mornings, a gale won't hurl you to the floor and rearrange the furniture.

That cold morning, orbiting one last time over the school before landing for the day, you decide to master flight. You have read *Jonathan Livingston Seagull*, and, even though you didn't quite understand it, you feel a yearning to fly like an eagle. To soar. Not so you can be like the other kids, though—this is not a conformist urge—but for the sheer joy of it. Also because you got tangled up in someone's television antenna the very first day you tried, and that was embarrassing. You still have scratches on your hands from the aluminum vanes.

You're finished with the last of your homework by the time homeroom begins. A television, bolted to the wall about seven feet up like a dead gray eye, flickers to life and your daily dose of commercial "news" begins. You hate it. Fifteen minutes of babble delivered by polished ageless androids whose vocabulary consists of one-syllable words. Today, they tell you the word "scud" used to be a verb, generally used to poetically convey the motion of clouds drifting across the sky. That was before it became a threat. The word "scud" now implies chemical weapons, great green clouds of gas that do not scud but ooze venomous across the ground.

The nearby Southwest Oklahoma State University is famous for its programs in agriculture and animal husbandry, which explains why you have to dig ditches and muck out stables in your horticulture class. Your advisor, a bony man who sweated while he talked, told you it was all learning about plants and stuff. Those were his words, "Plants and stuff." You seemed to be making him nervous so you agreed to the horticulture class. You've learned that horse shit is easier to pick up with a pitchfork than a shovel, and that after spending an hour in a dusty stable, your mucous will be black for the rest of the day. The rest of the class are the sorts of boys you avoid. The burly, surly sort who refer to all women as "bitches" and talk about which girl is a "ho" and which a "tease." They threaten one another with pitchforks and pruning shears. You give them a wide berth.

Instead of scattering clean straw in the stables, you duck outside and open your arms. You rise into the air, without a thought, like magic. From the height of a tree, nothing about the barn or the rusted barbed wire or the dead brown fields affects you in any way. You are on your own, self-sufficient. You're not sure, but you suspect your father feels this way in his desert camouflage. From a few hundred feet up, the world becomes an abstraction, a hieroglyph you can't read.

In the distance, you can see faint figures looping around the school. Escapees. You are closer to the sun, still cold, beset by paradoxes. You can fly, but do not belong in the air.

Not all your classes are as bad as horticulture, though. You're light-years ahead in the chemistry class, which is just now getting to polar and non-polar covalent bonds. You try not to yawn.

French is another story. You are far from bilingual, but thought you were progressing well in your former French class. In Norman High School the French teacher is from Quebec and only uses English when calling the roll. She gives the class instructions like she's swearing. Every word sounds vehement on her pouty lips. She's very pretty though: hair cut short like a movie star's, long arms and legs, round glasses. You're content to watch her while she writes *en francais* on the chalkboard and berates the class like a native Parisian.

Today, near the end of class, a blonde girl asks you for help in conjugating an irregular verb. She has blue eyes and a cute pug nose. Luckily you know the answer, and you assist her, thinking she's probably flirting with you. She's attractive, but, compared to the teacher, who is luscious, she's just another high school girl.

The flight home is far more difficult. This time the wind is in your face, forcing a fist past your teeth. To fly home, you must open your jacket and let the wind swell in it, ride high into the air, high enough you'd die if you panicked. You can see whole blocks from up there, can see the yards of people who've hired Arthur's Landscape Service to drive up in a truck and spraypaint their brown and dying grass lurid Easter-basket-green. This used to make you laugh. Once you get altitude, you fling your weight forward, spilling the air from your wings and plummet downward, headfirst.

You use your jacket as a control surface now and let your legs hang behind you as you fall, and wait until the last few feet that make your nuts cling tight to your skin until you turn, hold the jacket tight, let it fill with wind again and yank you away from the ground like a bungee cord, your internal organs firmly rattled by the close call. It takes about twenty climbs and dives to get home that way. Below you, people walk, not looking up, leaning heavily into the wind.

You plummet to the sidewalk outside your uncle's house, hitting hard enough to make your teeth clatter and your ankles ache. Each time you do this, fly home against the wind, you know you may die. You may plummet too far too fast and dig a trench in an unnaturally green yard with your forehead. You may impale yourself a dozen times on a television aerial. You may fly into power lines. It's dangerous. Usually you wouldn't do such things, but this is different. This is flying.

After dinner, you turn on CNN to check the progress of Operation Desert Shield, because your father is in Saudi Arabia right now, probably cleaning his M-16 or drinking instant coffee from a tin cup. You wish him well. Even though you're sure he doesn't understand an atom of you, you love your father and are proud of him for going across the ocean to live in a tent in the desert under the threat of attack. It seems noble, and, in a way you can't quite articulate, stupid at the same time. You tried to talk to your uncle about this once, but thoughts refused to coalesce into words and his active listening began to annoy you. It's easier just to keep quiet and watch the news. And drink instant coffee from a white ceramic mug with your uncle's company logo on the side.

There's a message on the machine from your mother. You call her back, dutiful son that you are, and she reads the letter she just got from your father. He stole some trucks from the port of Riyadh to help his unit move to the front lines. He walks between tents in his flak jacket and pot helmet, with his gas mask slung over his shoulder. It's very hot. Once you've hung up, you're amazed at your mother's audacity, to talk to you about the man she wants so fiercely to divorce. You don't understand her. But, after all, she's a woman. Just another inscrutable woman.

You go to your room and, using cardboard you snip from the boxes that held your books and clothing, you make control fins to strap onto your wrists and ankles. You're thinking, with more surface in the air, maybe you could steer better, be a little more nimble. You also realize that, by cutting up the boxes, you're surrendering your original hope of a blitzkrieg visit. You're here to stay. You will impress the neighborhood kids, these aerial acrobats whose names you don't know. You will get better at flying. You decide to practice until you can snatch dragonflies out of the air with your teeth. The weekend seems far away.

That night, in the single bed in your uncle's spare bedroom, you wonder about your life. If you had three futures, you'd be an astrophysicist, a writer and a fighter pilot. You shift under forty pounds of quilts that almost smother you (because your uncle keeps the house at a comfortable fifty degrees) and imagine dropping canisters of napalm on Iraqi soldiers, imagine GIs cheering as you fly low over their lines and strafe enemy tanks. A picture of yourself, thicker in the arms and chest, climbing into the cockpit of an F-16 plays before your eyes. You're wearing a green g-suit and your French teacher is waving a white handkerchief up at you. You strap yourself into the jet with a noble expression. But you're good at math and physics, which you think is very interesting, although you wonder about its relevance. And the writer thing, maybe then you could explain to your dad what it's like to catch the Oklahoma breeze in your jacket and fly toward the rising sun.

This morning there's a cold breeze blowing through your body as you brush your teeth. You think of the pug-nosed blonde with the unusual pendant—she is the source. You wonder if she'll speak to you today, again today, perhaps setting a precedent for the rest of the academic year.

The wind is erratic this morning; you can feel its caprice in the ruffles of your hair, the tugs on your jacket. Flying today might be more dangerous than usual. You spread your wings anyway. You are flung up and away like a frisbee. Glancing around, you notice far fewer in flight than yesterday. It is dangerous, you think, and cut straight for school.

The wind shifts, twitches, and you must keep your body alert and in constant motion. It's exhausting. Despite the cold, you're sweating by the time you reach the schoolyard, one quick orbit, and are just about to land when the wind dies. Your eyes go huge and you hear high shrieks from the entire neighborhood, then the roar of still air rushing past. Your own throat fills with tearing noise.

The cold hard ground reaches and slaps you with a flat hand. Silence, dark, and for a moment you can't breathe. You claw at the frozen dirt until air finally floods into your lungs. The wind of life. You open your eyes and see dead brown grass, huge. As you stand, slowly checking yourself for injuries, the wind again pushes at you. Your ribs feel pummeled and everything aches, especially the inside of one cheek where you bit yourself. You spit blood onto the dead grass and trudge toward the door.

Waiting, you see about a dozen kids walk by, some limping, all dirty. One boy in a grubby denim jacket has a strange angle to his right arm and you can see the gleam of tears on his cheeks. You can't even trust the wind.

After the daily French tirade, you're hunched over your notebook in class when the pug-nosed girl comes up and asks you to help her conjugate an -ir verb. She's wearing a red sweater today that nicely accents her gold necklace. You introduce yourself.

"I'm Elizabeth," she says.

"Nice necklace," you say. She cups the gold helicopter in her hand and smiles.

"Why do you bring all your books to class?"

"I can't always find my locker." She grins.

After you correct her faulty French, Elizabeth explains that her father is a lieutenant in the army, a helicopter pilot. Apache. You nod, and tell her about your father, a sergeant in the infantry. You don't remember the battalion number but you describe the shoulder insignia to her:

a white sword with blue and red flames. She nods, her hair bobbing. You tell her about your father stealing trucks, and she laughs. Encouraged by her laughter to a pitch of courage you've never known, you ask her to come to your house that evening. To watch CNN together. She says Yeah, sure, and the rest of your day passes in a haze.

On the flight home, you dive toward the convenience store, buy a six-pack of Cokes and some chips with your allowance money. You feel like you're riding the fastest wind ever, even though you walk the rest of the way home. You're flying so fast the breath is being ripped out of your mouth, exhilarating. You're smiling so wide your mouth hurts.

Two hours later, Elizabeth rings the doorbell. The Cokes are cold, the chips are in a bowl, and you are sitting on the floor in front of the television. A stranger in Baghdad is describing the sounds of explosions, tracer bullets cutting the air and leaving glowing streaks, a missile the size of an airplane that flew past his window. With your new flier's eyes, you can see a path through the streams of bullets and missiles—a narrow one. You might not be able to do it with your backpack on. You've been staring so long your eyes are dry and red.

Elizabeth lets herself in, glares at you, then notices your expression. Mouth open, she rushes to sit beside you and she gasps, then stares. Maybe, you think, both of you hoping, praying hard enough, together, will be enough. Enough to stop it all or at least to protect two fathers who were now in a war. War. Chills run up your arms and you shiver— Elizabeth puts her arm around you. You reach around and support her lower back with your own arm, and your chills are warmed away. Her sweater feels as soft as a kitten.

CNN cuts to Wolf Blitzer, the man with a tricolor beard, who stands in front of a huge map of Iraq, pointing to red silhouettes of airplanes, missiles, tanks. His words don't sink into you but the red does. Jets, Scuds, T-42s all just waiting to. . . . Elizabeth eats a chip. The crunch startles you from reverie into the present.

"It's about time." You nod and go to the refrigerator for Cokes. You crack hers open, set the cool can down beside her.

"Is the floor okay, or should we sit on, uh, something else?" you ask.

"Floor's fine." Elizabeth sips her Coke and gives a ladylike belch. "My dad'll be the first in. Just like Panama. Helicopter pilots always are."

"It's going to be a long night," you say, even though the sun's still up, and sit down beside her. Soon you will tell her how terrified you are, how you've never been separated from your family before, how you want all this, well, *most* of this, to be a dream you'll wake up from. But for the moment the TV is showing live images from midnight Baghdad, and all you can do is watch.

Your Uncle Ted comes in soon after. His forehead wrinkles and he walks over, squeezes your shoulder, then disappears into his room.

Your back is sore. Your eyes hurt, all the Coke is gone, and your lips tingle from the salt on the chips. Elizabeth still sits beside you. You look at her, examine her profile in the TV light. You stand and take her hand. She looks up at you, eyes wide. You walk together to the front door and open it, step onto the porch. You leave the door open.

The moon is a silver crescent above. The stars look like tracers frozen in place. The breeze plucks at your sleeves and, together, you raise your arms, but your feet stay hard on the ground.

GLOSSARY

Hopi kivas (144): The Hopi are Southwestern Indians who live in pueblos made of stone and sand, standing several stories high. Kivas are underground chambers in the pueblo home used for community gatherings and religious ceremonies.

Jonathan Livingston Seagull **(144):** a fable/novella by Richard Bach, first published in 1970, about a seagull who learns about life, flight, and self-determination.

M-16 (147): U.S. military designation for a family of assault rifles used in the Vietnam, Gulf, and Iraq wars.

port of Riyadh (147): Riyadh is the capital of and the largest city in Saudi Arabia, situated in the center of the Arabian Peninsula. A railway links Riyadh with Dammam, a port on the Persian Gulf, making Riyadh known as a "dry port."

blitzkrieg (148): German for "lightning war"; an attack tactic based on speed and surprise used by the Nazis.

napalm (148): flammable liquid used in warfare; often jellied gasoline used in bombs.

strafe (148): to fire upon with a machine gun from low-flying airplanes.

F-16 (148): also known as a Flying Falcon or Viper, a multirole jet fighter.

g-suit (148): worn by aviators and astronauts undergoing high levels of acceleration; it is designed to prevent blackouts due to blood pooling in the lower part of the body.

tracer bullets (150): special bullets modified to ignite upon firing, making their trajectory visible to the naked eye.

T-42 (150): a single-engine military aircraft usually used for instrument training.

just like Panama (151): Known as Operation Just Cause, the United States invasion of Panama deposed general and military dictator Manuel Noriega in December 1989, during the administration of President George H.W. Bush.

Crisis

The stories in this section offer reflections on the deepest kinds of losses—parents, siblings, countries and cultures of origin, the self. Sometimes these losses are the result of history or accident, "bad luck"; more often, they are part of the process of discovering how life presses inexorably forward, pulling us in tow, toward a denial or an assertion of identity. In crisis, who we turn out to be becomes the greatest challenge of our lives.

THE EVE OF THE SPIRIT FESTIVAL

by Lan Samantha Chang

Chang's story is framed by crisis. It opens immediately after a Chinese Buddhist cremation ceremony. Two young girls, drawn together by their mother's untimely death, must also endure their father's way of mourning, which is to ignore Chinese mourning traditions and focus exclusively on his ambition to become an American professor. Eleven-year-old Emily, the older of the two, blames him for letting her mother die. Our narrator, six-year-old Claudia, deals with her mother's death by assuming the defensive. She stands apart from this tragedy, as if she were watching a play unfold in which the characters seem both familiar and strange.

Claudia soon finds that with her family's retreat into its own private world of disappointment and anger, she has a hard time finding ways to recall her mother. While her father busies himself with the American custom of throwing after-work parties for his colleagues, Claudia observes Emily's increasing cynicism and hostility toward him.

A turning point occurs several years later, around Guijie, the Chinese Spirit Festival, marking a time "when the living are required to appease and provide for the ghosts of their ancestors." On the eve of this festival, Claudia begins to wonder whether her mother's ghost would be able to recognize her. She finds no solace in her scientist father or her sullen, contemptuous sister. She becomes the perfect, praiseworthy, stay-at-home daughter, waiting for her reward, while Emily succeeds in assimilating into American culture in all the ways that finally elude their father. But Emily undergoes this process far from home, on the West Coast. Even on occasional visits to New York, Emily refuses to see her father.

Their father's death precipitates the final crisis. Though Emily returns to New York for the funeral and, while dressed in traditional Chinese mourning clothes, insists on an American cremation, she cannot bring herself to give up the anger toward her father that defines and fills her life. Anger, and the sadness that informs and fuels it, will haunt Emily, leaving Claudia, considered to be the "lucky" daughter, to fulfill her father's expectations, empty-handed and empty-hearted for the ghost that never comes.

Lan Samantha Chang was born and raised in Appleton, Wisconsin, the daughter of parents who emigrated from China after World War II. Chang attended Yale University first as a premedical student and then as an East Asian Studies major. She went on to study at Harvard University's Kennedy School of Government and earned an MFA at the University of Iowa's Writers' Workshop, a program that she now directs. In addition to Hunger, *the collection from which this story is drawn, Chang has published a novel,* Inheritance.

Chang's story, with its focus on the fragility of family relationships, can be compared to several other stories in this section, particularly to Perabo's "Some Say the World" and Sharma's "Surrounded by Sleep." Generational conflict around traditional values can also be found in Delman's excerpt from Burnt Bread and Chutney, *Rodriguez's "The Boy Without a Flag," and Chen-Johnson's "Knuckles."*

After the Buddhist ceremony, when our mother's spirit had been chanted to a safe passage and her body cremated, Emily and I sat silently on our living room carpet. She held me in her arms; her long hair stuck to our wet faces. We sat as stiffly as temple gods except for the angry thump of my sister's heart against my cheek.

Finally she spoke. "It's Baba's fault," she said. "The American doctors would have fixed her."

I was six years old—I only knew that our father and mother had decided against an operation. And I had privately agreed, imagining the doctors tearing a hole in her body. As I thought of this, I felt a sudden sob pass through me.

"Don't cry, Baby," Emily whispered. "You're okay." I felt my tears dry to salt, my throat lock shut.

Then our father walked into the room.

He and Emily had grown close in the past few months. Emily was eleven, old enough to come along on his trips to the hospital. I had often stood in the neighbor's window and watched them leave for visiting hours, Emily's mittened hand tucked into his.

But now my sister refused to acknowledge him. She pushed the back of my head to turn me away from him also.

"First daughter—" he began.

"Go away, Baba," Emily said. Her voice shook. The evening sun glowed garnet red through the dark tent of her hair.

"You told me she would get better," I heard her say. "Now you're burning paper money for her ghost. What good will that do?"

"I am sorry," Baba said.

"I don't care."

Her voice burned. I squirmed beneath her hand, but she wouldn't let me look. It was something between her and Baba. I watched his black wingtip shoes retreat to the door. When he had gone, Emily let go of me. I sat up and looked at her; something had changed. Not in the lovely outlines of her face—our mother's face—but in her eyes, shadow-black, lost in unforgiveness.

They say the dead return to us. But we never saw our mother again, though we kept a kind of emptiness waiting in case she might come back. I listened always, seeking her voice, the lost thread of a conversation I'd been too young to have with her. I did not dare mention her to Emily. Since I could remember, my sister had kept her most powerful feelings private, sealed away. She rarely mentioned our mother, and soon my memories faded. I could not picture her. I saw only Emily's angry face, the late sun streaking red through her dark hair.

After the traditional forty-nine-day mourning period, Baba did not set foot in the Buddhist temple. It was as if he had listened to Emily: what good did it do? Instead he focused on earthly ambitions, his research at the lab.

At that time he aspired beyond the position of lab instructor to the rank of associate professor, and he often invited his American colleagues over for "drinks." Emily and I were recruited to help with the preparations and serving. As we went about our tasks, we would sometimes catch a glimpse of our father, standing in the corner, watching the American men and studying to become one.

But he couldn't get it right—our parties had an air of cultural confusion. We served potato chips on laquered trays; Chinese landscapes bumped against watercolors of the Statue of Liberty, the Empire State Building.

Nor were Emily or I capable of helping him. I was still a child, and Emily said she did not care. Since my mother's death, she had rejected anything he held dear. She refused to study chemistry and spoke in American slang. Her rebellion puzzled me, it seemed so vehement and so arbitrary.

Now she stalked through the living room, platform shoes thudding on the carpet. "I hate this," she said, fiercely ripping another rag from a pair of old pajama bottoms. "Entertaining these jerks is a waste of time."

Some chemists from Texas were visiting his department and he had invited them over for cocktails.

"I can finish it," I said. "You just need to do the parts I can't reach."

"It's not the dusting," she said. "It's the way he acts around them. 'Herro, herro! Hi Blad, hi Warry! Let me take your coat! Howsa Giants game?' " she mimicked, in a voice that made me wince, a voice alive with cruelty and pain. "If he were smart he wouldn't invite people over on football afternoons in the first place."

"What do you mean?" I asked, startled. Brad Delmonte was our father's boss. I had noticed Baba reading the sports pages that morning—something he rarely did.

"Oh, forget it," Emily said. I felt as if she and I were utterly separate. Then she smiled. "You've got oil on your glasses, Claudia."

Baba walked in carrying two bottles of wine. "They should arrive in half an hour," he said, looking at his watch. "They won't be early. Americans are never early."

Emily looked away. "I'm going to Jodie's house," she said.

Baba frowned and straightened his tie. "I want you to stay while they're here. We might need something from the kitchen."

"Claudia can get it for them."

"She's barely tall enough to reach the cabinets."

Emily stood and clenched her dustcloth. "I don't care," she said. "I hate meeting the people you have over."

"They're successful American scientists. You'd be better off with them instead of running around with your teenage friends, these sloppy kids, these rich white kids who dress like beggars."

"You're nuts, Dad," Emily said—she had begun addressing him the way an American child does. "You're nuts if you think these bosses of yours are ever going to do anything for you or any of us." And she threw her dustcloth, hard, into our New York Giants wastebasket.

"Speak to me with respect."

"You don't deserve it!"

"You are staying in this apartment! That is an order!"

"I wish you'd died instead of Mama!" Emily cried. She darted past our father, her long braid flying behind her. He stared at her, his expression oddly slack, the way it had been in the weeks after the funeral. He stepped toward her, reached hesitantly at her flying braid, but she turned and saw him, cried out as if he had struck her, and ran out of the room. His hands dropped to his sides.

Emily refused to leave our bedroom. Otherwise that party was like so many others. The guests arrived late and left early. They talked about buying new cars and the Dallas Cowboys. I served pretzels and salted nuts.

Baba walked around emptying ashtrays and refilling drinks. I noticed that the other men also wore vests and ties, but that the uniform looked somehow different on my slighter, darker father.

"Cute little daughter you have there," said Baba's boss. He was a large bearded smoker with a sandy voice. He didn't bend down to look at me or the ashtray that I raised toward his big square hand.

I went into our room and found Emily sitting on one of our unmade twin beds. It was dusk. Through the window I could see that the dull winter sun had almost disappeared. I sat next to her on the bed. Until that day, I think, it was Emily who took care of me and not the other way around.

After a minute, she spoke. "I'm going to leave," she said. "As soon as I turn eighteen, I'm going to leave home and never come back!" She burst into tears. I reached for her shoulder but her thin, heaving body frightened me. She seemed too grown up to be comforted. I thought about the breasts swelling beneath her sweater. Her body had become a foreign place.

Perhaps Emily had warned me that she would someday leave in order to start me off on my own. I found myself avoiding her, as though her impending desertion would matter less if I deserted her first. I discovered a place to hide while she and my father fought, in the living room behind a painted screen. I would read a novel or look out the window. Sometimes they forgot about me—from the next room I would hear one of them break off an argument and say, "Where did Claudia go?" "I don't know," the other would reply. After a silence, they would start again.

One of these fights stands out in my memory. I must have been ten or eleven years old. It was the fourteenth day of the seventh lunar month: the eve of Guijie, the Chinese Spirit Festival, when the living are required to appease and provide for the ghosts of their ancestors. To the believing, the earth was thick with gathering spirits; it was safest to stay indoors and burn incense.

I seldom thought about the Chinese calendar, but every year on Guijie I wondered about my mother's ghost. Where was it? Would it still recognize me? How would I know when I saw it? I wanted to ask

Baba, but I didn't dare. Baba had an odd attitude toward Guijie. On one hand, he had eschewed all Chinese customs since my mother's death. He was a scientist, he said; he scorned the traditional tales of unsatisfied spirits roaming the earth.

But I cannot remember a time when I was not made aware, in some way, of Guijie's fluctuating lunar date. That year the eve of the Spirit Festival fell on a Thursday, usually his night out with the men from his department. Emily and I waited for him to leave but he sat on the couch, calmly reading the *New York Times*.

I finished drying the dishes. Emily began to fidget. She had a date that night and had counted on my father's absence. She spent half an hour washing and combing her hair, trying to make up her mind. Finally she asked me to give her a trim. I knew she'd decided to go out.

"Just a little," she said. "The ends are scraggly." We spread some newspapers on the living room floor. Emily stood in the middle of the papers with her hair combed down her back, thick and glossy, black as ink. It hadn't really been cut since she was born. Since my mother's death I had taken over the task of giving it a periodic touch-up.

I hovered behind her with the shears, searching for the scraggly ends, but there were none.

My father looked up from his newspaper. "What are you doing that for? You can't go out tonight," he said.

"I have a date!"

My father put down his newspaper. I threw the shears onto a chair and fled to my refuge behind the screen.

Through a slit over the hinge I caught a glimpse of Emily near the foyer, slender in her denim jacket, her black hair flooding down her back, her delicate features contorted with anger. My father's hair was disheveled, his hands clenched at his sides. The newspapers had scattered over the floor.

"Dressing up in boys' clothes, with paint on your face—"

"This is nothing! My going out on a few dates is nothing! You don't know what you're talking about!"

"Don't shout." My father shook his finger. "The neighbors will hear you."

"Goddammit, Dad!" Her voice rose to a shriek. She stamped her feet to make the most noise possible.

"What happened to you?" he cried. "You used to be so much like her. Look at you—"

Though I'd covered my ears I could hear my sister's wail echo off the walls. The door slammed, and her footfalls vanished down the stairs.

Things were quiet for a minute. Then I heard my father walk toward my corner. My heart thumped with fear—usually he let me alone. I had to look up when I heard him move the screen away. He knelt down next to me. His hair was streaked with gray, and his glasses needed cleaning.

"What are you doing?" he asked.

I shook my head, nothing.

After a minute I asked him, "Is Guijie why you didn't go play bridge tonight, Baba?"

"No, Claudia," he said. He always called me by my American name. This formality, I thought, was an indication of how distant he felt from me. "I stopped playing bridge last week."

"Why?" We both looked toward the window, where beyond our reflections the Hudson River flowed.

"It's not important," he said.

"Okay."

But he didn't leave. "I'm getting old," he said after a moment. "Someone ten years younger was just promoted over me. I'm not going to try to keep up with them anymore."

It was the closest he had ever come to confiding in me. After a few more minutes he stood up and went into the kitchen. The newspapers rustled under his feet. For almost half an hour I heard him fumbling through the kitchen cabinets, looking for something he'd probably put there years ago. Eventually he came out, carrying a small brass urn and some matches. When Emily returned home after midnight, the apartment still smelled of the incense he had burned to protect her while she was gone.

I tried to be a good daughter. I stayed in every night and wore no makeup, I studied hard and got all A's, I did not leave home but went to college at NYU, right down the street. Jealously I guarded my small allotment of praise, clutching it like a pocket of precious stones. Emily snuck out of the apartment late at night; she wore high-heeled sandals with patched blue jeans; she twisted her long hair into graceful, complex loops and braids that belied respectability. She smelled of lipstick and perfume. Nothing I could ever achieve would equal my sister's misbehavior.

When Emily turned eighteen and did leave home, a part of my father disappeared. I wondered sometimes: where did it go? Did she take it with her? What secret charm had she carried with her as she vanished down the tunnel to the jet that would take her to college in California, steadily and without looking back, while my father and I watched silently from the window at the gate? The apartment afterwards became quite still—it was only the two of us, mourning and dreaming through pale-blue winter afternoons and silent evenings.

Emily called me, usually late at night after my father had gone to sleep. She sent me pictures of herself and people I didn't know, smiling on the sunny Berkeley campus. Sometimes after my father and I ate our simple meals or TV dinners I would go into our old room, where I had kept both of our twin beds, and take out Emily's pictures, trying to imagine what she must have been feeling, studying her expression and her swinging hair. But I always stared the longest at a postcard she'd sent me one winter break from northern New Mexico, a professional photo of a powerful, vast blue sky over faraway pink and sandy-beige mesas. The clarity and cleanness fascinated me. In a place like that, I thought, there would be nothing to search for, no reason to hide.

After college she went to work at a bank in San Francisco. I saw her once when she flew to Manhattan on business. She skipped a meeting to have lunch with me. She wore an elegant gray suit and had pinned up her hair.

"How's Dad?" she asked. I looked around, slightly alarmed. We were sitting in a bistro on the East Side, but I somehow thought he might overhear us.

"He's okay," I said. "We don't talk very much. Why don't you come home and see him?"

Emily stared at her water glass. "I don't think so."

"He misses you."

"I know. I don't want to hear about it."

"You hardly ever call him."

"There's nothing we can talk about. Don't tell him you saw me, promise?"

"Okay."

During my junior year at NYU, my father suffered a stroke. He was fifty-nine years old, and he was still working as a lab instructor in the chemistry department. One evening in early fall I came home from a class and found him on the floor, near the kitchen telephone. He was wearing his usual vest and tie. I called the hospital and sat down next to him. His wire-rimmed glasses lay on the floor a foot away. One-half of his face was frozen, the other half lined with sudden age and pain.

"They said they'll be right here," I said. "It won't be very long." I couldn't tell how much he understood. I smoothed his vest and straightened his tie. I folded his glasses. I knew he wouldn't like it if the ambulance workers saw him in a state of dishevelment. "I'm sure they'll be here soon," I said.

We waited. Then I noticed he was trying to tell me something. A line of spittle ran from the left side of his mouth. I leaned closer. After a while I made out his words: "Tell Emily," he said.

The ambulance arrived as I picked up the telephone to call California. That evening, at the hospital, what was remaining of my father left the earth.

Emily insisted that we not hold a Buddhist cremation ceremony. "I never want to think about that stuff again," she said. "Plus, all of his friends are Americans. I don't know who would come, except for us." She had reached New York the morning after his death. Her eyes were vague and her fingernails bitten down.

On the third day we scattered his ashes in the river. Afterward we held a small memorial service for his friends from work. We didn't talk much as we straightened the living room and dusted the furniture. It took almost three hours. The place was a mess. We hadn't had a party in years.

It was a warm cloudy afternoon, and the Hudson looked dull and sluggish from the living room window. I noticed that although she had not wanted a Buddhist ceremony, Emily had dressed in black and white according to Chinese mourning custom. I had asked the department secretary to put up a sign on the bulletin board. Eleven people came; they drank five bottles of wine. Two of his Chinese students stood in the corner, eating cheese and crackers.

Brad Delmonte, paunchy and no longer smoking, attached himself to Emily. "I remember you when you were just a little girl," I heard him say as I walked by with the extra crackers.

"I don't remember you," she said.

"You're still a cute little thing." She bumped his arm, and he spilled his drink.

Afterward we sat on the couch and surveyed the cluttered coffee table. It was past seven but we didn't talk about dinner.

"I'm glad they came," I said.

"I hate them." Emily looked at her fingernails. "I don't know whom I hate more: them, or him—for taking it."

"It doesn't matter anymore," I said.

"I suppose."

We watched the room grow dark.

"Do you know what?" Emily said. "It's the eve of the fifteenth day of the seventh lunar month."

"How do you know?" During college I had grown completely unaware of the lunar calendar.

"One of those chemistry nerds from Taiwan told me this afternoon."

I wanted to laugh, but instead I felt myself make a strange whimpering sound, squeezed out from my tight and hollow chest.

"Remember the time Dad and I had that big fight?" she said. "You know that now, in my grown-up life, I don't fight with anyone? I never had problems with anybody except him."

"No one cared about you as much as he did," I said.

"I don't want to hear about it." She twisted the end of her long braid. "He was a pain, and you know it. He got so strict after Mama died. It wasn't all my fault."

"I'm sorry," I said. But I was so angry with her that I felt my face turn red, my cheeks tingle in the dark. She'd considered our father a nerd as well, had squandered his love with such thoughtlessness that I could scarcely breathe to think about it. It seemed impossibly unfair that she had memories of my mother as well. Carefully I waited for my feelings to go away. Emily, I thought, was all I had.

But as I sat, a vision distilled before my eyes: the soft baked shades, the great blue sky of New Mexico. I realized that after graduation I could go wherever I wanted. A rusty door swung open and filled my mind with sweet freedom, fearful coolness.

"Let's do something," I said.

"What do you mean?"

"I want to do something."

"What did we used to do?" Emily looked down at the lock of hair in her hand. "Wait, I know."

We found newspapers and spread them on the floor. We turned on the lamps and moved the coffee table out of the way, brought the wine-glasses to the sink. Emily went to the bathroom, and I searched for the shears a long time before I found them in the kitchen. I glimpsed the in-cense urn in a cabinet and quickly shut the door. When I returned to the living room it smelled of shampoo. Emily stood in the middle of the papers with her wet hair down her back, staring at herself in the reflec-tion from the window. The lamplight cast circles under her eyes.

"I had a dream last night," she said. "I was walking down the street. I felt a tug. He was trying to reach me, trying to pull my hair."

"Just a trim?" I asked.

"No," she said. "Why don't you cut it."

"What do you mean?" I snipped a two-inch lock off the side.

Emily looked down at the hair on the newspapers. "I'm serious," she said. "Cut my hair. I want to see two feet of hair on the floor."

"Emily, you don't know what you're saying," I said. But a pleasur-able, weightless feeling had come over me. I placed the scissors at the nape of her neck. "How about it?" I asked, and my voice sounded low and odd.

"*I don't care.*" An echo of the past. I cut. The shears went *snack*. A long black lock of hair hit the newspapers by my feet.

The Chinese say that our hair and our bodies are given to us from our ancestors, gifts that should not be tampered with. My mother herself had never done this. But after the first few moments I enjoyed myself, pressing the thick black locks through the shears, heavy against my thumb. Emily's hair slipped to the floor around us, rich and beautiful, lying in long graceful arcs over my shoes. She stood perfectly still, staring out the window. The Hudson River flowed behind our reflections, bearing my father's ashes through the night.

When I was finished, the back of her neck gleamed clean and white under a precise shining cap. "You missed your calling," Emily said. "You want me to do yours?"

My hair, browner and scragglier, had never been past my shoulders. I had always kept it short, figuring the ancestors wouldn't be offended by my tampering with a lesser gift. "No," I said. "But you should take a shower. Some of those small bits will probably itch."

"It's already ten o'clock. We should go to sleep soon anyway." Satisfied, she glanced at the mirror in the foyer. "I look like a completely different person," she said. She left to take her shower. I wrapped up her hair in the newspapers and went into the kitchen. I stood next to the sink for a long time before throwing the bundle away.

The past sees through all attempts at disguise. That night I was awakened by my sister's scream. I gasped and stiffened, grabbing a handful of blanket.

"*Claudia*," Emily cried from the other bed. "Claudia, wake up!"

"What is it?"

"I saw Baba." She hadn't called our father Baba in years. "Over there, by the door. Did you see him?"

"No," I said. "I didn't see anything." My bones felt frozen in place. After a moment I opened my eyes. The full moon shone through the window, bathing our room in silver and shadow. I heard my sister sob and then fall silent. I looked carefully at the door, but I noticed nothing.

Then I understood that his ghost would never visit me. I was, one might say, the lucky daughter. But I lay awake until morning, waiting; part of me is waiting still.

ORDINARY PAIN

by Michael Lowenthal

*For a teenager, "average" often translates as "mediocre." Twelve-
going-on-thirteen-year-old Larry Blank, the protagonist of Lowenthal's story, flies so far under the radar that he fears he is as
"nondescript as his name." At his privileged private school, status
comes from a "heritage of oppression" that few students can claim;
Larry, son of completely assimilated, mostly nonobservant, upper-
middle-class Jews, certainly cannot make such a claim. But his upcoming bar mitzvah provides him with a golden opportunity to
single himself out for what turns out to be a devastating distinction.*

*Larry's experiences in Hebrew school begin uneventfully. He
learns some Hebrew and Jewish history. During these classes, others
recount engaging, often tragic stories involving distant relatives,
but never Larry—until the class studies the Holocaust. Then,
Larry can tell of his German grandfather Ludwig who never made
it to America. That this grandfather died of diabetes, well cared
for in a Berlin hospital before the Nazis started rounding up Jews,
seems like an insignificant detail. It becomes irrelevant to Larry's
wildly successful invented heritage: shot while trying to escape
from an extermination camp.*

*At Mooretown Friends, Larry, the best marketer of his newly
minted Hebrew-school celebrity, instantly becomes the most popular student on campus. Even his skeptical best friend, a remote*

descendent of Vanzetti (the early twentieth-century Italian American anarchist who, along with fellow laborer Sacco, was falsely accused of theft and murder and executed largely as the result of xenophobia), cannot poke holes in Larry's story, though he's never heard it before. As the day of his bar mitzvah draws near, Larry senses that his fame is about to peak. His speech, unlike the speeches of his Hebrew school classmates that offer only a gloss on their Torah portions, will comment broadly on the significance of the Holocaust and on the importance of remembering the suffering of those who experienced it. His parents and their friends will be none the wiser about Larry's version of Grandfather Ludwig's death, but his own classmates and friends will connect Larry's words with his glorious fabrication.

The crisis point for a lie often occurs where it unexpectedly intersects with a truth. In the case of "Ordinary Pain," that truth comes in the form of a wizened old guest cantor from New York, whose tattooed numbers are revealed when he helps Larry locate his Torah reading. The cantor's response to his speech, and the phrase that Larry remembers hearing from a real camp survivor—"If you could lick my heart, it would poison you"—leave him with a Holocaust memory all his own.

Michael Lowenthal, unlike his protagonist Larry Blank, did lose a great-grandfather and half-uncle in Nazi extermination camps; he claims to have written this story in response to what he has called the "spotlight of suffering" that many American Jews yearn nostalgically—if unconsciously—for, now that a number of them have become "disproportionately powerful insiders" in American culture. He is the author of three novels, and his short stories have been widely anthologized, appearing in such literary journals as The Southern Review *and* The Kenyon Review. *He currently lives in Boston where he serves on the executive board of PEN New England.*

"Ordinary Pain," with its emphasis on creating and using a fiction, can be contrasted with Packer's "Drinking Coffee Elsewhere"; while Larry wishes to attract attention to himself with his

*fiction about his grandfather denying his good fortune to have es-
caped the tragic events of the Holocaust, Dina wishes to pretend to
others and to herself that her mother's death and her own confusing sexual feelings are insignificant blips in an ordinary black girl's
life. It can also be compared to Erdrich's "The Shawl," in which a
real-life event is treated like fiction, capable of revision and rein-
terpretation. The thematic emphasis on lies intersecting with
truths is also reflected in Levithan's "The Alumni Interview."*

L arry Blank feared he was as nondescript as his name. His nose was
normal, not hawkish or wide, his hair the shade of soggy cardboard. He had dirt-brown eyes, freckleless skin. Each year he measured
just what the growth charts would predict, so that in all of his class
photographs—arranged by height—he was lost in the middle of the
middle row.

If Larry wasn't particularly unpopular, it was because disfavor required being noticed. He had an official "best friend," Vance—who, as
son of Larry's parents' bridge partners, couldn't shirk the obligation—
but other than that, no one much talked to him. Like the Muzak piped
into department stores, or the pastel wallpaper of doctors' waiting
rooms, Larry seemed fashioned to elude people's awareness.

Above everything, it was the name: Larry Blank. The joke was so
boring, his fellow seventh-graders didn't bother teasing him. They had
names with history, badges of pride. Vance was short for Vanzetti, the
wrongly executed anarchist, Vance's first cousin three times removed.
Tanisha Jefferson's ancestors had been slaves at Monticello, and people
shushed deferentially when she spoke of them.

At Mooretown Friends, where no one lacked for Volvos or summer
homes, true status came from underprivilege. More valuable than country club credentials was the ability to claim membership in the
disadvantaged—the groups lauded by their social studies text. Larry, resigned to his own blandness, wished at least for a heritage of oppression.
But his name meant nothing—literally.

He complained to his parents. "Blank? What kind of a name is that?"

"Ours," his father said. "That's what kind."

"Okay, so maybe you were stuck with that. But Larry? It doesn't stand for anything."

"You're named after your grandfather," his mother explained, "but we didn't want kids to make fun. If we called you Ludwig, you'd have griped we didn't name you something normal."

"I wouldn't have," Larry insisted.

"Yes you would."

Larry knew little about his grandparents, who had died before his birth. They were German, he dimly sensed; they'd sold insurance. He asked if there were photos, and his mother produced a single snapshot, from Marienbad in 1929: his grandfather strolling on the promenade. The man was huge—three hundred pounds at least—but the bulk only added to his elegance. His pants flared up like a funnel, the trashcan-width waist hoisted by dainty suspenders.

Larry pictured himself as fat as Ludwig, so fat that strangers would stare. He climbed into his father's too-big pants and shirt, padded them with pillows until his mirror image bulged. It gave him an idea.

He went to the kitchen and wolfed half a package of Chips Ahoy! At the point when he thought he would be sick, he dunked two tablespoons of strawberry Quik into a glass, then filled it with half-and-half. He guzzled until his lips glowed pink.

Larry decided to forge a career as the fat kid. Obesity would make him the butt of bathroom graffiti, the target of playground taunts. He'd be the underdog; everyone would know his name.

And so he ate. He ate and ate, sneaking downstairs each night after his parents had gone to bed and gobbling cinnamon grahams smeared with peanut butter. He stuffed himself with Snickers bars. Beer Nuts became a secret breakfast. He studied the fat content on nutritional labels, calculating how to ingest four and five hundred percent of his daily requirement.

But no matter how much he gorged, Larry didn't gain. Every day he weighed in on his mother's digital scale. One hundred four pounds, one hundred three—how could he lose in the midst of his pigging?! His metabolism defied all logic, a perpetual motion machine. It burned up everything he offered it.

After three weeks Larry quit, cursing his body as he'd cursed his name. He was a prisoner of his normalcy.

In a year he would be due for a bar mitzvah. His parents enrolled him in Hebrew school.

Larry had never thought of himself as Jewish. He didn't have curly hair like Jonah Greenberg. He didn't have the honking schnozz. And the Blanks were hardly observant. Once or twice they'd erected a Chanukah bush; most years they didn't go that far.

But a bar mitzvah, his father said, was nonnegotiable. He had done it, as had his father and his father, too, and now it was Larry's turn. Larry was perplexed by the sudden bow to tradition, annoyed that it would claim his time. With the fat project a resounding failure, he needed to find other avenues to distinction, and Hebrew school didn't seem a winning bet. Jews were plentiful at Mooretown Friends, probably more so than birthright Quakers.

But what choice did a twelve-year-old have? Hebrew school met Wednesday nights and Saturdays at the synagogue bordering the golf course. His parents gave him money for the cab.

Mrs. Hershman, the teacher, taught the "aleph-bet" and made them sing it to the tune of the "A-B-Cs." The language was difficult. Larry's voice cracked. He lip-synched and tried to look convincing.

The second hour of each class was modern Jewish history. They started with the Inquisition, then fast-forwarded to pogroms. "Can anyone tell me what a pogrom was?" asked Mrs. Hershman. She rolled the r with an Old World accent, as if relishing an ethnic delicacy.

Miriam Goodman, a froggy little girl whose eyes floated on the verge of being crossed, raised her hand. "A pogrom is when they massacre a whole town of Jews just because they're Jews. It's a kind of unfair prosecution."

"Persecution," corrected Mrs. Hershman.

"Yeah, persecution. My great-uncle Boris was in a pogrom in Latvia. He and his sister were the only ones who survived. They hid in an outhouse for three days with no food or water and rats biting at their toes. But they escaped, and they saved the family candlesticks. My mom's going to give me them when I get married."

Mrs. Hershman walked over to Miriam and placed a reverent hand on her shoulder. "You should be proud of such tradition in your family. That kind of courage has allowed the Jewish people to survive through the centuries."

Other kids piped up with questions. "Were they down inside the outhouse holes?" "Didn't the rat bites get infected?" Miriam responded with the patient largesse of a movie star doling autographs. She told and retold the tale of Uncle Boris until it was time for class to end.

Slinking out, Larry seethed with jealousy. Even here, the spotlight shone away from him.

The next week was Zionism, and the week after that, the Holocaust. Mrs. Hershman passed out time lines of Hitler's rise. A glossary defined *Judenrein, Reichstag, yellow star*. The students had secured parental signatures to see "a film of disturbingly explicit nature." In grainy black and white, they viewed corpses stacked like cordwood, heaps of shoes and eyeglasses and shorn hair. Women stood shivering before the camera, their naked breasts shrunken bags of skin.

When the movie ended, Larry heard sounds that might be crying. "Six million murdered," Mrs. Hershman said. "Think how lucky we are to be alive."

"Did you know anyone who was killed?" asked Ethan Taub. He was the only one in the class worse than Larry at the aleph-bet. In elementary school he'd been held back two grades.

"I'm too young," said the teacher, turning on the lights. "But my parents lost many loved ones. I'm sure your parents and grandparents did, too. Later, we'll be doing oral histories. But does anyone know right now what happened to their families in the Holocaust?"

No one raised a hand, not even Miriam Goodman. The fluorescent tubes ticked expectantly.

"Well, thank HaShem if no one here has tragedy in their family. But this is still our collective tragedy, as Jews." Mrs. Hershman tugged the movie screen's cord so that it snapped up with a ghostly vinyl shriek.

Larry thought of the living ghosts in the wartime footage, stick-thin men with grotesque blowfish stomachs. He thought of the paunch he had tried to cultivate. "My grandfather was from Germany," he blurted.

Mrs. Hershman's eyebrows perked. "Your grandfather? When did he come over?"

"He didn't," Larry said. "He died there."

The lack of sound that greeted this announcement was louder than any gasp. Larry felt tendrils of attention stretching for him. The room's walls seemed to tilt in his direction.

"I'm so sorry," said Mrs. Hershman. "It must be hard to talk about. Do you know which camp?"

Larry's pulse clogged the veins in his neck. His brain felt wobbly and wonderful. He picked a name from the movie: "Buchenwald."

"Yes," said the teacher, as if she'd known.

There were stirrings of amazement from his classmates. Ethan Taub asked tactlessly, "Was he gassed?"

"Now class, remember," warned Mrs. Hershman, "this isn't Twenty Questions. We're talking about a real person's life."

"It's okay," Larry said. "It's just, you know . . . I'm not used to saying stuff."

He was stalling. The truth was, Ludwig had died of diabetes in 1935, well tended in a Berlin hospital. Larry's father had been a year old at the time; his uncle Gene, two-and-a-half. Within six months, their mother had the family settled in Connecticut.

"He wasn't gassed," Larry said. "He was shot. In an escape attempt." He recalled Miriam's pogrom account, how each new particular burnished her gleaming aura. "My grandfather made it outside the fence," he went on, "but then he turned back to help his brother through, and the guards shot both of them. His name was Ludwig. That's how come my parents called me Larry—the same first letter and all. I guess I'm his namesake, or whatever."

"That's quite a legacy to live up to," said Mrs. Hershman.

"I know," Larry said, "I know it is."

After class, not wanting to squander his success all at once, he rushed past his thronging classmates to the street. He imagined the cab that drove him home a limousine.

Riding to regular school the next morning, already in need of another fix, Larry schemed ways to export his celebrity. In homeroom, he doodled Stars of David on his spiral notebook. *Jude,* he wrote in block letters, remembering the previous night's film. *Achtung, Shoah, Buchenwald.* He added approximations of Hebrew characters.

Nobody was biting, so finally Larry knocked his notebook on the floor. Tanisha Jefferson handed it back to him.

"What's all that mumbo-jumbo?" she asked.

"What?" Larry said, playing dumb.

"This. These stars. These words in Jewish."

"Oh, that. Just stuff about the Holocaust. Today's the anniversary of when my grandfather was killed."

Tanisha's jaw dropped so wide she almost lost her Bubble Yum. "Your grandfather got killed in the Holocaust?"

"Yeah," Larry said. "He was shot."

Two other kids screeched their chairs around to listen.

Larry followed the same script he'd invented at Hebrew school, only this time with added details. Ludwig had been the ringleader of an underground rebellion. Because of his cunning, seventeen men escaped, but then the guard they'd bribed ratted on them. That's when they made a run for it. Alone; Ludwig could have managed, but he had to carry his sick brother, who was so weak he couldn't support himself. They caught him at the fence and gunned him down.

By lunchtime, everyone knew. People fought for space at the cafeteria table. Trays of American chop suey almost overturned.

Larry maintained a pose of superiority. He would tell them—yes, he would—but first they had to settle down, because this was no circus sideshow attraction. This was history. This was remembrance.

Larry added backstory to his fantasy. To the gathered crowd he explained that Ludwig hadn't gone easily. When the Nazis came for him, he refused; he wouldn't open the door for a band of thugs. The Nazis broke in and found him in the kitchen, holding on to the massive stove. "I'm not leaving," he told them. "This is my home." An SS officer tried to pull him free, but Ludwig in his anger was too strong. A second Nazi grabbed him, then a third, but still Ludwig wouldn't budge. "I am not leaving," he repeated. "I won't let go." Finally, the officer grabbed a meat cleaver from the wall. With one clean chop he severed Ludwig's thumb. "What happened?" he mocked. "Why'd you let go?"

Larry paused to let the horror sink in. He took a bite of his American chop suey, now congealed to a gloppy mass. Its sliminess in his throat inspired him further.

"This might not be appropriate for mealtime," he warned. He was a genius. He couldn't stop himself. "There was this time in Buchenwald—that's the concentration camp they took him to. My grandfather felt sick, probably from the soup they were fed, made with nasty sewage water. After dinner, when they got back to the bunkhouse he threw up. His hunk of bread wasn't digested yet, so the other prisoners dove and tried to steal it. That's how starving they were. My grandfather had to get down on the floor, too, and fight them for a piece of his own puke."

"Eew," Tanisha groaned, and dropped her fork. "I don't think I can take any more of this."

Someone assented, but everyone stayed put. Larry was now the sun around which they all revolved; they leaned phototropically for more.

"It's not pretty," Larry said, "but it's the truth."

Vance sat across from him, glumly gnawing a carrot from his brown-bag lunch. Larry figured he was peeved, because as his best friend, Vance expected first dibs on information. Later, Larry would apologize, explaining that he'd never mentioned Ludwig because the subject was too touchy in his family. He hadn't planned to blab, but then Tanisha asked.

Vance crumpled his empty lunch bag and hook-shot it into a trashcan. He stared at Larry. "I don't believe you," he said.

"What?" Larry said, even though he'd heard.

"I don't believe you. You're making it up."

"Oh shit," said Tanisha. "He's telling you about his people getting murdered, and you're calling him a liar? Oh shit."

Larry gripped the table's edge, so invested in the story that his rage at being doubted was genuine. "What don't you believe?" he said. "You think the Holocaust didn't happen?"

"Of course it happened. That doesn't mean your grandfather ate his own puke."

"What, you want a doctor's report?"

Larry chortled, hoping to persuade the others that Vance was ridiculous. But no one joined in. Vance's skepticism had tainted their credulity.

"Tell me this," Vance said. "Your grandfather died, right?"

"Yeah."

"And so did his brother. So how do you know exactly what happened in the camp?"

It was a good question. Larry wanted to shoot back with "How do you know about your dead cousin what's-his-name?" But Sacco and Vanzetti were pictured in their history book. Vance's claim could be fully documented.

Like spark plugs in a cold engine, Larry's synapses strained to fire. "There was a guy . . ." he said, out of nowhere, "a schoolteacher. He kept a diary of everything. He wrote it down on the backs of envelopes."

"Uh-huh," Vance said. "I bet. And what happened to the envelopes?"

"They're . . . in the museum. The Holocaust Museum in the Smithsonian."

The name cast a hush over the crowd. The Smithsonian was the destination of the annual eighth-grade trip, the sparkling Oz that teachers dangled before them—mere seventh-graders—as inducement to two years of good behavior.

"I told you so," said Tanisha, plucking a walnut from her brownie. "The Smithsonian? No way could he be faking."

Larry shrugged as if to say, "Go ahead, check it out"—his triumph poisoned already with the terror that someone might.

But after that, no one challenged him. Even Vance deferred to his authority. What Larry discovered in the following weeks and months was that people didn't want to doubt their celebrities. They wanted, more than anything, to believe.

His renown was unprecedented. Calamity had visited their circle previously—one girl's father had nearly died two winters earlier until doctors gave him someone else's liver; Tanisha's Brooklyn cousin had lost two fingers in a drive-by shooting—but these were nothing compared to Larry's story. He found that Ludwig's misfortune, despite its distance of decades, was an endlessly potent narrative, and that merely setting a given episode in the concentration camp exponentially increased its profoundness. Pain inflicted by the Nazis hurt more than ordinary pain. The Holocaust was the ultimate trump card.

Word of Larry's heritage spread. Kids he didn't even know found him at his locker and asked to hear the story of the cleavered thumb. Mr. Tisch, his social studies teacher, kept him after class to say, "Your grandfather would be proud of you."

Larry tattooed his wrist with a blue felt-tip pen: 6-14-42. This was Ludwig's number, he confided to Tanisha, knowing she'd have the whole school talking by fourth period. He made sure to roll up his sleeves.

The ploy worked so well that he forgot to wash the ink. At home that night, his mother grabbed his arm. "What on earth?" she demanded. "What is this?"

Larry had told her nothing of his concoction, so he simply confessed the truth: the number was his locker combination. She insisted he scrub clean before dinner. But the next morning he reapplied the numerals. He fended off teenage paparazzi all day.

People called him now. He got invited. Rob Swann, the soccer team captain, asked him to his birthday slumber party. The redhead from Life Science made a bid to be his lab partner.

Walking down the corridors, Larry felt fluorescent with importance. He was a tycoon of tragedy.

As the bar mitzvah neared, Larry grew studious. He possessed no knack for the material, but Mrs. Hershman suggested he dedicate the occasion to Ludwig's memory, and this incentive kept his focus sharp. His grandfather had been killed for his faith, the teacher said; learning the liturgy was the least Larry could do.

He labored over his Torah portion and his haftorah. He warbled the ancient melodies seemingly composed to taunt a boy at his change of voice. He practiced donning the tallis and tefillin—a silly-looking costume, but one, he realized, well suited as a conversation piece.

Each bar and bat mitzvah candidate was expected to prepare a speech. Mrs. Hershman advised that the students stick to a gloss on their allotted scripture, but she pulled Larry aside separately. For his recitation, she said, comments on the Holocaust might be movingly appropriate. She loaned him books to read: Anne Frank's *Diary of a Young Girl; Night,* by Elie Wiesel.

After boning up on the Final Solution, Larry decided that his choice of Buchenwald had been astute. When Mrs. Hershman first put him on the spot, he'd almost claimed Theresienstadt as the site of Ludwig's death; the lilting name felt good on his tongue. But now he learned that Theresienstadt, with its art classes and orchestras, was hardly even a concentration camp. Buchenwald wielded far greater prestige.

He was thrilled to find, in an oral history of Holocaust survivors, the line that he knew would make his presentation's high point. "If you could lick my heart," one survivor said, "it would poison you." Who could compete with such agony?

Larry's parents would be attending, of course, as would his uncle Gene, and he worried about their reaction to his zeal. Knowing the banality of the actual family past, might they question Larry's sincerity? But if he kept his comments general, without mentioning specific relatives, they should welcome his ethnic empathy. That was the whole point of a bar mitzvah! He rehearsed his cadence, his swell to the finale. Before the mirror, he nearly brought himself to tears.

When the day came, Larry was ready. His mother had bought him a suit at Brooks Brothers, a charcoal gray miniature of what his father wore to work. He had new black lace-up shoes, and his first-ever pair of non-tube socks.

In the car on the way to the synagogue, he sang to himself his memorized Torah portion. He understood now that the trick was to let your voice crack. He didn't flub a single word.

He felt the crisply folded pages of his speech, tucked into his jacket's inside pocket. The corners jabbed with his slightest bend or shift, but the twinge was good—it allowed him to practice wincing.

And then they were there, and Rabbi Kahn ushered them in, and all of a sudden it was time. Larry sat on the bimah, tiny in the plush high-backed chair. The sanctuary fanned before him, the same sloping shape as his school auditorium and with a similar choky carpet-cleanser smell.

Larry gazed across the banks of seats: his parents and their friends and Uncle Gene in the front row; then behind them, the regulars from the congregation; and in back, dozens and dozens of kids from school. Weeks earlier, addressing invitations, Larry's mother had questioned his guest list's length. She didn't know of the new voguish Larry, only the quietly unremarkable boy she'd raised. "Honey," she said, "having so many friends is wonderful. But do you really think all of them will come?" Larry had been stricken with uncertainty.

But scanning the crowd, he saw that his fears had been unfounded. Vance was here, and Tanisha, and Rob Swann. His whole homeroom had come, and most of social studies. Everyone was here to see him.

The service dawdled like a tape recorder on low batteries. Stand up, sit down; stay silent, please repeat. Larry watched his schoolmates, some respectful in their monkey suits, others joking and trying not to laugh. If the wait was too long, Larry might lose them. Performance was such a delicate balance, he had learned, a dance of delivery and delay. Every audience had its breaking point.

Yes, he knew he was performing. And if at times his act had been so heartfelt that he himself almost believed it, he was aware, too, that there must come an end. Even if he managed somehow never to be debunked, the fact was that people got bored. Even the Holocaust, if overused, grew mundane. But what Larry hoped was that this day would be the cresting of the wave. He would surf the glorious edge, riding for all it was worth, and then, just before the crash, turn out to chase another swell.

At last it was time for the Torah reading. There were seven segments, of which Larry would chant only the last. The first six would be sung by the cantor.

There was a special cantor today, Rabbi Kahn explained, visiting from a congregation in New York. It was an honor to have such a distinguished guest. The man who'd been sitting on the far left of the bimah, whom Larry had barely noticed, rose and approached the podium.

He was short in the way of old people, as if a lifetime of exposure had shrunk him down. Everything was too big on him, his tweed jacket swallowing his arms, his *tallis* like a child's costume cape. In order to see the Torah, he mounted the wooden stool usually reserved for bar mitzvah boys.

And yet when he opened his mouth, the cantor was anything but small. He sang with the rough-hewn authority of a shepherd beckoning his flock, the kind of voice that makes microphones redundant. Larry wondered where, in that tiny chest, it came from.

The countdown began. Before each Torah segment, a different man was called to recite the blessing. The first two required special lineage and went to synagogue regulars, but the rest had been apportioned by the family: Larry's father's boss; Dave Foster, their next-door neighbor; Uncle Gene; Larry's father; and finally Larry.

Up the men came, offering handshakes like cigars, then down again when each portion ended. As his turn neared, Larry woozed with adrenaline. He slowed his breath, trying to locate a meditative calm. *"Om,"* he hummed silently, a mantra copied from the movies. *"Om, om."* He repeated the sound, again and again, until he sang, "I'm, I'm."

Then the wait that had seemed infinite abruptly found its end, when the cantor summoned him with an operatic flourish. Larry stood and straightened his jacket. He squared his jaw, as he had trained himself. He puffed his chest like Ludwig in the photograph.

Staring out into the congregation, Larry saw only a vague scrim of light and dark. The rabbi flashed a hidden thumbs-up below the podium. His father managed a nervous nod. Larry pretended not to know any of them. They were mere fans; he was the superstar.

He began the preliminary prayer, the rote formula locked on its perfect pitch. If he concentrated, he knew he could nail this. He would chant the blessing and the Torah portion, displaying his impressive competence. And then the real test: the pages tucked next to his hurried heart. He would speak of cruelty and devastation, but also of enduring hope and faith. He would explain the responsibility he felt—to history, to memory, to truth. He'd be fervent and unforgettable.

At the blessing's conclusion, the congregation called "Amen," their voices like a spotlight trained on him. Now the tiny cantor leaned in close. The man was even older than Larry had first imagined, his skin scored with lines that evoked the underside of an autumn leaf. "You'll be fine," the cantor whispered. "Follow along with me."

Until now, Larry had heard only the cantor's Hebrew. His English was edged with a foreign accent, so that "with me" became "viss me," a whip.

"Ready?" he asked.

Larry nodded firmly, he'd never felt more ready in his life.

Like a conductor preparing to cue the orchestra, the cantor lifted his *yod,* the miniature silver hand with which he'd guide Larry through the text. The antique was delicate, precise in its semblance of flesh. Larry fixed his sights on the metal finger. Focus, he thought. Full voice. Confidence.

The cantor scanned the Torah scroll for the portion's first word. Because Larry had now claimed the wooden stool, the old man had to

stretch on tiptoe. He reached to his arm's limit, his wrist extending
turtlelike from his jacket sleeve, and that's when Larry saw the numerals.

They looked fake at first. Mine were more real than that, he
thought. But then he could see the depth of the tattoo, its dye etched
into the wrinkled skin. After half a century the numbers were still clear,
the dull purple of the stamp on a slab of beef.

"Go ahead," the cantor urged. "You can begin." He smiled, but in
his face Larry saw the hollow-eyed victims from the Hebrew school documentary. The *yod*'s disembodied hand was a ghastly skeleton.

Larry tried to retrieve his voice, but it disobeyed. He slumped
against the podium. A folded corner of his speech poked his ribs.

"You can do it," his father coached. "Mrs. Hershman says you know
it cold."

Larry glanced up and saw his teacher. He saw his mother, too, Uncle
Gene, the kids from school. He wished he could erase himself.

"Please," said the cantor. "We must begin."

And then, somehow, because the show must go on, Larry did
begin—shakily at first, his voice reedy and small. The cantor's pointing
hand accused him and Larry closed his eyes to banish it, chanting the
rest from memory. He missed a phrase, backpedaled, got it right on the
second try. He eked the tune word by word from his tightened throat.

In a blink he was finished; he'd only made the one mistake. The
rabbi pumped his hand with a hearty "mazel tov."

Now the speech was all that remained. Larry cleared his throat and
began to read from his laser printout. He was aware of the words, but
not of speaking them, as if he were a ventriloquist's dummy. He came
to the section about the concentration camps. Buchenwald, Treblinka,
Westerbork—the names must have sounded ludicrous in his trumped-
up accent. He thought he heard a snicker, but it was only someone's
sneeze. The audience sat rapt, credulous.

He pressed on, trying to ignore the cantor behind him, trying not to
imagine what he'd endured. "To remember," Larry said, "is a never-
ending duty. If we forget, then survival is meaningless." The congregation,
spellbound, restored his confidence. He surged to the heart-swelling conclusion. "They say we're the Chosen People, but I think we should be a

choosing people. Today I choose to remember what happened to our ancestors, and I choose to risk the same fate by standing up to say: I'm a Jew."

In the kiddush room downstairs, after the challah and wine were blessed, Larry was swarmed by awestruck well-wishers. There were hundreds, it seemed; they all wanted to shake his hand.

Mrs. Hershman requested a Xerox of the speech, saying it would be a model for years to come. "Totally cool," gushed Tanisha. "You made me feel it. It was almost worse than slavery." Vance offered a hug, and said, "Way to go, man. That speech should be in the Smithsonian."

And then, after Rabbi Kahn and some cousins from Florida, Larry looked up to the cantor's wizened face. On his chin shone a lurid dab of wine. Tears muddled his weary, knowing eyes.

"Son," he said, "I've seen more than I care to in my life. Humans doing inhuman things."

Larry braced himself. He feared his luck was spent.

"Sometimes," the cantor went on, "many times, I wished to die. But this, today. To hear a sensitive young man like you—it just makes me want to live and live!"

He drew Larry down, his hand gripping Larry's jaw, and pushed a wet kiss onto his mouth. The lips were rancid with kiddush wine and nicotine. If you could lick my heart, Larry thought, it would poison you.

His vision sizzled and shrank like a TV screen in a storm. He withered. He was going to be sick.

Excusing himself, he bolted to the bathroom, and wasn't quite to the sink when he threw up. He choked off his throat and swallowed back the bile, but specks of challah spattered the linoleum. A second retch, then only grueling air.

When the heaving subsided and Larry found his breath, he bent to the sink to rinse his mouth. Grains of vomit clung inside his cheeks. Larry washed and washed, even gargled liquid soap, but every swallow tasted just as bitter.

GLOSSARY

pogrom (173): from the Russian, to wreak havoc; a form of riot against a particular group (historically, Jews) characterized by the destruction of homes, businesses, and religious centers, sometimes even involving murder and massacre.

Zionism (174): an international political movement that supports a homeland for the Jewish people in Israel.

Holocaust (174): also known as Ha-Shoah or the Shoah; the term is generally used to describe the killing of approximately six million European Jews during World War II as a part of a deliberate extermination plan conceived of and executed by the German Nazis under Hitler.

Judenrein (174): German, meaning free of Jews.

Reichstag (174): the original parliament of the German empire.

yellow star (174): the yellow patch—compulsory during the Middle Ages and revived by the Nazis—that Jews were ordered to sew on their clothing to mark them publicly as Jews.

HaShem (174): the term used when referring to God to avoid pronouncing that word.

Jude (176): German for Jew.

tallis (180): a large rectangular prayer shawl.

Anne Frank's *Diary of a Young Girl; Night* by Elie Wiesel (180): first-person witness narratives about living in hiding (Anne Frank's *Diary*) and experiencing the Holocaust (*Night*).

Final Solution (180): refers to the Nazi plan to engage in systematic genocide against the European Jewish population during World War II.

bimah (181): elevated area or platform in a Jewish synagogue where the person reading the Torah stands.

kiddush room (185): room where blessing is said over the wine to sanctify the Sabbath or a holiday.

challah (185): special braided egg bread eaten on the Sabbath and on Jewish holidays.

SOME SAY THE WORLD

by Susan Perabo

In this story, a recovering teenage pyromaniac, zonked on Xanax, lives with her recently remarried mother who continues a weekly tryst with the teenager's father. At age eleven, she discovers that fire is "like blood, water, shelter," and that once a fire grows out of control, she must relinquish the illusion of her own power over it. The fire in her heart, the first sentence of the story, becomes an ongoing metaphor for this addiction. She cannot control her mother's narcissism; she could not control her parents' split. Instead of following the pattern of developing a desire for control, she opts for a life where the goal is to create chaos and destruction, what human beings seem destined to do anyway, from her perspective. Hospitalizations over the years have not helped; they only serve to remind her that "no one is going to help me in any way whatsoever."

Perabo's story provides a unique narrative viewpoint. The narrator gives the impression of—like her mother's new husband, Mr. Arnette—a depressed adult, dealing with a rebellious and duplicitous teenage-like mother. Neither she nor Mr. Arnette is fooled by her mother's ridiculous claim that she is studying poetry at the local college (the cover-up for the affair). Though Mr. Arnette once ran a successful windshield safety-glass company, he now plays endless games of Parcheesi with the narrator and drives her to see her psychiatrist twice a week. His passive acceptance of his lot mimics the narrator's own tranquilized stupor. They resemble an old married couple, while the narrator's mother appears to be living out some teenage fantasy, with her not-so-secret affair and her cosmetics counter job at Neiman Marcus.

Can things get worse? Yes—when the Parcheesi players suddenly decide to take action. The narrator throws her Xanax down the toilet so that she can feel "awake," and she and Mr. Arnette follow her mother to a nearby motel to be flies on the wall "together." What they see is the only predictable moment in the story; how they react and where they plan their next move (atop a Ferris wheel that the narrator views as "dangerous") testify to the ways in which the narrator might come to understand the full meaning of fire as an experience worth not just succumbing to, but surviving.

Susan Perabo graduated from Webster University in Missouri, which didn't have a women's softball team. Perabo landed a spot on the men's Division III team, and in so doing was the first woman ever to play NCAA baseball, a fact commemorated on a plaque in the Baseball Hall of Fame. Perabo never knew about the plaque until her parents came across it while visiting Cooperstown. She holds an MFA from the University of Arkansas and currently is writer in residence and associate professor of English at Dickinson College in Carlisle, Pennsylvania. Often compared to the writer Lorrie Moore, Perabo creates stories with no easy answers at the end. "Some Say the World" is part of her collection of stories entitled Who I Was Supposed to Be.

This story's rebellious narrator can be compared to ZZ Packer's Dina in "Drinking Coffee Elsewhere." Her sense of alienation and abandonment, and her eccentric way of dealing with it, can be read in conjunction with Tucker's narrator in "How I Learned to Fly." Perabo's use of symbols, such as fire and safety glass that is not shatterproof, can also be compared to the way in which Packer and Tucker use symbols in their stories.

There is fire in my heart. I do what I can.

I sleep deep sleep. I sit in my bedroom window, bare feet on the roof, and scratch dry sticks across the slate. In the two months I've been living here, though, I've spent most of my time playing board games with Mr. Arnette, my mother's new husband. He seems to have an unending supply of them in his basement from when his kids lived at home. My mother isn't around very often. She works at the makeup counter at Neiman Marcus, although she really hasn't needed to since she and Mr. Arnette were married. Mr. Arnette retired a few years ago, at forty, when he sold the windshield safety-glass company he had started right out of high school for what my mother described as "a fancy sum, for something that still shatters." It was right after that that she met and married him. But she works anyway, only now she calls it a hobby.

It's early March; more importantly, Monday night, the night my mother pretends to be in class at community college. This semester it's poetry, but she's run the gamut. Two summers ago she thought she had me convinced she'd taken up diving.

When she comes in the door a little after nine she sets her clearly untouched poetry book on the end table next to where I am on the couch.

"How was it?" Mr. Arnette asks, smacking his gum and not looking up from the board.

"Oh my," my mother said. "You wouldn't believe the things those people wrote then."

"Who'd you do tonight?" I ask her. It is a game that I have worked up. Sometimes I suspect that Mr. Arnette is playing it as well, but other times I think he's just being duped by her. You can never tell with Mr. Arnette. Sometimes I imagine he has a secret life, although he rarely leaves the house. He seems the type of guy who might have boxes of knickknacks buried all over the world for no reason.

"What's that?" my mother asks, separating the lashes over one eye, which have been caked with sweat-soaked mascara.

"Who'd you do tonight?" I put a cigarette in my mouth, wait for one of them to light it.

"Oh, Browning," my mother says.

"Which one?" Mr. Arnette asks. He looks up at me, not her, then takes the lighter from his shirt pocket and snaps on the flame in front of my face, so close I could reach out and swallow it.

"Which *one?*" she asks.

"Which Browning," Mr. Arnette says. The lighter disappears back into his shirt.

My mother misses a beat, then says, "All of them."

She hovers over the Parcheesi board, feigning interest in the game, and her mink stole knocks one of my pieces to the floor. Mr. Arnette makes a disgusted sigh, although it was him, I know, who bought her the thing. She likes to wear it to work, along with a lot of expensive jewelry. She does not work *for* her customers, she recently explained to me, she works *with* them.

She pats my head. "About your bedtime," she says, as if I am twelve and have to get up early to catch the school bus, not eighteen and drugged beyond understanding anything much more difficult than Parcheesi and knowing that my mother, at forty, is sneaking around in motel rooms.

My parents were divorced when I was five. I have not seen my father since then, but even so I've been able to keep track of his moods. If my mother is irritable on Monday nights I know that my father is considering calling everything off. If she is sad I know that he has asked for her back. If she is her usual perky self, like tonight, I know that things have gone as planned. They have met every Monday in the same motel since I was in the sixth grade and playing with lighters under my covers after bedtime. I used to find motel receipts, not even torn or wadded up, but just lying in the kitchen wastebasket next to orange peels and soggy cigarettes, with "Mr. and Mrs." and then my father's name following. Still, my mother, through eight years and two more husbands, has never spoken of it to me, and acts as if I could not possibly have figured it out. Thus over the years I have been forced to make up my own story of them: passionate but incompatible, my father a dashing and successful salesman, only through town once a week, only able (willing?) to give my mother three hours. Other times I think it is she who insists on being home each Monday by nine, she that likes doling herself out on her terms, only in small doses. I imagine that they do not talk, that their clothes are strewn around the room before there is time to say anything, and back on by the time they catch their breath. It is easier for me to think of it this way, because I can't imagine what they might possibly say to each other.

At Neiman Marcus, where my mother works, they found me in a dressing room last winter with a can of lighter fluid and my pockets stuffed with old underwear and dishtowels. This incident was especially distressing because everyone finally thought that after nearly eight years I had been cured, that the fire was gone, that I was no longer a threat to society. The police led me out of the store handcuffed, first through women's lingerie and then smack past the makeup counter, where my mother was halfway pretending not to know me, or to know me just well enough to be interested in what was taking place. They put me away for almost a year for that one, my third time in the hospital since the first fire. The length of my stay was caused by pure frustration, I'm convinced, on the part of my doctors. The "we'll teach her" philosophy of psychology. Two months ago they let me out again, into a different world where my mother is married yet again, and I spend my days spitting on dice with her husband and asking politely for matches to light my cigarettes. Either the doctors think I am cured or they have given in, the way I have, the way I did when I was only eleven, when I realized the fire was like blood, water, shelter. Essential.

The thing about fire is this: it is yours for one glorious moment. You bear it, you raise it. The first time, in the record store downtown, I stood over the bathroom trash can, thinking I would not let it grow, that I would love it only to a point, and then kill it. That is the trick with fire. For that thirty seconds, you have a choice: spit on it, step on it, douse it with a can of Coke. But wait one moment too long, get caught up in its beauty, and it has grown beyond your control. And it is that moment that I live for. The relinquishing. The power passes from you to it. The world opens up, and you with it. I cried in the record store when the flame rose above my head: not from fear, but from ecstasy.

I sleep sixteen hours a day, more if it's rainy. Another rationale: enough Xanax and I will be too tired to start fires. I am in bed by ten and don't get up till nearly noon. Usually I take a nap before dinner. The rest of the time is game time. It's a murky haze, more often than not. Me forgetting which color I am, what the rules are. Sometimes Mr. Arnette corrects me; other times he lets it go and it is three turns later by the time I realize I have moved my piece the wrong way on a one-way board.

We are on a Parcheesi kick now. Seven or eight games a day. We don't talk much. Mostly we just talk about the game, about the pieces as if they are real people, with spouses and children waiting in some tiny house for them to return from their endless road trips. "In a slump. You're due," Mr. Arnette will say to his men. Sometimes he whispers to the dice. I suspect this is all to entertain me, because he is always checking my reaction. Usually I smile.

Twice a week Mr. Arnette drives me across town to see my psychiatrist. He reads magazines in the waiting room while I explain to the doctor that I am fine except for the fact that I take so much Xanax I feel my brain has been rewired for a task other than real life. The doctor always nods at this, raising his eyebrows as if I have given him some new information that he will get right on, and then tells me the medication will eventually remedy any "discomfort" I might be feeling. I am used to this, and have learned not to greet with great surprise the fact that no one is going to help me in any way whatsoever.

It's Friday, and on the way home from the doctor's we drive by a Lions Club carnival that has set up in a park near Mr. Arnette's house. It is twilight, and my mother will be waiting for us at home, but for some reason Mr. Arnette follows the waving arms of a fat clown and pulls into the carnival parking lot.

"What do you say?" he says. He takes a piece of gum from his pocket and puts it in his mouth.

I look out the window at the carnival. I don't get out much. Grocery stores are monumental at this point, and the sight of all these people milling around, the rides, the games, frightens me. A Ferris wheel directly in front of me is spinning around and around, and it makes me dizzy just watching it.

"I'm kinda tired," I say.

Mr. Arnette chews louder, manipulates the gum into actually sounding frustrated.

"I think it'd be good for you," he says. He has never said such a thing before, but instead of causing me to feel loved and comforted it makes me nauseous. I've been told everything from shock treatments to making lanyards would be "good for me," and in practically this same tone.

I feel like crying, and know if I do that he will panic and take me home. But I don't have the time. He is out of the car before I can well up any tears, and I continue to sit, my seat belt still on, staring out the window into the gray sky. Mr. Arnette stands in front of the fender, gesturing for me to join him.

The last time I was at a carnival was the Freshman Fair at my high school, five thousand years ago. I went on a Saturday night with a boy named Dave who took pictures for the school paper. He held my hand as we walked through the crowds of people and he was sweaty—greasy, almost. He stuck his tongue in my ear in the Haunted House ride and I barely noticed because they had a burning effigy of our rival school's mascot on the wall. The fire licked along the walls and I realized with absolute glee that they had set up one hell of a fire hazard.

Mr. Arnette gets back into the car with a sigh, but does not drive away.

"You need to get out more," he says, and I wonder what has changed, wonder if he had a fight with my mother, or sex with my mother, or some other unlikely thing.

"Used to take the kids here," he says, spinning the keys around his finger. I don't even know his kids' names. They call occasionally, but he speaks so rarely when he's on the phone with them that I can't pick up very much information. I imagine them jabbering away somewhere about work and weather and the price of ground round while he sits on the kitchen stool, picking his fingernails and nodding into the phone.

"I'm not exactly a kid," I say.

"You don't like carnivals?"

"I just don't feel like it."

"If she doesn't feel like it then she doesn't feel like it," he says, as if there is someone else in the car, another part of him, maybe, who he is arguing with.

We continue our drive home in silence. When we stop at a red light he says, "Why do you take all that shit if it makes you feel so bad?"

I laugh at him. It is a question so logical that it pegs him for a fool, and I can't believe I'm really sitting here with him.

"It's not quite that simple," I say.

He shrugs, gives it up, continues the drive home. He is not a fighter, not a radical. Once I came upon him in my bedroom, looking through a photo album of people he had never met. I stood in the doorway and watched him for nearly ten minutes, as he smiled slightly, turning the pages, and I imagined him making up lives for the people in my life. He is that way. Content not to get the whole picture.

I'm standing in the bathroom, trying to stir up enough nerve to just dump them, the whole bottle. My mother taps lightly on the door. I spend more than two minutes in the bathroom and she gets edgy.

"Honey?"

"Just a second," I say. I'm holding them in my hand, all of them. There must be a million of them, at least, enough to confuse me until I hit menopause.

"Are you sick?"

I close my hand around the pills and open the door just far enough for her to get her foot in it.

"Mother," I say. "I'm fine. I'm just putting on a little makeup."

This gets her, physically sends her back a step. She wants to believe it so much that I can see her talking herself into it.

"But it's almost time for bed," she says.

"Just to see how it looks," I say, giving her a big smile through the crack and inching the door closed again. I hear Mr. Arnette's heavy footsteps come tromping up the stairs.

"What's the fuss?" he asks.

"She's putting on makeup," my mother says in a stage whisper. "Maybe she's trying to look cute for you."

That takes care of my clenched hand. It opens of its own accord at my mother's words, and the pills sink to the bottom of the toilet, falling to pieces as they go.

"I think she's really just feeling up to it, starting to feel better," I hear my mother say. It is a new tone for her, and this time it's really a whisper, really some sentiment she doesn't want me to hear. I put my ear against the door. "I'd do anything to make her happy," she says. It makes my chest hurt, she believes it so much.

Sunday has come and my eyes can't stay open wide enough. I feel as if I have gotten glasses and a hearing aid over the weekend; colors are brighter and words sharper. No echoes. Words stop when mouths stop. My mother looks at me suspiciously when she comes into the kitchen early in the morning and finds me cooking bacon.

"What's gotten into you?" she asks, pleasantly enough, but with a flicker of panic in her face. Me around the oven means bad news for her. But the heat rising from the burners is only making me warm, and the smell of the bacon is so good that I can't think of much else.

"Just feeling awake," I say.

She smiles, nods, then studies me.

"I'm fine," I tell her.

Mr. Arnette drags into the kitchen, his hair mussed and his robe worn. I have never seen him in the morning.

"Well look who's up," he says. He winks at me.

"Why don't I finish up and you two go in and start a game," my mother says brightly. Mr. Arnette sits down at the table and opens the newspaper.

"I don't feel like it," I say. "Why don't we do something today?"

"We have to go to a party later," my mother says, glancing at Mr. Arnette for support. "I don't think you'd have very much fun there."

I set a plate of eggs and bacon in front of Mr. Arnette.

"Where's mine?" my mother asks.

"You hate eggs," I say.

"We don't *have* to go to the party," Mr. Arnette says.

My mother frowns, looks from him to me.

"Well I do," she says. "And I think it would be right for you to come with me. She can take care of herself."

I see my mother now, like she has been stripped down out of her clothes and her skin and even her bones. Her soul is steamed over and dripping fat droplets.

"You all go on," I say. "I don't mind."

I spend the day with my father. I sit out on the porch with the old photo album. The pictures make sense now, fit into an order I have never seen before. My father as a young man raises a tennis racket over his head. He is swinging at something: a butterfly or a bug, though, not a ball. In another he stares away into the distance while my mother pulls his arm, trying to get him to look at the camera. They are so clear now, my father and his bird nose. In one picture he holds me on his lap. I am crying, screaming, and my father is looking at me perplexed. He is barely twenty, I know, and cannot believe that I am his.

My mother and Mr. Arnette do not come home until late. I've lost track of time, still sitting with the photo album when the headlights swim into the driveway. They get out of the car and my mother takes Mr. Arnette's hand, swings it wildly around.

"Oh, darling!" my mother exclaims. I am not sure if it is to me or Mr. Arnette.

They are both drunk. My mother stumbles going through the door and Mr. Arnette catches her, leads her inside. Then he comes back out, grunts, and sits down on the porch step.

"What have you been doing all night?" he asks.

"Looking through this," I say, holding up the album.

He is quiet for a moment. Then he says: "You ever see your father?"

He says it almost as an afterthought, but to something that wasn't said. He says it like we've been on the porch together all night, discussing my father for hours like he was really one of the family.

"Just in here," I say.

"Think he's still a good-looking guy?"

"Dashing, I imagine," I say.

He snorts out a laugh.

"Why'd you marry her?" I hear myself ask.

He leans back, rests his head on the wood inches from my feet.

"Company," he says. He yawns. And I can see him now, too. Safety glass that still shatters. He begins to snore.

"Mr. Arnette?" I say. I reach down and just barely touch the top of his head. He doesn't move.

I go into the house and up the stairs. Their bedroom door is closed, and I imagine my mother is in about the same shape as he is, but that they will sleep it off in different places, with dreams of different people's arms.

When I open my door, my mother is standing in my room, the empty bottle of Xanax in one hand, the other hand palm up, as if she were questioning someone even before I arrived.

"Wait a minute," I say. "Just wait."

"I knew it," she says. "I knew there was something wrong."

"Nothing's wrong," I say. "What are you doing in my room? You scared me, standing there like that."

Her mouth opens. "I scared you?"

"I don't think I need those anymore," I say.

"Forgive me if I find it difficult to trust your judgment," she says.

I want a cigarette bad. I had to go all night without them, and I go to the dresser for my pack.

"A light," I say. "Do you have a light?"

"Not on your life," she says.

"I'm fine," I say. I accidentally break the cigarette between my fingers and reach for another one.

She sits down on the bed. "You hurt people," she says quietly. "Not just me. You think you take those pills because I don't want you to hurt me?"

"I never hurt anybody," I say.

"You are so lucky," she says. "You could have killed both of us five times over. In the dressing room, did you ever think about the woman in the next one?"

"I wasn't trying to hurt anybody," I say. "You don't understand."

"You're right about that," she says. She sets the empty bottle on the bed and stands up. "I'm sorry," she says. "I can only live with this for so long."

She leaves. I hear her bedroom door close. The house is silent. Below me, Mr. Arnette sleeps on the porch.

I sit down on the bed. I am crazy, all right. I have always been crazy. I see my mother standing on the front porch as I get out of my first police car, only fourteen, braces squeezing my teeth. She stares at me in disbelief when the police tell her that I have caused over a thousand dollars in damage at the record store, a thousand dollars with only one match. It is then that she begins to look at me like a stranger.

It's Monday again, and she is in her bedroom preparing. Mr. Arnette sits in the rocking chair watching a basketball game. I am on the couch. Cheers from the crowd.

"She wants you to go back into the hospital," he says. He doesn't look at me. He moves his glasses from hand to hand.

"I know," I say. "It's O.K. It's not so bad there."

"Anybody play Parcheesi?"

A man on the court has lost his contact lens. Players are on their knees, hunting.

"Cards mostly," I say. "Lots of jigsaw puzzles."

He nods. "You take those drugs today?"

"No," I say. "Soon enough. It's funny, being able to see so well. But not great so much."

My mother comes into the room and picks up her purse. "Have a good game," she says. She kisses Mr. Arnette on the top of the head, presses her lips into his hair for a long time, until he moves away.

"What was that for?" he asks. He really wants to know, I can tell.

"It doesn't have to be for anything, does it?" she says. She smiles at

me, lingers for a moment as if she has something to add but cannot remember what it could have been, and then she leaves.

Mr. Arnette swings the rocking chair around and faces me. "You
don't have to go," he says. "Imagine me here, all by myself."

"You'll do O.K.," I say. "Come visit."

He nods, picks up the poetry book from the coffee table where my
mother has left it, absently flips through it.

"She didn't even think to take it along," he says.

"She doesn't try so hard anymore," I say. "To fool anybody."

He stops on a page, squints at it, puts on his glasses. "Here's one
you'd like," he says, smiling. "*Some say the world will end in fire, others
say in ice.*" He stops, looks up at me and raises his eyebrows.

"I'd like to see them," I say. I hear my mother's car start up in the
driveway. "Just one time, see them together. Be a fly on the wall."

"We can be flies together," he says.

It is not a long drive, only a few miles, much too close as far as I'm con-
cerned, for something that seems like it must be another world. Mr. Arnette stays a few cars behind her, then drives past the motel after she
pulls into the lot. He drives around the block twice, then three times.

"What are you waiting for?" I ask him.

"A reason not to do this," he says. He presses down the accelerator
and we speed past the motel again. We drive around the city, looking at
closed-down stores, empty streets. We don't talk, act as if we really have
nowhere to go. He finally makes his way back to the motel, and this
time he pulls into the lot. We park at the far end and walk along the row
of empty spaces, toward my mother's car. The motel is nearly empty,
but the room next to her car is occupied. The shade on the window is up
a couple of inches. Mr. Arnette squats down, then reaches for me.

I close one eye and look inside. The bathroom light is on, the door
open, and I can see my mother gingerly applying her eye shadow in
front of the mirror. There is a man in the bed, sitting up, yawning. He
stretches his skinny arms. He is nearly bald, but has a small mustache
under his pointed nose. It is a stranger, no one I have ever seen before.

"He looks a lot different than the pictures," Mr. Arnette whispers.

"It's not him," I say, but as soon as I say this I know that it is.

Mr. Arnette looks at me. "Sweetheart . . ." he says.

My mother shuts off the bathroom light and I can see her silhouette move to the edge of the bed. She sits down and touches the man on the chest, running her finger from his throat to his waist. He takes her hand and puts the finger in his mouth. It is like watching shadows. She says something I cannot make out. Is it about me? Of course, I realize, it is not.

I shiver in the cold. Mr. Arnette takes off his sweater and sets it around my shoulders.

The man begins to put his clothes on, slowly. Next to me, I hear Mr. Arnette's breath catch.

"What is it?" I whisper. I wonder if he can be jealous, if he cares that much.

He only shakes his head. "Chilling," he whispers.

"What?" I say.

"What happens to people."

They are sitting on the edge of the bed together. My mother fumbles for her purse, takes out a pack of cigarettes, gives one to my father and takes one for herself. She lights them both.

"Where will we go?" Mr. Arnette whispers.

"What?" I say.

They are holding hands on the bed. The shadow of smoke drifts above them, the tiny circles of fire all that light the room.

"Where will we go?" he says again. I lean in against him. He is warm.

Inside the room is quiet. Together the man and the woman raise the cigarettes to their mouths. For a moment, the faces of my parents glow in the darkness. Then Mr. Arnette takes me by the arm and actually lifts me off the ground.

"Wait," I say. "Wait." But I don't fight him. I want him to take me away, finally. I have seen enough.

We are three blocks from the motel before he remembers to turn on his headlights.

"Slow down," I say. "You're gonna kill us both." I take out a cigarette and push the car lighter in.

"Jesus Christ," he says. "What would she do then?" For a moment he is insane, so much more than I ever could have hoped to be.

There are lights up ahead. Music. It is the carnival, its last night, in full swing. The car wildly spits up gravel as Mr. Arnette rumbles across the lot. He jumps out of the car, dashes forward a few feet, then turns and slams his fist into the hood. Then he is perfectly still. He looks straight at me, and I am afraid to move. The cigarette lighter clicks out. A father rushes his children into the back of the station wagon next to us, where they look at us through the big back window, mouths open.

I pull the lighter out, touch my fingers close enough to the middle to feel the raw heat. Then I light my cigarette and blow smoke into the windshield. Mr. Arnette watches me. I know now that he will never go back to my mother, will probably never lay eyes on her again. Something about seeing them, even though he knew. Something about seeing them.

He turns and starts walking toward the ticket booth. I get out of the car and follow him, stand behind him smoking while he buys two tickets.

"Ferris wheel," he says, turning to me. He smiles slightly. "None of those puke rides. Slow. Slow rides tonight."

We get into a car that I'm sure is broken. It swings differently than the others, crooked somehow. I start to say something, but a girl with yellow teeth and matching hair closes the bar over us and we are suddenly moving in a great lurch forward.

"Hey, hey!" Mr. Arnette says, squeezing the bar and looking down onto the park.

"These things are dangerous," I say.

"Bullshit," he says. "We're safer up here than anywhere else in the world."

We screech to a halt near the top, for the loading of passengers into the cars below us. We swing crookedly over the game booths, and I can see us, crashing down into the middle of the ring toss. So many ways to buy it, so few to stay alive.

"I've always liked the looks of Canada," Mr. Arnette says. He is smiling pleasantly, innocent as the dawn.

We start moving again. The motion is hypnotizing, and I no longer feel sick, but only strange, detached.

"Nice night for driving," I hear myself say.

He doesn't answer. He is looking at my hands, which are open, palms up on my lap, as if I am waiting for something on this ride. He reaches into his sweater pocket and takes out his pack of gum. He sets it in my hand, and my fingers close around it.

We swing around again. Below me, I see a circle of teenagers standing around a small bonfire, warming their hands. Sparks pop around them and die in the grass as the flame reaches higher. The Ferris wheel whips us toward it, and then away again, up into the night.

GLOSSARY

lanyards (193): a rope or woven cord often worn around the neck or wrist to carry something; in this story, "lanyard" may refer to the common camp craft, in which plastic or fabric strings are woven together to construct a decorative band, such as a keychain.

"Some say the world will end in fire; some say in ice" **(199):** the first two lines from a Robert Frost poem entitled "Fire and Ice," originally published in *Harper's Magazine* in 1920.

SURROUNDED BY SLEEP

by Akhil Sharma

Ten-year-old Ajay's life as he knows it comes to a crashing halt on an August afternoon when his fourteen-year-old brother Aman, frolicking at a nearby public pool, dives in and strikes his head on the pool's cement bottom. Three minutes later, he's brain-dead. Sharma's devastating story tells of the ripple effect that Aman's accident has on Ajay's parents and on Ajay in particular.

Dominating the story is the metaphor of sleep: whether coma-induced or symbolic, sleep represents a hauntingly strange emptiness and unrest. Ajay's family has recently moved from India to New York; the tragedy occurs in Arlington, Virginia, where the boys are visiting relatives. His mother's response to the fact that her elder son Aman will never be the same is to revert to Hindu prayer. Her "attempts to sway God" are mirrored by Ajay's animated conversations with a God who looks like Clark Kent. Both Ajay and his mother want to have returned the three minutes it took to snatch Aman from his already well-mapped future beginning at the Bronx High School of Science. Even Ajay's father, who commutes back and forth to Arlington from his job in New York where his son remains hospitalized, cannot help from falling victim to, as Ajay sees it, the coma-like existence that they are all now condemned to live caused by hospital life.

As Ajay's conversations with God escalate in intensity, they emphasize his desperation. He begins fifth grade in Arlington, rather than returning to New York, since his family is waiting for a space in a good, long-term health-care facility to open for Aman. Ajay fears his own selfishness yet offers astonishing insight into his family's confusing and often conflicting values, understanding that his mother requires both his success and any sacrifice he can make in exchange for Aman's speedy recovery. He slowly allows himself to feel the accident's unreality—how, back in India, this whole scenario would be impossible to imagine. He learns that his parents are separate, vulnerable people, not a single entity; he experiences doubt in the nonnegotiable God that he has created out of his fear and guilt; and he begins to recognize different expressions of grief, not the least of which is his own, at first adult-like and stoic, and finally ageappropriately tearful. In the end, he considers that Aman's sheer bad luck may have provided the opportunity for his own growth.

Akhil Sharma was born in Delhi in 1971, emigrating to the United States with his family at the age of eight. He grew up in Edison, New Jersey, attending Princeton University and several other graduate programs, including a stint at Harvard Law School, before deciding on a career in banking. Sharma's stories have appeared in such publications as Best American Short Stories, *the* O. Henry Award Winners Anthology, The Atlantic Monthly *and* The New Yorker, *where "Surrounded by Sleep" was originally published. He is also the author of the novel* The Obedient Father *and was named one of GRANTA's best young American novelists in 2007. He lives in New York City.*

With its emphasis on a young boy's attempt to fathom and survive his own and his family's despair, "Surrounded by Sleep" can be read in conjunction with Louise Erdrich's "The Shawl"; in that story, as in Sharma's, deep sadness brings with it a larger and possibly not so narrow and depressing vision of the spoils of sacrifice. Sharma's use of Ajay's rich fantasy life as a coping mechanism can also be compared to the way that Tucker employs his narrator's fantasy life in "How I Learned to Fly."

One August afternoon, when Ajay was ten years old, his elder brother, Aman, dove into a pool and struck his head on the cement bottom. For three minutes, he lay there unconscious. Two boys continued to swim, kicking and splashing, until finally Aman was spotted below them. Water had entered through his nose and mouth. It had filled his stomach. His lungs collapsed. By the time he was pulled out, he could no longer think, talk, chew, or roll over in his sleep.

Ajay's family had moved from India to Queens, New York, two years earlier. The accident occurred during the boys' summer vacation, on a visit with their aunt and uncle in Arlington, Virginia. After the accident, Ajay's mother came to Arlington, where she waited to see if Aman would recover. At the hospital, she told the doctors and nurses that her son had been accepted into the Bronx High School of Science, in the hope that by highlighting his intelligence she would move them to make a greater effort on his behalf. Within a few weeks of the accident, the insurance company said that Aman should be transferred to a less expensive care facility, a long-term one. But only a few of these were any good, and those were full, and Ajay's mother refused to move Aman until a space opened in one of them. So she remained in Arlington, and Ajay stayed too, and his father visited from Queens on the weekends when he wasn't working. Ajay was enrolled at the local public school and in September he started fifth grade.

Before the accident, Ajay had never prayed much. In India, he and his brother used to go with their mother to the temple every Tuesday night, but that was mostly because there was a good *dosa* restaurant nearby. In America, his family went to a temple only on important holy days and birthdays. But shortly after Ajay's mother came to Arlington, she moved into the room that he and his brother had shared during the summer and made an altar in a corner. She threw an old flowered sheet over a cardboard box that had once held a television. On top she put a clay lamp, an incense-stick holder, and postcards depicting various gods. There was also a postcard of Mahatma Gandhi. She explained to Ajay that God could take any form; the picture of Mahatma Gandhi was there because he had appeared to her in a dream after the accident and told her that

Aman would recover and become a surgeon. Now she and Ajay prayed for
at least half an hour before the altar every morning and night.

At first she prayed with absolute humility. "Whatever you do will be
good because you are doing it," she murmured to the postcards of Ram
and Shivaji, daubing their lips with water and rice. Mahatma Gandhi
got only water, because he did not like to eat. As weeks passed and
Aman did not recover in time to return to the Bronx High School of
Science for the first day of classes, his mother began doing things that
called attention to her piety. She sometimes held the prayer lamp until it
blistered her palms. Instead of kneeling before the altar, she lay face
down. She fasted twice a week. Her attempts to sway God were not so
different from Ajay's performing somersaults to amuse his aunt, and
they made God seem human to Ajay.

One morning as Ajay knelt before the altar, he traced an Om, a cru-
cifix, and a Star of David into the pile of the carpet. Beneath these he
traced an S, for Superman, inside an upside-down triangle. His mother
came up beside him.

"What are you praying for?" she asked. She had her hat on, a thick
gray knitted one that a man might wear. The tracings went against the
weave of the carpet and were darker than the surrounding nap. Pretending to examine them, Ajay leaned forward and put his hand over
the S. His mother did not mind the Christian and Jewish symbols—they
were for commonly recognized gods, after all—but she could not toler-
ate his praying to Superman. She'd caught him doing so once several
weeks earlier and had become very angry, as if Ajay's faith in Superman
made her faith in Ram ridiculous. "Right in front of God," she had said
several times.

Ajay, in his nervousness, spoke the truth. "I'm asking God to give
me a hundred percent on the math test."

His mother was silent for a moment. "What if God says you can
have the math grade but then Aman will have to be sick a little while
longer?" she asked.

Ajay kept quiet. He could hear cars on the road outside. He knew
that his mother wanted to bewail her misfortune before God so that
God would feel guilty. He looked at the postcard of Mahatma Gandhi.

It was a black-and-white photo of him walking down a city street with an enormous crowd trailing behind him. Ajay thought of how, before the accident, Aman had been so modest that he would not leave the bathroom until he was fully dressed. Now he had rashes on his penis from the catheter that drew his urine into a translucent bag hanging from the guardrail of his bed.

His mother asked again, "Would you say, 'Let him be sick a little while longer'?"

"Are you going to tell me the story about Uncle Naveen again?" he asked.

"Why shouldn't I? When I was sick, as a girl, your uncle walked seven times around the temple and asked God to let him fail his exams just as long as I got better."

"If I failed the math test and told you that story, you'd slap me and ask what one has to do with the other."

His mother turned to the altar. "What sort of sons did you give me, God?" she asked. "One you drown, the other is this selfish fool."

"I will fast today so that God puts some sense in me," Ajay said, glancing away from the altar and up at his mother. He liked the drama of fasting.

"No, you are a growing boy." His mother knelt down beside him and said to the altar, "He is stupid, but he has a good heart."

Prayer, Ajay thought, should appeal with humility and an open heart to some greater force. But the praying that he and his mother did felt sly and confused. By treating God as someone to bargain with, it seemed to him, they prayed as if they were casting a spell.

This meant that it was possible to do away with the presence of God entirely. For example, Ajay's mother had recently asked a relative in India to drive a nail into a holy tree and tie a saffron thread to the nail on Aman's behalf. Ajay invented his own ritual. On his way to school each morning, he passed a thick tree rooted half on the sidewalk and half on the road. One day Ajay got the idea that if he circled the tree seven times, touching the north side every other time, he would have a lucky day. From then on he did it every morning, although he felt embarrassed and always looked around beforehand to make sure no one was watching.

One night Ajay asked God whether he minded being prayed to only in need.

"You think of your toe only when you stub it," God replied. God looked like Clark Kent. He wore a gray cardigan, slacks, and thick glasses, and had a forelock that curled just as Ajay's did.

God and Ajay had begun talking occasionally after Aman drowned. Now they talked most nights while Ajay lay in bed and waited for sleep. God sat at the foot of Ajay's mattress. His mother's mattress lay parallel to his, a few feet away. Originally God had appeared to Ajay as Krishna, but Ajay had felt foolish discussing brain damage with a blue god who held a flute and wore a dhoti.

"You're not angry with me for touching the tree and all that?"

"No. I'm flexible."

"I respect you. The tree is just a way of praying to you," Ajay assured God.

God laughed. "I am not too caught up in formalities."

Ajay was quiet. He was convinced that he had been marked as special by Aman's accident. The beginnings of all heroes are distinguished by misfortune. Superman and Batman were both orphans. Krishna was separated from his parents at birth. The god Ram had to spend fourteen years in a forest. Ajay waited to speak until it would not appear improper to begin talking about himself.

"How famous will I be?" he asked finally.

"I can't tell you the future," God answered.

Ajay asked, "Why not?"

"Even if I told you something, later I might change my mind."

"But it might be harder to change your mind after you have said something will happen."

God laughed again. "You'll be so famous that fame will be a problem."

Ajay sighed. His mother snorted and rolled over.

"I want Aman's drowning to lead to something," he said to God.

"He won't be forgotten."

"I can't just be famous, though. I need to be rich too, to take care of Mummy and Daddy and pay Aman's hospital bills."

"You are always practical." God had a soulful and pitying voice, and God's sympathy made Ajay imagine himself as a truly tragic figure, like Amitabh Bachchan in the movie *Trishul*.

"I have responsibilities," Ajay said. He was so excited at the thought of his possible greatness that he knew he would have difficulty sleeping. Perhaps he would have to go read in the bathroom.

"You can hardly imagine the life ahead," God said.

Even though God's tone promised greatness, the idea of the future frightened Ajay. He opened his eyes. There was light coming from the street. The room was cold and had a smell of must and incense. His aunt and uncle's house was a narrow two-story home next to a four-lane road. The apartment building with the pool where Aman had drowned was a few blocks up the road, one in a cluster of tall brick buildings with stucco fronts. Ajay pulled the blanket tighter around him. In India, he could not have imagined the reality of his life in America: the thick smell of meat in the school cafeteria, the many television channels. And, of course, he could not have imagined Aman's accident, or the hospital where he spent so much time.

The hospital was boring. Vinod, Ajay's cousin, picked him up after school and dropped him off there almost every day. Vinod was twenty-two. In addition to attending county college and studying computer programming, he worked at a 7-Eleven near Ajay's school. He often brought Ajay hot chocolate and a comic from the store, which had to be returned, so Ajay was not allowed to open it until he had wiped his hands.

Vinod usually asked him a riddle on the way to the hospital. "Why are manhole covers round?" It took Ajay half the ride to admit that he did not know. He was having difficulty talking. He didn't know why. The only time he could talk easily was when he was with God. The explanation he gave himself for this was that just as he couldn't chew when there was too much in his mouth, he couldn't talk when there were too many thoughts in his head.

When Ajay got to Aman's room, he greeted him as if he were all right. "Hello, lazy. How much longer are you going to sleep?" His mother was always there. She got up and hugged Ajay. She asked how school had been, and he didn't know what to say. In music class, the teacher sang a song about a sailor who had bared his breast before jumping into the sea. This had caused the other students to giggle. But Ajay could not say the word *breast* to his mother without blushing. He had also cried. He'd been thinking of how Aman's accident had made his own life mysterious and confused. What would happen next? Would Aman die or would he go on as he was? Where would they live? Usually when Ajay cried in school, he was told to go outside. But it had been raining, and the teacher had sent him into the hallway. He sat on the floor and wept. Any mention of this would upset his mother. And so he said nothing had happened that day.

Sometimes when Ajay arrived his mother was on the phone, telling his father that she missed him and was expecting to see him on Friday. His father took a Greyhound bus most Fridays from Queens to Arlington, returning on Sunday night in time to work the next day. He was a bookkeeper for a department store. Before the accident, Ajay had thought of his parents as the same person: MummyDaddy. Now, when he saw his father praying stiffly or when his father failed to say hello to Aman in his hospital bed, Ajay sensed that his mother and father were quite different people. After his mother got off the phone, she always went to the cafeteria to get coffee for herself and Jell-O or cookies for him. He knew that if she took her coat with her, it meant that she was especially sad. Instead of going directly to the cafeteria, she was going to go outside and walk around the hospital parking lot.

That day, while she was gone, Ajay stood beside the hospital bed and balanced a comic book on Aman's chest. He read to him very slowly. Before turning each page, he said, "Okay, Aman?"

Aman was fourteen. He was thin and had curly hair. Immediately after the accident, there had been so many machines around his bed that only one person could stand beside him at a time. Now there was just a single waxy yellow tube. One end of this went into his abdomen; the other, blocked by a green bullet-shaped plug, was what his Isocal milk was poured through. When not being used, the tube was rolled up and bound by a rubber band and tucked beneath Aman's hospital gown. But even with the tube hidden, it was obvious that there was something wrong with Aman. It was in his stillness and his open eyes. Once, in their house in Queens, Ajay had left a plastic bowl on a radiator overnight and the sides had drooped and sagged so that the bowl looked a little like an eye. Aman reminded Ajay of that bowl.

Ajay had not gone with his brother to the swimming pool on the day of the accident, because he had been reading a book and wanted to finish it. But he heard the ambulance siren from his aunt and uncle's house. The pool was only a few minutes away, and when he got there a crowd had gathered around the ambulance. Ajay saw his uncle first, in shorts and an undershirt, talking to a man inside the ambulance. His aunt was standing beside him. Then Ajay saw Aman on a stretcher, in blue shorts with a plastic mask over his nose and mouth. His aunt hurried over to take Ajay home. He cried as they walked, although he had been certain that Aman would be fine in a few days: in a Spider-Man comic he had just read, Aunt May had fallen into a coma and she had woken up perfectly fine. Ajay had cried simply because he felt crying was called for by the seriousness of the occasion. Perhaps this moment would mark the beginning of his future greatness. From that day on, Ajay found it hard to cry in front of his family. Whenever tears started coming, he felt like a liar. If he loved his brother, he knew, he would not have thought about himself as the ambulance had pulled away, nor would he talk with God at night about becoming famous.

When Ajay's mother returned to Aman's room with coffee and cookies, she sometimes talked to Ajay about Aman. She told him that when Aman was six he had seen a children's television show that had a character named Chunu, which was Aman's nickname, and he had thought the show was based on his own life. But most days Ajay went into the lounge to read. There was a TV in the corner and a lamp near a window that looked out over a parking lot. It was the perfect place to read. Ajay liked fantasy novels where the hero, who was preferably under the age of twenty-five, had an undiscovered talent that made him famous when it was revealed. He could read for hours without interruption, and sometimes when Vinod came to drive Ajay and his mother home from the hospital it was hard for him to remember the details of the real day that had passed.

One evening when he was in the lounge, he saw a rock star being interviewed on *Entertainment Tonight*. The musician, dressed in a sleeveless undershirt that revealed a swarm of tattoos on his arms and shoulders, had begun to shout at the audience, over his interviewer, "Don't watch me! Live your life! I'm not you!" Filled with a sudden desire to do something, Ajay hurried out of the television lounge and stood on the sidewalk in front of the hospital entrance. But he did not know what to do. It was cold and dark and there was an enormous moon. Cars leaving the parking lot stopped one by one at the edge of the road. Ajay watched as they waited for an opening in the traffic, their brake lights glowing.

"Are things getting worse?" Ajay asked God. The weekend before had been Thanksgiving. Christmas soon would come, and a new year would start, a year during which Aman would not have talked or walked. Suddenly Ajay understood hopelessness. Hopelessness felt very much like fear. It involved a clutching in the stomach and a numbness in the arms and legs.

"What do you think?" God answered.

"They seem to be."

"At least Aman's hospital hasn't forced him out."

"At least Aman isn't dead. At least Daddy's Greyhound bus has never skidded off a bridge." Lately Ajay had begun talking much more quickly to God than he used to. Before, when he had talked to God, Ajay would think of what God would say in response before he said anything. Now Ajay spoke without knowing how God might respond.

"You shouldn't be angry at me." God sighed. God was wearing his usual cardigan. "You can't understand why I do what I do."

"You should explain better, then."

"Christ was my son. I loved Job. How long did Ram have to live in a forest?"

"What does that have to do with me?" This was usually the cue for discussing Ajay's prospects. But hopelessness made the future feel even more frightening than the present.

"I can't tell you what the connection is, but you'll be proud of yourself."

They were silent for a while.

"Do you love me truly?" Ajay asked.

"Yes."

"Will you make Aman normal?" As soon as Ajay asked the question, God ceased to be real. Ajay knew then that he was alone, lying under his blankets, his face exposed to the cold dark.

"I can't tell you the future," God said softly. These were words that Ajay already knew.

"Just get rid of the minutes when Aman lay on the bottom of the pool. What are three minutes to you?"

"Presidents die in less time than that. Planes crash in less time than that."

Ajay opened his eyes. His mother was on her side and she had a blanket pulled up to her neck. She looked like an ordinary woman. It surprised him that you couldn't tell, looking at her, that she had a son who was brain-dead.

In fact, things were getting worse. Putting away his mother's mattress and his own in a closet in the morning, getting up very early so he could use the bathroom before his aunt or uncle did, spending so many hours in the hospital—all this had given Ajay the reassuring sense that real life was in abeyance, and that what was happening was unreal. He and his mother and brother were just waiting to make a long-delayed bus trip. The bus would come eventually to carry them to Queens, where he would return to school at P.S. 20 and to Sunday afternoons spent at the Hindi movie theater under the trestle for the 7 train. But now Ajay was starting to understand that the world was always real, whether you were reading a book or sleeping, and that it eroded you every day.

He saw the evidence of this erosion in his mother, who had grown severe and unforgiving. Usually when Vinod brought her and Ajay home from the hospital, she had dinner with the rest of the family. After his mother helped his aunt wash the dishes, the two women watched theological action movies. One night, in spite of a headache that had made her sit with her eyes closed all afternoon, she ate dinner, washed dishes, sat down in front of the TV. As soon as the movie was over, she went upstairs, vomited, and lay on her mattress with a wet towel over her forehead. She asked Ajay to massage her neck and shoulders. As he did so, Ajay noticed that she was crying. The tears frightened Ajay and made him angry. "You shouldn't have watched TV," he said accusingly.

"I have to," she said. "People will cry with you once, and they will cry with you a second time. But if you cry a third time, people will say you are boring and always crying."

Ajay did not want to believe what she had said, but her cynicism made him think that she must have had conversations with his aunt and uncle that he did not know about. "That's not true," he told her, massaging her scalp. "Uncle is kind. Auntie Aruna is always kind."

"What do you know?" She shook her head, freeing herself from Ajay's fingers. She stared at him. Upside down, her face looked unfamiliar and terrifying. "If God lets Aman live long enough, you will become a stranger too. You will say, 'I have been unhappy for so long because of Aman, now I don't want to talk about him or look at him.' Don't think I don't know you," she said.

Suddenly Ajay hated himself. To hate himself was to see himself as the opposite of everything he wanted to be: short instead of tall, fat instead of thin. When he brushed his teeth that night, he looked at his face: his chin was round and fat as a heel. His nose was so broad that he had once been able to fit a small rock in one nostril.

His father was also being eroded. Before the accident, Ajay's father loved jokes—he could do perfect imitations—and Ajay had felt lucky to have him as a father. (Once, Ajay's father had convinced his own mother that he was possessed by the ghost of a British man.) And even after the accident, his father had impressed Ajay with the patient loyalty of his weekly bus journeys. But now his father was different.

One Saturday afternoon, as Ajay and his father were returning from the hospital, his father slowed the car without warning and turned into the dirt parking lot of a bar that looked as though it had originally been a small house. It had a pitched roof with a black tarp. At the edge of the lot stood a tall neon sign of an orange hand lifting a mug of sudsy golden beer. Ajay had never seen anybody drink except in the movies. He wondered whether his father was going to ask for directions to somewhere, and if so, to where.

His father said, "One minute," and they climbed out of the car.

They went up wooden steps into the bar. Inside, it was dark and smelled of cigarette smoke and something stale and sweet. The floor was linoleum like the kitchen at his aunt and uncle's. There was a bar with stools around it, and a basketball game played on a television bolted against the ceiling, like the one in Aman's hospital room.

His father stood by the bar waiting for the bartender to notice him. His father had a round face and was wearing a white shirt and dark dress pants, as he often did on the weekend, since it was more economical to have the same clothes for the office and home.

The bartender came over. "How much for a Budweiser?" his father asked.

It was a dollar fifty. "Can I buy a single cigarette?" He did not have to buy; the bartender would just give him one. His father helped Ajay up onto a stool and sat down himself. Ajay looked around and wondered what would happen if somebody started a knife fight. When his father had drunk half his beer, he carefully lit the cigarette. The bartender was standing at the end of the bar. There were only two other men in the place. Ajay was disappointed that there were no women wearing dresses slit all the way up their thighs. Perhaps they came in the evenings.

His father asked him if he had ever watched a basketball game all the way through.

"I've seen the Harlem Globetrotters."

His father smiled and took a sip. "I've heard they don't play other teams, because they can defeat everyone else so easily."

"They only play against each other, unless there is an emergency— like in the cartoon, when they play against the aliens to save the Earth," Ajay said.

"Aliens?"

Ajay blushed as he realized his father was teasing him.

When they left, the light outside felt too bright. As his father opened the car door for Ajay, he said, "I'm sorry." That's when Ajay first felt that his father might have done something wrong. The thought made him worry. Once they were on the road, his father said gently, "Don't tell your mother."

Fear made Ajay feel cruel. He asked his father, "What do you think about when you think of Aman?"

Instead of becoming sad, Ajay's father smiled. "I am surprised by how strong he is. It's not easy for him to keep living. But even before, he was strong. When he was interviewing for high school scholarships, one interviewer asked him, 'Are you a thinker or a doer?' He laughed and said, 'That's like asking, "Are you an idiot or a moron?"' "

From then on they often stopped at the bar on the way back from the hospital. Ajay's father always asked the bartender for a cigarette before he sat down, and during the ride home he always reminded Ajay not to tell his mother.

Ajay found that he himself was changing. His superstitions were becoming extreme. Now when he walked around the good-luck tree he punched it, every other time, hard, so that his knuckles hurt. Afterward, he would hold his breath for a moment longer than he thought he could bear, and ask God to give the unused breaths to Aman.

In December, a place opened in one of the good long-term care facilities. It was in New Jersey. This meant that Ajay and his mother could move back to New York and live with his father again. This was the news Ajay's father brought when he arrived for a two-week holiday at Christmas.

Ajay felt the clarity of panic. Life would be the same as before the accident but also unimaginably different. He would return to P.S. 20, while Aman continued to be fed through a tube in his abdomen. Life would be Aman's getting older and growing taller than their parents but having less consciousness than even a dog, which can become excited or afraid.

Ajay decided to use his devotion to shame God into fixing Aman. The fact that two religions regarded the coming December days as holy ones suggested to Ajay that prayers during this time would be especially potent. So he prayed whenever he thought of it—at his locker, even in the middle of a quiz. His mother wouldn't let him fast, but he started throwing away the lunch he took to school. And when his mother prayed in the morning, Ajay watched to make sure that she bowed at least once toward each of the postcards of deities. If she did not, he bowed three times to the possibly offended god on the postcard. He had noticed that his father finished his prayers in less time than it took to brush his teeth. And so now, when his father began praying in the morning, Ajay immediately crouched down beside him, because he knew his father would be embarrassed to get up first. But Ajay found it harder and harder to drift into the rhythm of sung prayers or into his nightly conversations with God. How could chanting and burning incense undo three minutes of a sunny August afternoon? It was like trying to move a sheet of blank paper from one end of a table to the other by blinking so fast that you started a breeze.

On Christmas Eve his mother asked the hospital chaplain to come to Aman's room and pray with them. The family knelt together beside Aman's bed. Afterward the chaplain asked her whether she would be attending Christmas services. "Of course, Father," she said.

"I'm also coming," Ajay said.

The chaplain turned toward Ajay's father, who was sitting in a wheelchair because there was nowhere else to sit.

"I'll wait for God at home," he said.

That night, Ajay watched *It's a Wonderful Life* on television. To him, the movie meant that happiness arrived late, if ever. Later, when he got in bed and closed his eyes, God appeared. There was little to say.

"Will Aman be better in the morning?"

"No."

"Why not?"

"When you prayed for the math exam, you could have asked for

Aman to get better, and instead of your getting an A, Aman would have woken."

This was so ridiculous that Ajay opened his eyes. His father was sleeping nearby on folded-up blankets. Ajay felt disappointed at not feeling guilt. Guilt might have contained some hope that God existed.

When Ajay arrived at the hospital with his father and mother the next morning, Aman was asleep, breathing through his mouth while a nurse poured a can of Isocal into his stomach through the yellow tube. Ajay had not expected that Aman would have recovered; nevertheless, seeing him that way put a weight in Ajay's chest.

The Christmas prayers were held in a large, mostly empty room: people in chairs sat next to people in wheelchairs. His father walked out in the middle of the service.

Later, Ajay sat in a corner of Aman's room and watched his parents. His mother was reading a Hindi women's magazine to Aman while she shelled peanuts into her lap. His father was reading a thick red book in preparation for a civil service exam. The day wore on. The sky outside grew dark. At some point Ajay began to cry. He tried to be quiet. He did not want his parents to notice his tears and think that he was crying for Aman, because in reality he was crying for how difficult his own life was.

His father noticed first. "What's the matter, hero?"

His mother shouted, "What happened?" and she sounded so alarmed it was as if Ajay were bleeding.

"I didn't get any Christmas presents. I need a Christmas present," Ajay shouted. "You didn't buy me a Christmas present." And then, because he had revealed his own selfishness, Ajay let himself sob. "You have to give me something. I should get something for all this." Ajay clenched his hands and wiped his face with his fists. "Each time I come here I should get something."

His mother pulled him up and pressed him into her stomach. His father came and stood beside them. "What do you want?" his father asked.

Ajay had no prepared answer for this.

"What do you want?" his mother repeated.

The only thing he could think was "I want to eat pizza and I want candy."

His mother stroked his hair and called him her little baby. She kept wiping his face with a fold of her sari. When at last he stopped crying, they decided that Ajay's father should take him back to his aunt and uncle's. On the way, they stopped at a mini-mall. It was a little after five, and the streetlights were on. Ajay and his father did not take off their winter coats as they ate, in a pizzeria staffed by Chinese people. While he chewed, Ajay closed his eyes and tried to imagine God looking like Clark Kent, wearing a cardigan and eyeglasses, but he could not. Afterward, Ajay and his father went next door to a magazine shop and Ajay got a bag of Three Musketeers bars and a bag of Reese's peanut butter cups, and then he was tired and ready for home.

He held the candy in his lap while his father drove in silence. Even through the plastic, he could smell the sugar and chocolate. Some of the houses outside were dark, and others were outlined in Christmas lights.

After a while Ajay rolled down the window slightly. The car filled with wind. They passed the building where Aman's accident had occurred. Ajay had not walked past it since the accident. When they drove by, he usually looked away. Now he tried to spot the fenced swimming pool at the building's side. He wondered whether the pool that had pressed itself into Aman's mouth and lungs and stomach had been drained, so that nobody would be touched by its unlucky waters. Probably it had not been emptied until fall. All summer long, people must have swum in the pool and sat on its sides, splashing their feet in the water, and not known that his brother had lain for three minutes on its concrete bottom one August afternoon.

GLOSSARY

dosa (205): a savory South Indian crepe.

Mahatma Gandhi (205): 1869–1948, a major political and spiritual leader of India and the Indian Independence Movement; Gandhi pioneered the resistance of tyranny through nonviolent civil disobedience.

Ram and Shivaji (206): Ram refers to the seventh incarnation of Vishnu, the central figure of the Ramayana, the Hindu epic; Ram was said to have freed the earth from the cruelty and sins of the demon king Ravena. Shivaji refers to the Indian folk hero, founder of the Maratha empire in Western India; an ancient freedom fighter, he represents the struggle against great imperial power.

Om (206): mystical or sacred syllable in the Hindu religion, placed at the beginning of most Hindu texts to be uttered at the beginning and end of sacred readings or any prayer.

Krishna (208): an incarnation of Vishnu, the supreme Hindu god; a heroic warrior and teacher, Krishna is usually depicted as a young cowherd, playing a flute to symbolize his pastoral childhood.

The god Ram had to spend fourteen years in a forest (208): refers to Ram's exile from his father's court as a result of intrigue; the exile was happily undertaken by Ram as a representation of his complete devotion and filial piety.

Amitabh Bachchan in the movie _Trishul_ (209): about an estranged father and son. The son, raised in the country by his mother and played by Bachchan, comes to the city to claim his patrimony; the film depicts his struggles to make himself known to his father and to gain a foothold in a strange and new environment.

LA LLORONA/WEEPING WOMAN

by Alma Luz Villanueva

*Behind Villanueva's story is the Mexican folk legend of La
Llorona, the weeping woman whose ghost wanders along water-
ways, crying out for her dead children. Like most folk literature,
different versions suggest different causes for her grief, and most of
them involve betrayal by a man, but in all versions La Llorona
chooses to sacrifice her children to the waters and then spends her
afterlife mourning and searching for them, sometimes with the
aim of sharing her suffering by threatening the lives of others.*

*Villanueva was born in Lompoc, California, in 1944, grew up
in the Mission district of San Francisco, and until she was eleven
lived with her grandmother, a Yaqui Indian from Mexico. Her
grandmother's version of the La Llorona story may well have included a connection with La Malinche, the Native American
woman who served as Hernán Cortés's interpreter (and mistress)
and was said to have betrayed Mexico to the Spanish conquista-
dores. According to this version, once La Malinche bears Cortés's
child, Cortés abandons her. Although it is unclear whether or not
she kills her child, the tale compares the Spanish invasion of
Mexico—and the demise of indigenous culture after the conquest—
to La Malinche's loss—of her child, perhaps, but certainly her
soul. In general, La Llorona's restless spirit and ghostly nature—in
some versions of the tale, she is an eerie, skeletal figure, carrying the*

head of a horse—signals a victim, and it is that part of the tale that Villanueva's story develops.

The women of Villanueva's story are all victims. Isidra, the grandmother, must live in perpetual displacement, far from her child-hood Mexico, where the stark desert provided the backdrop for singing birds and cool rivers. There, legends became part of the landscape, while California provides a poor substitute. It is a place where she must endure the dismissive contempt of Carmen, her only surviving child, and where she can only recall from earlier years the weeping and singing of La Llorona. Carmen herself leads the hardscrabble life of a prostitute; she brings home clients that are gringos and demands that her mother change the sheets on her bed. She seems thoroughly uninterested in her seven-year-old daughter Luna, the apple of her grandmother's eye. When Luna is assaulted by a teenage boy posing as a policeman, Carmen does take her to a clinic; however, once she is assured that Luna's hymen is still intact, her callous disregard for the impact of this experience on Luna is as chilling as the assault itself.

For Isidra, a visitation from La Llorona offers victims retribu-tion for what happened when "the terrible men from the great ocean came"; for Luna, La Llorona becomes the focal point of her entry into the adult world, with its cruelty and betrayal. Vil-lanueva creates, between grandmother and grandchild, a secret, cross-generational bond of understanding as Isidra uses Luna's fas-cination with the La Llorona figure to offer her the chance to dis-cover both the worst and the best in herself.

After her grandmother's death, Villanueva was raised by her mother and aunt during her adolescent years. She dropped out of school in the tenth grade to have her first child and had her second at age seventeen. Living on welfare in a San Francisco housing project and married to a violent man, Villanueva struggled to survive her early adulthood. She went on to complete her education, eventually earning an MFA from Vermont College. She has held writer-in-residence positions at Cabrillo College, University of California at Irvine, San Francisco State University, and University of California at Santa Cruz. She currently teaches writing at Antioch University in Los Angeles and has published six books of poetry, three novels, and a collection of short fiction. Villanueva is the recipient of an American Book Award, a Latin American Writers Poetry Prize, and a PEN Oakland fiction award.

With its folkloric underpinnings, this story can be compared to Erdrich's "The Shawl" and to Kantner's excerpt from Ordinary Wolves. *Luna's relationship with her grandmother can be read alongside Delman's relationship with her Nana-bai in the excerpt from* Burnt Bread and Chutney *and Lovey's fantasies about her maternal grandmother in Yamanaka's excerpt from* Wild Meat and the Bully Burgers.

All conversation between the child, Luna, and her grandmother, Isidra, is in Spanish.

Luna looked out the rain-streaked window with sadness and boredom at the wet, gray street. "Will it ever stop raining, Mamacita? I hate the rain." Her voice was a murmur, fogging a small patch of glass in front of her. Luna was seven years old, and she resented being locked in with her grandmother for the third day. Her brand-new roller skates that allowed her to skate to the end of the block stood in a dark corner by the front door of the chilly flat. Only the kitchen was truly warm, where her grandmother stood rolling out handmade tortillas and a huge pot of beans simmered on the stove, sealed with fresh onions, fresh tomatoes, ground beef, cilantro, and a whole, bright red chorizo.

"If it keeps raining this way the water will rise, Niña. It'll rise up to the windows, maybe more." The old woman's dark face looked down at her dark hands rolling the white flour in perfect circles without any expression, though a faint, extremely faint, humor reflected, briefly, as a pinpoint of light in her large, dark Indian eyes that seemed to take in all light like a sponge. Like the Earth.

"Do you mean we could float away? Like a flood?" Luna's voice rose with excitement and fear.

"San Francisco is surrounded by water. The great ocean on one side, no? If it continues to rain this way, why not?" She walked over to the hot griddle and placed a perfect tortilla on it and flipped it by hand as gentle bubbles appeared on its floury surface.

"Are you scared, Mamacita?" Luna managed to ask. Where the day had been boring, watching the endless rain, now each drop was a threat, and it terrified her to think of the wild ocean getting closer. And if her grandmother was so calm, that meant there was no escape.

"If I were to hear La Llorona crying, then I'd be afraid, Niña."

Luna's eyes flew open and her small, pink mouth opened slightly, but she couldn't speak.

"All my life, in Mexico"—the child in front of her disappeared, and instead the old woman, Isidra, saw the stark desert landscape running, running to meet the wide, cool river, the cactus, the flowers, the birds, bright and plentiful, she could hear them singing—"when it rained too long, we could hear her, La Llorona, crying for her children down by the river. Crying and lamenting, with her beautiful black shawl over her head. Not for protection from the rain, no, but because she was either too beautiful, or perhaps too ugly, to behold."

A large yellow butterfly grazed her head, floating in the Sonoran heat, and Isidra remembered the tortillas. She placed the finished ones in a clean, worn towel, wrapping them tightly, and began rolling out a new white circle.

Normally, Luna would insist on a fresh, hot, buttered tortilla sprinkled with salt, but she was too absorbed by the image of a Weeping Woman who was too beautiful, or too ugly, to look at, and the rain was coming down, harder now, making the windows tremble as the wind in four loud gusts threatened the huge house, made into separate flats, with extinction. Only this kitchen is safe, Luna hoped. "Why was she crying, Mamacita?"

"For her children, Niña. When the great flood came, and the terrible men from the great ocean came, she turned her children into fish." Isidra paused to wet her dry lips. "It was the only way to save them," the old woman added, seeing the terror on her granddaughter's face.

"Were they fish forever?" Luna whispered. She imagined the house floating now out to the great ocean.

"When La Llorona cried like that, so loudly"—the old woman, Isidra, saw the river again; she longed to step in it, to touch it, to bathe—"they would come to her if her sorrow was so great. Then, she'd take the black shawl from her head, making sure no human being was nearby to witness her magic, and scooping it into the river like a net, her children would appear one by one."

The yellow butterfly, huge in the bright Sonoran sun, floated in front of her granddaughter, and Isidra thought of her three children who'd survived their infancy. The ones who'd lived long enough to hear about La Llorona. And then only one survived to adulthood: Luna's mother. May she not be like her mother, the old woman prayed for the child silently. I have no daughter, she added with her familiar sense of perpetual grief. Just the little fish the river took away, and I have no magic. No, not anymore.

The butterfly vanished into the chill San Francisco air and the child was speaking. "How many children did La Llorona have?"

"No one knows for certain, but, as far as I know, there were four like the four winds and all of them daughters. You see, Luna, she saved her daughters from the terrible men, but her sons stayed and fought and died. They were real Indians then, and the gringos just looked like plucked chickens to them." She began to laugh softly, revealing strong, square teeth. "The Indians knew they were evil when they killed even the little children for nothing, sending them to the dark side of the moon, so that the mothers couldn't even see their little ones in the Full Moon Face. Evil!" she spat.

"Why does it scare you, Mamacita, to hear her crying? Is she crying now? Can you hear her now, Mamacita?" The child drew up to her grandmother, resting herself against that fragile strength. Her grandmother.

Isidra rarely touched the child. That's the way she'd been brought up. After infancy she was rarely touched or pampered. But this was her granddaughter and who would know, she mused, as she smoothed the thick, curling hair from the child's wondering, frightened eyes. She looks like my mother, she thought. The same eyes. The same kind of pride and something ancient like mi mamá.

"No, Niña, I don't hear her now, but if I did I'd be prepared to leave this place because if her children will not be scooped into her shawl, La Llorona kills as many people as she can. Mostly men, but one never knows." Isidra squeezed the child once with her left arm and gently pushed her away.

"I don't blame her. She has her reasons to be so angry, and she has every reason to weep." The old woman sighed deep in her belly, in her old worn-out womb. "Since coming to this country," now she spoke in a low, secretive voice, "I have yet to hear her." Her eyes watered.

Quickly, she reached up and adjusted her red headband, the one she always wore in the house, but never, ever, in the street. Then, the old woman stiffened her body and spit into the air: "Too many gringos here, mi Luna, and no room for La Llorona. No, no, she'll have nothing to do with them. Nor I."

In one swift movement she undid the towel, took a warm tortilla from the stack, buttered and salted it, and handed it to the child.

It was delicious, and the beans smelled wonderfully good now, and the rain outside seemed sad but bearable. "Do you miss La Llorona sometimes, Mamacita? She sounds awful, but I think I like her." Luna paused, glancing at the rain. "A little bit."

"What a question! Who could miss La Llorona?" Isidra laughed to herself. "Let's just hope you never hear her. But if you do, prepare yourself, Niña."

Luna's heart began to race again.

"Prepare to live or die. Yes, that's her message." As Isidra lifted the lid from the simmering beans, the brilliant yellow butterfly melted into the palm of her hand. She smiled as she scooped the beans into a bowl and placed it in front of Luna. "Now eat, Niña. Eat it all."

Thunder struck in the distance and lightning flashed, turning the kitchen window white with light, but Luna couldn't hear La Llorona. She ate without speaking, listening for the sounds of her unspeakable grief.

In the middle of the night, Luna woke to the loud voices. She froze, upright, in her bed, looking over to her grandmother's. Then she heard her grandmother's voice: "Don't treat me this way, Carmen, God will punish you. Yes, God will punish you for this." Her voice held no emphasis or threat; it was like a lament, a pleading.

"Make the bed, vieja! I feed you and put up with you. Now, make the goddamned bed, do you hear me, vieja?"

"It's a sin what you're doing. It's a sin, making me make the bed for you and that man." Then her voice changed as it rose to her old fury: "You aren't a daughter of mine! *My* children are dead!"

Luna heard her grandmother cry out, and she ran into the dimly lit front room where her mother stood over her cowering grandmother, her fist raised again. Carmen's harsh red hair shone dully in the faint light, but her eyes were bright with violence—the kind of violence that maims, or kills, the vulnerable. The kind of violence that's forgotten how to love.

"Don't touch her or I'll kill you! I'll kill you if you touch her again! I'll kill you!" Luna screamed hysterically, grabbing onto her grandmother's arm. It was as fragile and soft as a child's.

"See what you've started? I should throw you out! Out in the street! Out in the street where you belong, with this brat!" Carmen shrieked, hating the sight of the two of them together. Together against her.

There was a knock at the door and a man's voice. "Hey, Carmen, are you in there?" The voice was low pitched and impatient. He knocked again.

"Just a minute, Frank!" Instantly Carmen switched her fury to a false, feminine charm. She ran to the bathroom and hurriedly applied some bright red lipstick, checking her light-skinned makeup for streaks. She pushed back her hair in an angry gesture and ran to open the door.

"Go to bed, Niña. I'll be right there. Go to bed. "Would you like some cinnamon chocolate? I'll bring you some." Isidra touched the child's shoulders, guiding her toward their bedroom, and then she went to start the milk, putting it on a low heat. It would be ready when she was finished changing the sheets.

Carmen was making the man comfortable as he handed her a bottle of wine. "Oh, I pay her room and board, some extra money, to watch the kid for me. Got to work day and night, you know," she laughed knowingly. "I found her through a friend. Just relax and I'll get some glasses, baby." Carmen bent over to kiss him, offering her breasts to him. He cupped one, hungrily, as she giggled. Then he cupped them both and squeezed them a little too hard, but she said nothing, bringing her teeth down to taste the bright red lipstick.

It was late afternoon and Luna knew her grandmother was looking for her and calling her. "LUNA!" she'd be shouting in a thin, high-pitched voice from the second-story kitchen window. "LUNA!" as though the moon would know where her granddaughter was. "LUNA!" she sang to the setting sun, but no child sang back. Some boys in the distance jeered her, laughing, "Luuunaaaa!"

Pat, Luna's older friend, had talked her into coming to the park. No one would know, she'd said. Pat swung as high as she could and leaped to the sand, screaming.

"Do you want me to get you started? Come on, I'll push you." Pat's face was flushed with excitement as she held the swing for Luna.

"What're you kids doing here so late?" a male voice said, interrupting their play. He was a teenager, but he looked like a man to the girls. They stared at him quietly.

"Don't you know it's against the law to be here this late?" He showed them a badge. "I'm a policeman and I'm going to have to take one of you in. I'm going to have to call your parents."

"She'll go!" Pat said, running down the cement path.

As the boy hurt Luna, he said, "If you scream, I'll kill you." She didn't scream or cry, but she did hear La Llorona weeping very close by.

"The hymen's intact, so he didn't rape her, and there's no trace of semen," the doctor told Luna's mother. Pat had run home, and Carmen was getting ready to go to her night job as a waitress. By the time Luna got home Carmen had called the police.

The doctor was hurting her again where the boy had put his finger, and she had to tell them about how he touched her everywhere. She looked at her mother, but she seemed only angry at the nuisance, as though Luna had staged everything to annoy her.

"So, she wasn't raped?" Carmen asked the doctor once more.

"There's no evidence of it."

"Well, nothing happened to you, Luna, so stop that trembling act. Do you hear me?"

"Excuse me," the doctor interjected, "she's been through quite an ordeal for a seven-year-old. She'll need to talk about it . . ."

"Well, I don't have time for all that. As it is I'm late for work." Carmen rushed Luna into her coat, pulling on her to be quick.

"Here's the number for a *free* clinic." The doctor, an older woman, handed it to her, though she knew it was useless.

As Luna and her mother settled into their seats on the bus, Carmen told her, "Keep this to yourself. Nothing happened to you anyway, crybaby." She kept her voice low in the bus, but Luna heard the hatred anyway. "The old woman makes a big deal out of nothing as it is."

"Where are we going, Mamacita?" Luna asked, looking out the bus window at the beginning darkness and the rain blurring the streets going by. They never went out at night except to go to church once a week, and then someone always picked them up in their car and brought them back home. So, Luna had no idea where they were going.

"We're going to the great ocean." Isidra had her old, dark wool coat on and a plastic scarf over her head, her going-out dress, and many pairs of stockings to keep her legs warm, but her shoes, unsuited for the rain, were wet. The umbrella rested, closed, between them, dripping a long, thin puddle towards the feet in front.

"Why?" was all Luna could say. Isidra put her hand on top of Luna's small, cold hand. Years later, Luna would remember her grandmother's touch was like dry, loose feathers. Comfort without pain. Strange, irrational—a silent comfort.

Luna had to help her grandmother off the bus because the step to the street was so high and the driver hadn't pulled close enough to the curb. There was a fast-food place a block from the beach. They entered the front door with fear and excitement. They rarely went out to eat. Luna told her grandmother the menu in Spanish and waited for her to decide. Some people came and got in front of them, but it didn't matter. Luna ordered in a shy, proud voice. No one paid the least bit of attention to them as they sat by themselves eating. And they hardly spoke as the rain came in gusts.

"Come, walk quickly, Niña," Isidra commanded, holding the umbrella up over their heads with her right hand and Luna with her left. They rushed across the street, as fast as they could go, to the roar.

It was absolutely dark now except for the flickering streetlight behind them. The immense white waves frothed at their peaks, a terrible darkness beneath them, and then, suddenly, in long, smooth lines, they'd decide to meet the earth, angrily, with their roars. Luna wanted to turn and run, she was so terrified, but her grandmother held her hand lightly. She looked up at her grandmother and her eyes looked far away as though she were straining to see something.

"There she is," Isidra hissed. "There she is!"

"Who?"

"You can't hear her because of the ocean, but there she is!" Isidra drew Luna close to her, feeling the smallness of her body. She felt the trembling stop.

There was a dark figure moving along the beach, slowly. Her shawl covered her head. She looked tall and strong as she came toward them, weeping and singing.

GLOSSARY

Sonoran (225): refers to the Sonoran Desert area, an arid region covering 120,000 square miles in northwestern Mexico, southwestern Arizona, and southeastern California, including around Palm Springs; sometimes known as the Colorado Desert.

TRIAD

by Danzy Senna

A mother's death from cancer and its immediate aftermath in a young woman's life is the subject of Senna's "Triad." Told from three different racial perspectives, the stories repeat many of the same details, but each family dynamic is distinctive. Senna adheres to the same plot pattern and to the same standard characters—daughter, mother, hospice nurses, father, aunt and uncle, imagined passerby, supermarket promotion employee, family dog in gastric distress—yet she manages through small, subtle nuances to make all three accounts equally poignant in deeply unexpected ways.

Each story revolves around the mother's last expressed desire and a vision of "Happy Family? American Dream?" culled from the daughter's imagination and represented through the imagined passerby. For the white mother of the white family, it's blood-red sweet cherries juxtaposed with the violent, alcoholic father; the abused, "slightly haggard" wife; the pudgy daughter named Laura who always believed that her mother "would die a bloody death at her father's hand." For the black mother of the black family, it's blushed, cool sweet peaches in contrast to the successful, middle-class doctor-father with two faces, healer by day and angry drinker and dispenser of cruel tirades by night; the chronically depressed and embarrassed mother wishing that she were dead; the pudgy girl in cornrows named Yvette who always feared that her mother would commit suicide. Each of these families seems to use its own racial stereotype as a disguise.

The final family is mixed; the mother is white, a "zaftig red-haired woman" who obsesses about the blue-red skin of a plum and the "sweet messiness" of its juice; the father, a black professor with unfulfilled dreams who, though alcoholic and physically abusive, joins AA and cleans himself up to keep the marriage going; the daughter, Soledad, who, from her imagined stranger's perspective, looks adopted, and who is able to see her parents survive their difficulties and start to resemble each other a little, their "sweet messiness" having pulled them through. No stereotype exists to hide behind here.

Other characterizing details distinguish each version, but just as interesting is what remains the same, especially the immutable reality of death itself, along with the fear that even the heaviness of this reality will fade over time.

Danzy Senna was born in Boston, Massachusetts, and is the daughter of Afro-Mexican poet Carl Senna and Irish American writer and poet Fanny Howe; her aunt is the poet Susan Howe. Both parents were activists during the civil rights movement. Senna attended Stanford University and received an MFA from the University of California at Irvine, where she won several writing awards. She is the author of the novel Caucasia *and contributed a significant essay, "The Mulatto Millennium," for a collection of writing entitled* Half and Half, *edited by Claudine Chiawei O'Hearn. "Triad" represents Senna's effort to break down traditional expectations of racial and ethnic authenticity; though the emotional experience of losing a mother is nearly identical in each version of the same story, Senna's refusal to be categorized as a "mixed" writer or a writer of color can be seen in the equivalent power of all three narratives.*

"Triad's" focus on the outcome of a mother's absence or death can be compared with several stories in this collection, notably Lee's "Casual Water," Erdrich's "The Shawl," Tucker's "How I Learned to Fly," the excerpt from Kantner's Ordinary Wolves, *and, perhaps*

most effectively, Packer's "Drinking Coffee Elsewhere" and Chang's "The Eve of the Spirit Festival." Of particular interest might be a comparison of the experiences here and in "Drinking Coffee Elsewhere," where race as well as sexual identity are factors. Another fruitful comparison can be made between the fear of losing the reality of loss in "Triad" and in "The Eve of the Spirit Festival."

1. Cherries in Winter

Laura smells what's happening under the table, but she doesn't say anything. It doesn't seem appropriate to mention, given the circumstances. Nobody else says a word either. They just eat their food in silence. A new one floats up, and Laura tries to hold her breath as she takes another bite of turkey. It's more difficult than she imagined, to eat without breathing.

Laura's mother died yesterday. She died quietly, all drugged up, in a white room surrounded by black nurses. It was a planned death, like a planned pregnancy. Everybody had plenty of time to mourn before the official end actually came. Relatives from both sides have come to town for the funeral tomorrow, and the aura at the table now is one of suppressed relief and impatience for the ceremony to be over.

The last time Laura saw her mother was two weeks ago, in the hospice in New Haven. Her breasts were gone and she wore a bandana over her head so that she looked like a young boy. So pale, she looked almost see-through. She drifted in and out of awareness, but when she was awake, all she could talk about were cherries: the blood red of them, the sweetness of them, the coolness of them, the sensation of the pit rolling over her tongue. Laura went everywhere that cold gray day looking for cherries, but they were out of season and when she came back to the hospice her mother was not talking about cherries anymore. Her eyes were closed and it was time for Laura to catch the train back to campus.

A new smell wafts up from under the table. It's unbelievable that such a small dog could make such a big impact on the world. Laura holds a napkin over her mouth and eyes the other guests. They scrape at their plates unhappily.

"Pass the gravy, Laura," her father says, nodding his big head toward the bowl. Her father looks fatter than he did two weeks ago. The weight sits on his chest where it's supposed to be most deadly. She hands him the gravy.

Aunt Mabel made all the food. She and Gus drove from Syracuse this morning with a whole trunk-load of steamy Tupperware containers.

"Have you chosen a major?" Uncle Gus asks her from across the table.

"Fine arts."

"Better than crude arts." Uncle Gus snorts with laughter after he says it.

Laura just nods and takes another sip of wine.

Through the window above Gus's head, she can see it has begun to snow. Soft flakes drift down and make a home on the branches of the apple tree where she used to sit, hiding from the world. She went there for many reasons, but the one she remembers most is her father. Once, it was her runny nose that made him angry. He couldn't stand the sight of it. He saw it as evidence of stupidity. He came after her one day, holding a car key wrapped in toilet paper. He wanted to pick her nose, but he didn't want to use his actual finger so he'd made this prosthesis. Laura shrieked and sobbed and squirmed out of his grip, and made it up that apple tree before he could catch her.

Now that Laura was an adult, her nose-running had turned into chronic nasal congestion, sinusitis, as it were. A wan vegetarian in her dormitory at school suggested that she might be allergic to wheat and dairy. Last month she'd stopped eating both and her nose was now a clear and easy passageway. She thinks that if her nose were still blocked she wouldn't be able to smell the stench under the table. Another one floats up just then, a real doozy. Aunt Mabel coughs into her napkin.

"Jesus fucking Christ," her father says, rising. His chair falls to the floor behind him. "Where is that damn dog?"

He reaches under the table and she hears the yelp of Atticus, being dragged out from his hiding place. Atticus is old, nearly toothless. He was her mother's dog, a replacement baby for when Laura got too old to hold. Her mother used to take that dog everywhere. Now he sleeps almost all the time. Her father grips the dog by the scruff and belts him once, twice, across his rump. The dog scurries away whimpering, his tail between his legs.

Her father picks up his fallen chair, looks down at the table, daring anybody to say a word.

Uncle Gus snorts with laughter. "I thought it was you all that time, Bob."

Aunt Mabel laughs a little and everybody goes back to their food.

Except Laura. She stares out the window, where the snow is falling harder. When she was a kid, Laura used to play a game at dinner. She would imagine that she was a passerby on the street out front, somebody who just happened to glance in through their picture window at this dinner scene. She would imagine herself and her family through that stranger's eyes: a red-faced and bearded fat man at the head of the table, a slightly haggard wife serving food from the kitchen, a pudgy girl with braces feeding scraps to the dog under the table. Would they see this scene and think, Happy Family? The American Dream? Or would they notice the details: the swiftness with which the father belted back his glasses of scotch? And the way his voice grew louder and more slurred with each course? Would they know just from looking that some nights after dinner, his rage ended with that small mother bloody and bruised and weeping? On those nights, Laura would lie in the dark holding her pillow and praying to some faceless Sunday school God that her mother not die tonight. Because she always believed her mother would die a bloody death at her father's hand. She never guessed her mother's death would come from the inside out—a pedestrian passing of the most common and blameless variety.

Laura lies in the dark of her bedroom staring at the embers of her teenaged self. A poster of Harrison Ford still hangs above her bed, another one of Jennifer Beals from *Flashdance* beside her dresser mirror. Her stomach makes unhappy sounds. Aunt Mabel's turkey isn't sitting well with her, but somehow she drifts off to sleep.

She wakes sometime later in the darkness to the sound of beeping garbage trucks outside.

Her mother looked almost beautiful in that hospice bed, androgynous and tiny, translucent. The last thing she said to Laura: "What I wouldn't do for a nice cold bowl of cherries."

Laura gets up and goes to the bathroom off the hall with the puffy pink toilet seat that makes a sighing noise when she sits down on it. It's only four-thirty A.M. She heads back to her room but instead of getting back into bed she dresses in the dark, then goes outside and sits in her father's Chevy, letting it warm up before she rolls slowly out of the driveway.

Connecticut is an embalmed state. The houses sit like taxidermy, animals stuffed and hung, their marble eyes watching her as she cruises past. The Star Market is open. She doesn't know if it's been open all night or if it has just now opened for the morning. The only other person she sees as she moves through the aisles is a man behind a table. Over him hangs a sign that says ENSURE: COMPLETE BALANCED NUTRITION FOR A HEALTHIER YOU. Behind him is a sculpture of bottles with the same words on them. When she moves past, he holds up a Dixie cup with white fluid in it. It reminds her of the hospital, the fluids that flowed in and out of her mother. "Would you like to try Ensure?" She shakes her head and moves on toward the produce department.

The fruit is piled neatly, identical apples and identical pears, not a mark on their waxy skins.

There are cherries too, imported in the winter from Peru. The sign says 5.99/LB. She fills a bag until it can't hold any more.

Outside, the parking lot is still empty, but the sky has begun to brighten. She sits in the Chevy with the motor running, eating the cherries. They don't taste very sweet. They are dry, rubbery things, and after a few tries she sets them on the seat next to her.

When her mother came home that afternoon so many years ago, she found Laura perched in the tree, still hiding from her father. Her mother put her hands on her hips and laughed at the sight of her daughter. "Is that a monkey up there?" she called up. "Come on down, Sweetie Pie, I need your help."

That same evening, Laura sat at the kitchen table and snapped green beans and watched her mother move around, cooking dinner and humming to the sound of Billie Holiday on the radio. Or, no. Maybe it was Johnny Cash. She isn't sure. And as she thinks about it, she isn't sure about any of the details. She can't remember what her mother was wearing, whether she was thin or fat, how she wore her hair, in a bun or down around her face. She can't remember what she looked like before the illness. Hard as she tries, she can't conjure up her face. It's slipping away already. And she knows there will come a day when she won't miss her mother anymore—a day when she only misses the feeling of missing. But she's not quite there yet. She still feels something of the dead hovering inside her. It lives for a moment in her chest, misshapen and bruised as a backyard fruit. She closes her eyes and lets it hang inside her. Then it falls away, too heavy to hold. She starts up the engine and heads on toward home.

2. Peaches in Winter

Yvette smells what's happening under the table, but she doesn't say anything. It doesn't seem appropriate to mention, given the circumstances. Nobody else says a word either. They just eat their food in silence. A new one floats up, and Yvette tries to hold her breath as she takes another bite of turkey. It's more difficult than she imagined, to eat without breathing.

Yvette's mother died yesterday. She died quietly, all drugged up, in a white room surrounded by a bevy of island nurses. It was a planned death, like a planned pregnancy. Everybody had plenty of time to mourn before the official end actually came. Relatives from both sides have come to town for the funeral tomorrow, and the aura at the table now is one of suppressed relief and impatience for the ceremony to be over.

The last time Yvette saw her mother was two weeks ago in the hospice in New Haven. Her breasts were gone and she wore a bandana over her head so that she looked like a young boy. Her skin seemed to grow darker the closer she got to the other side, as if she was turning to wood before Yvette's very eyes. She drifted in and out of awareness, but when she was awake, all she could talk about were peaches: the swirling blush of them, the sweetness of them, the coolness of them, the final sensation of the pit against her tongue. Yvette went all around New Haven that cold gray day looking for peaches, but they were out of season and when she came back to the hospice her mother was not talking about peaches anymore. Her eyes were closed and it was time to catch the train back to campus.

A new smell wafts up from under the table. It's unbelievable that such a small dog could make such a big impact on the world. Yvette holds a napkin over her mouth and eyes the other guests. They scrape at their plates unhappily.

"Pass the gravy, Yvette," her father says, nodding his big head toward the bowl. Her father looks fatter than he did two weeks ago. The weight sits on his chest where it's supposed to be most deadly. She hands him the gravy.

Aunt Grace made all the food. She and Byron drove all the way up from the city this morning with a whole trunk-load of steamy Tupperware containers.

"Have you chosen a major?" Uncle Byron asks her from across the table.

"Fine arts."

"Better than crude arts." Byron snorts with laughter after he says it.

Yvette just nods and takes another sip of wine.

Through the window above Byron's head, she can see it has begun to snow. Soft flakes drift down and make a home on the branches of the apple tree where she used to sit, hiding from the world. She went there for many reasons, but the one she remembers most is her father. Once, it was her runny nose that made him angry. He couldn't stand the sight of it. He saw it as evidence of stupidity. He came after her one day, holding a car key wrapped in toilet paper. He wanted to pick her nose, but he didn't want to use his actual finger so he'd made this prosthesis. Yvette shrieked and sobbed and squirmed out of his grip, and made it up that apple tree before he could catch her.

Now that Yvette was an adult, her nose-running had turned into chronic nasal congestion, sinusitis, as it were. A wan vegetarian in her dormitory at school suggested that she might be allergic to wheat and dairy. Last month she'd stopped eating both and her nose was now a clear and easy passageway. She thinks that if her nose were still blocked she wouldn't be able to smell the stench under the table. Another one floats up just then, a real doozy. Aunt Grace coughs into her napkin.

"Jesus fucking Christ," her father says, rising. His chair falls to the floor behind him. "Where is that damn dog?"

He reaches under the table and she hears the yelp of Rex being dragged out from his hiding place. Rex is old, nearly toothless. He was her mother's dog, a replacement baby for when Yvette got too old to hold. Her mother used to take that dog everywhere. Now he sleeps almost all the time. Her father grips the dog by the scruff and belts him once, twice, across his rump. The dog scurries away whimpering, his tail between his legs.

Her father picks up his fallen chair, looks down at the table, daring anybody to say a word.

Byron snorts with laughter. "I thought it was you all that time, James."

Aunt Grace chuckles a little and everybody goes back to their food.

Except Yvette. She stares out the window, where the snow is falling harder. When she was a kid, Yvette used to play a game at dinner. She would imagine she was a passerby on the street out front, somebody who just happened to glance in through their picture window at this dinner scene, and she would imagine her family through that stranger's eyes: a bespectacled light-skinned man with a goatee, a slim, nervous, brown-skinned woman serving food, a pudgy preteen girl in cornrows feeding scraps to the dog under the table. Would they see this scene and think, Happy Family? The American Dream? Would they see this scene as evidence of progress? Would they think, how wonderful, a black family living in this neighborhood? Or would they understand that the father, the good doctor, wore two faces? A healer by day could become cruel by night, wounding with the scotch flowing through his veins. Would they know just from looking that some nights after dinner, his tirades ended with her mother weeping at his invectives, wishing aloud that she were dead? On those nights, Yvette would lie in the dark holding her pillow and praying to some faceless preacher God that her mother not take her own life. Because in her heart, she always believed her mother would die at her own hand. She never guessed her mother's death would come from the inside out—a pedestrian death of the most common and blameless variety.

Yvette lies in the dark of her bedroom staring at the embers of her teenaged self. A poster of Michael Jackson still hangs above her bed, another one of Jennifer Beals from *Flashdance* beside her dresser mirror. Her stomach makes unhappy sounds. Grace's turkey isn't sitting well with her, but somehow she drifts off to sleep.

She wakes sometime later in the darkness to the sound of beeping garbage trucks outside.

Her mother looked almost beautiful in that hospice bed, androgynous and tiny, like a dark, fragile doll imported from a distant land. The last thing she said to Yvette: "What I wouldn't do for a peach."

Yvette gets up and goes to the bathroom off the hall with the puffy pink toilet seat that makes a sighing noise when she sits down on it. It's only four-thirty A.M. She heads back to her room, but instead of getting into bed she dresses in the dark, then goes outside and sits in her father's Chevy, letting it warm up before she rolls slowly out of the driveway.

Connecticut is an embalmed state. The houses sit like taxidermy, animals stuffed and hung, their marble eyes watching her as she cruises past. The Star Market is open. She doesn't know if it's been open all night or if it has just now opened for the morning. The only other person she sees as she moves through the aisles is a man sitting behind a table. The sign over his head says ENSURE: COMPLETE BALANCED NUTRITION FOR A HEALTHIER YOU. Behind him is a sculpture of bottles with the same words on them. When she moves past, he holds up a Dixie cup with white fluid in it. "Would you like to try Ensure?" She takes the cup and sips from it. The drink tastes like chalk. It reminds her of the hospice, the fluids that flowed in and out of her mother in her last year. She hands it back, wipes her lip, and moves on toward the produce department.

The fruit is piled neatly, identical apples and identical pears, not a mark on their waxy skins.

There are peaches too, imported in the winter from Peru. The sign says $2.99/LB. She fills a bag with five of the heaviest, ripest ones she can find.

Outside, the parking lot is still empty, but the sky has begun to brighten. She sits in the Chevy with the motor running holding a peach. It's perfectly round and perfectly soft, but when she takes a bite, it doesn't taste sweet. It is a mealy, tasteless thing, and after a few nibbles she sets it on the seat next to her.

When her mother came home that afternoon so many years ago, she found Yvette in the tree, still hiding from her father. Her mother put her hands on her hips and laughed at the sight of her daughter. "Is that a monkey I see up there?" she called up. "Come on down, Sugar Pie, I need your help."

That same evening, Yvette sat at the kitchen table and snapped green beans and watched her mother move around, cooking dinner and humming to the sound of Billie Holiday on the radio. Or, no. Maybe it was Johnny Cash. She isn't sure. And as she thinks about it, she isn't sure about any of the details. She can't remember what her mother was wearing, whether she was thin or fat, how she wore her hair, in an Afro or braids. She can't remember what she looked like before the illness. Hard as she tries, she can't conjure up her face. It's slipping away already. And she knows there will come a day when she won't miss her mother anymore— a day when she only misses the feeling of missing. But she's not quite there yet. She still feels something of the dead hovering inside her. It lives for a moment in her chest, misshapen and bruised as a backyard fruit. She closes her eyes and lets it hang inside her. Then it falls away, too heavy to hold. She starts up the engine and heads on toward home.

3. Plums in Winter

Soledad smells what's happening under the table, but she doesn't say anything. It doesn't seem appropriate to mention, given the circumstances. Nobody else says a word either. They just eat their food in silence. A new one floats up, and Soledad tries to hold her breath as she takes another bite of turkey. It's more difficult than she imagined, to eat without breathing.

Soledad's mother died yesterday. She died quietly, all drugged up, in a white room surrounded by stern-faced nurses. It was a planned death,

like a planned pregnancy. Everybody had plenty of time to mourn before the official end actually came. Relatives from both sides have come
to town for the funeral tomorrow, and the aura at the table now is one
of suppressed relief and impatience for the ceremony to be over.

The last time Soledad saw her mother was two weeks ago, in the hospice in New Haven. Her breasts were gone and she wore a bandana over
her head so that she looked like a young boy. Her green eyes had the
frosted sheen of sea glass as she writhed under the hospital sheets. She
drifted in and out of awareness, but when she was awake, all she could
talk about were plums: their blue-red skin, the sweet messiness of their
juice, their coolness, the final sensation of the pit against her tongue.
She talked about how there was no other word to describe the color of a
plum than the word for the thing itself. *Plum.* And wasn't that remarkable? Soledad went all around New Haven that cold gray day looking for
plums, but they were out of season and when she came back to the hospice her mother was not talking about plums anymore. Her eyes were
closed and it was time to catch the train back to campus.

A new smell wafts up from under the table. It's unbelievable that
such a small dog could make such a big impact on the world. Soledad
holds a napkin over her mouth and eyes the other guests. They scrape at
their plates unhappily.

"Pass the gravy, Soledad," her father says, nodding his big head toward the bowl. Her father looks fatter than he did two weeks ago. The
weight sits on his chest where it's supposed to be most deadly. She hands
him the gravy.

Aunt Rose made all the food. She and Uncle Izzy drove down from
Boston this morning with a whole trunk-load of steamy Tupperware
containers.

"Have you chosen a major?" Izzy asks her from across the table.

"Fine arts."

"Better than crude arts." Izzy snorts with laughter after he says it.

Soledad just nods and takes another sip of wine.

Through the window above Izzy's head, she can see it has begun to
snow. Soft flakes drift down and make a home on the branches of the
apple tree where she used to sit, hiding from the world. She went there

for many reasons, but the one she remembers most is her father. His temper. Once, it was her runny nose that made him angry. He saw her runny nose as evidence of stupidity. He couldn't stand looking at it. He came after her one day, holding a car key wrapped in toilet paper. He wanted to pick her nose, but he didn't want to use his actual finger so he'd made this prosthesis. Soledad shrieked and sobbed and squirmed out of his grip, and made it up that apple tree before he could grab her.

Now that Soledad was an adult, her nose-running had turned into chronic nasal congestion, sinusitis, as it were. A wan vegetarian in her dormitory at school suggested that she might be allergic to wheat and dairy. Last month she'd stopped eating both and her nose was now a clear and easy passageway. She thinks that if her nose were still blocked she wouldn't be able to smell the stench under the table. Another one floats up just then, a real doozy, followed by the dog's satisfied lip-smacking. Aunt Rose coughs into her napkin.

"Jesus fucking Christ," her father says, standing. His chair falls to the floor behind him. "Where's that damn dog?"

He reaches under the table and she hears the yelp of Blue being dragged out from his hiding place. He was her mother's dog, a replacement baby for when Soledad got too old to hold. Her mother took Blue everywhere with her when he was a puppy. Now Blue is old, nearly toothless. He sleeps almost all the time. Her father grips the dog by the scruff and belts him once, twice, across his rump. The dog scurries away whimpering, his tail between his legs.

Her father picks up his fallen chair, looks down at the table, daring anybody to say a word.

Izzy snorts with laughter. "I thought it was you all that time, Melvin."

Aunt Rose chuckles a little and everybody goes back to their food.

Except Soledad. She stares out the window, where the snow is falling harder. When she was a kid, Soledad used to play a game at dinner. She would imagine she was a passerby on the street out front, somebody who just happened to glance in through their picture window at this dinner scene, and she would imagine her family through that stranger's eyes: a portly black man at the head of the table, a zaftig red-haired woman in a peasant blouse serving food from the kitchen, a surly teenaged girl with corkscrew curls feeding scraps to the dog under the table. Would they see this scene and think, Happy Family? The American Dream? Would they even understand that this was a family? People got confused sometimes. They made up complicated explanations for the family—the man must be foreign, the woman must have adopted the kid from Brazil—rather than going with the obvious. Would they guess that the good professor liked to bellow when he was drunk? Would they guess that the good professor, with all his Poitier dreams, had a problem with his temper? Would they see that the mother wore makeup sometimes to hide her bruises? Not only would they guess it, but they would assume it. And so the girl, the corkscrew-curls girl, always smiled hard and wide on picture day, so wide her jaw hurt a little, hoping that her smile could save them all from the assumptions. Behind the smile, she always believed back then that her mother would die at her father's hand. But her father went to a meeting one day in the basement of a church and got sober a year later; and eventually, the hitting disappeared along with that bottle of scotch. And somehow her parents stayed together, started to look a little alike. And in the end, her mother's death came from the inside out—a pedestrian passing of the most common and blameless variety.

Later, Soledad lies in the dark of her bedroom staring at the embers of her teenaged self. A poster of Public Enemy still hangs above her bed, another one of Jennifer Beals from *Flashdance* beside her dresser mirror. Her stomach makes unhappy sounds. Aunt Rose's turkey isn't sitting well with her, but somehow she drifts off to sleep.

She wakes sometime later in the darkness to the sound of beeping garbage trucks outside.

Her mother looked almost beautiful in that hospice bed, androgynous and finally thin, the girl-woman a thousand diets had failed to make her. The last thing she said to Soledad: "What I wouldn't do for a nice cold plum."

Soledad gets up and goes to the bathroom off the hall with the puffy pink toilet seat that makes a sighing noise when she sits down on it. It's only four-thirty A.M. She heads back to her room, but instead of getting into bed she dresses in the dark, then goes outside and sits in her father's Chevy, letting it warm up before she rolls slowly out of the driveway.

Connecticut is an embalmed state. The houses sit like taxidermy, animals stuffed and hung, their marble eyes watching her as she cruises past. The Star Market is open. She doesn't know if it's been open all night or if it's just now opened for the morning. The only other person she sees as she moves through the aisles is a man sitting behind a table. The sign over his head says ENSURE: COMPLETE BALANCED NUTRITION FOR A HEALTHIER YOU. Behind him is a sculpture of bottles with the same words on them. When she moves past, he holds up a Dixie cup with white fluid in it. "Would you like to try Ensure?" She stares into the cup, always tempted by free lunches, but it reminds her of the hospice, the opposite of plums. She shakes her head and moves on toward the produce department.

The fruit is piled neatly, identical apples and identical pears, not a mark on their waxy skins.

There are plums too, imported in the winter from Peru. The sign says 3.99/LB. They are mostly hard, the gold of their youth still showing under the purple. She fills a bag with six of the ripest she can find.

Outside the parking lot is still empty, but the sky has begun to brighten. She sits in the Chevy with the motor running, eating a plum. It doesn't taste sweet or messy. It is a hard, clean, bitter thing, and after a few tries she sets it on the seat next to her.

When her mother came home that afternoon so many years ago, she found Soledad in the tree, still hiding from her father. Her mother put her hands on her hips and laughed at the sight of her daughter. "Is that a monkey up there?" she called up. "Come on down, Babe, I need your help."

That same evening, Soledad sat at the kitchen table and snapped green beans and watched her mother move around, cooking dinner and humming to the sound of Billie Holiday on the radio. Or, no. Maybe it was Johnny Cash. She isn't sure. And as she thinks about it, she isn't sure about any of the details. She can't remember what her mother was wearing, whether she was thin or fat, how she wore her hair back then, in a braid down her back or frizzed up and wild around her face. She can't remember what she looked like before the illness. Hard as she tries, she can't conjure up her face. It's slipping away already. And she knows there will come a day when she won't miss her mother anymore—a day when she only misses the feeling of missing. But she's not quite there yet. She still feels something of the dead hovering inside her. It lives for a moment in her chest, misshapen and bruised as a backyard fruit. She closes her eyes and lets it hang inside her. Then it falls away, too heavy to hold. She starts up the engine and heads on toward home.

GLOSSARY

zaftig (243): from the Yiddish, meaning a full-figured.
Poitier dreams (244): refers to Sidney Poitier, a Bahamian American actor, film director, and activist known for having consciously defied racial stereotyping through his dignity, suave style, and intelligence.

Discovering Relationships

These stories explore how we find our "place" in a culture that may complicate our efforts and even marginalize our identity. Whether that "place" involves learning the complex social signals of dating, positioning ourselves in relation to those closest to us, appreciating the learned pleasures of cultural bias, or beginning the process of creating a home, discovering relationships represents a crucial step.

HOW TO DATE A BROWNGIRL, BLACKGIRL, WHITEGIRL, OR HALFIE

by Junot Diaz

Diaz's dating guide for the Dominican American teenage male takes on the authority of experience by employing a narrator speaking in second person, similar to Tucker's narrator in "How I Learned to Fly." In his piece, Diaz creates a progressive set of instructions, starting with how to evict family members from an apartment and eliminate all vestiges of obvious Dominican "ghetto" culture (like government cheese, photos of family back in DR, a wastebasket full of soiled toilet paper) in readiness for a date.

Next, Diaz moves on to more specifics for whether or not the girl is a local or an "outsider"—someone from another neighborhood—and whether she's brown, black, white, or mixed ("halfie"). These categories come with Diaz's observations about the girl's parents (such as what kind of car they drive), the best place to go for dinner (a Dominican restaurant if she's "from around the way," Wendy's if she's not), what to talk about at dinner, what to do if threatened by the local bully on the walk there or back, and what to expect as her response to this bully. They also come with Diaz's philosophical asides, ranging from why to avoid a fight with this bully who could "eat you if he wanted," to the special needs of "halfies" whose parents are probably refugees from the civil rights movement and whose complicated self-hatred will not

*allow "attention-grabbing" behavior in school to translate into per-
missive behavior in private. It seems as if this narrator has developed a casebook on all possible scenarios, with allowances for
different outcomes.*

*Diaz is not afraid to include small gestures that reveal cultural
attitudes, even if these attitudes do not put Dominicans in the best
light. Not only does his narrator hide his origins when he gets rid of
the Dominican artifacts in his apartment; he instructs reticence
about insider knowledge, such as what tear gas smells like—
something that his mother's generation would recognize from "the
year the United States invaded your island." He also recommends
running a hand through your hair "like the whiteboys do" when
you want to appear calm, cool, and collected, even though "the only
thing that runs easily through your hair is Africa."*

*While it could be argued that this piece provides evidence for a
stereotypical machismo attitude toward women, Diaz's narrator
never allows his quips to outstrip his recognition that a date, with
all of its possible successes, disasters, and confusing moments,
ends—and then you are left alone, as you were—perhaps even less
than you were. As his final instruction, Diaz's narrator warns,
"Don't go downstairs. Don't fall asleep. It won't help."*

*Junot Diaz moved to the United States from the Dominican
Republic when he was six years old, settling in New Jersey. This
piece is from his short story collection* Drown *and was originally
published in* The New Yorker, *which placed him on a list of the
top twenty writers for the twenty-first century. He recently published his first novel,* The Brief Wondrous Life of Oscar Wao, *to
great critical acclaim. Diaz is currently a professor of creative
writing at MIT.*

*Diaz's "dating guide" bears an obvious "casebook" resemblance
to Alexie's "Indian Education." In addition to its second-person
narrative, its tone, seemingly assertive and confident but actually
self-deprecating and anxious, resembles that of Tucker's narrator
in "How I Learned to Fly."*

Wait for your brother and your mother to leave the apartment. You've already told them that you're feeling too sick to go to Union City to visit that tía who likes to squeeze your nuts. (He's gotten big, she'll say.) And even though your moms knows you ain't sick you stuck to your story until finally she said, Go ahead and stay, malcriado.

Clear the government cheese from the refrigerator. If the girl's from the Terrace stack the boxes behind the milk. If she's from the Park or Society Hill hide the cheese in the cabinet above the oven, way up where she'll never see. Leave yourself a reminder to get it out before morning or your moms will kick your ass. Take down any embarrassing photos of your family in the campo, especially the one with the half-naked kids dragging a goat on a rope leash. The kids are your cousins and by now they're old enough to understand why you're doing what you're doing. Hide the pictures of yourself with an Afro. Make sure the bathroom is presentable. Put the basket with all the crapped-on toilet paper under the sink. Spray the bucket with Lysol, then close the cabinet.

Shower, comb, dress. Sit on the couch and watch TV. If she's an outsider her father will be bringing her, maybe her mother. Neither of them want her seeing any boys from the Terrace—people get stabbed in the Terrace—but she's strong-headed and this time will get her way. If she's a whitegirl you know you'll at least get a hand job.

The directions were in your best handwriting, so her parents won't think you're an idiot. Get up from the couch and check the parking lot. Nothing. If the girl's local, don't sweat it. She'll flow over when she's good and ready. Sometimes she'll run into her other friends and a whole crowd will show up at your apartment and even though that means you ain't getting shit it will be fun anyway and you'll wish these people would come over more often. Sometimes the girl won't flow over at all and the next day in school she'll say sorry, smile and you'll be stupid enough to believe her and ask her out again.

Wait and after an hour go out to your corner. The neighborhood is full of traffic. Give one of your boys a shout and when he says, Are you still waiting on that bitch? say, Hell yeah.

Get back inside. Call her house and when her father picks up ask if

she's there. He'll ask, Who is this? Hang up. He sounds like a principal
or a police chief, the sort of dude with a big neck, who never has to
watch his back. Sit and wait. By the time your stomach's ready to give
out on you, a Honda or maybe a Jeep pulls in and out she comes.

Hey, you'll say.

Look, she'll say. My mom wants to meet you. She's got herself all
worried about nothing.

Don't panic. Say, Hey, no problem. Run a hand through your hair
like the whiteboys do even though the only thing that runs easily
through your hair is Africa. She will look good. The white ones are the
ones you want the most, aren't they, but usually the out-of-towners are
black, blackgirls who grew up with ballet and Girl Scouts, who have
three cars in their driveways. If she's a halfie don't be surprised that her
mother is white. Say, Hi. Her moms will say hi and you'll see that you
don't scare her, not really. She will say that she needs easier directions to
get out and even though she has the best directions in her lap give her
new ones. Make her happy.

You have choices. If the girl's from around the way, take her to El
Cibao for dinner. Order everything in your busted-up Spanish. Let her
correct you if she's Latina and amaze her if she's black. If she's not from
around the way, Wendy's will do. As you walk to the restaurant talk about
school. A local girl won't need stories about the neighborhood but the
other ones might. Supply the story about the loco who'd been storing canisters of tear gas in his basement for years, how one day the canisters
cracked and the whole neighborhood got a dose of the military-strength
stuff. Don't tell her that your moms knew right away what it was, that she
recognized its smell from the year the United States invaded your island.

Hope that you don't run into your nemesis, Howie, the Puerto Rican kid with the two killer mutts. He walks them all over the neighborhood and every now and then the mutts corner themselves a cat and tear
it to shreds, Howie laughing as the cat flips up in the air, its neck
twisted around like an owl, red meat showing through the soft fur. If
his dogs haven't cornered a cat, he will walk behind you and ask, Hey,
Yunior, is that your new fuckbuddy?

Let him talk. Howie weighs about two hundred pounds and could eat you if he wanted. At the field he will turn away. He has new sneakers, and doesn't want them muddy. If the girl's an outsider she will hiss now and say, What a fucking asshole. A homegirl would have been yelling back at him the whole time, unless she was shy. Either way don't feel bad that you didn't do anything. Never lose a fight on a first date or that will be the end of it.

Dinner will be tense. You are not good at talking to people you don't know. A halfie will tell you that her parents met in the Movement, will say, Back then people thought it a radical thing to do. It will sound like something her parents made her memorize. Your brother once heard that one and said, Man, that sounds like a whole lot of Uncle Tomming to me. Don't repeat this.

Put down your hamburger and say, It must have been hard.

She will appreciate your interest. She will tell you more. Black people, she will say, treat me real bad. That's why I don't like them. You'll wonder how she feels about Dominicans. Don't ask. Let her speak on it and when you're both finished eating walk back into the neighborhood. The skies will be magnificent. Pollutants have made Jersey sunsets one of the wonders of the world. Point it out. Touch her shoulder and say, That's nice, right?

Get serious. Watch TV but stay alert. Sip some of the Bermúdez your father left in the cabinet, which nobody touches. A local girl may have hips and a thick ass but she won't be quick about letting you touch. She has to live in the same neighborhood you do, has to deal with you being all up in her business. She might just chill with you and then go home. She might kiss you and then go, or she might, if she's reckless, give it up, but that's rare. Kissing will suffice. A whitegirl might just give it up right then. Don't stop her. She'll take her gum out of her mouth, stick it to the plastic sofa covers and then will move close to you. You have nice eyes, she might say.

Tell her that you love her hair, that you love her skin, her lips, because, in truth, you love them more than you love your own.

She'll say, I like Spanish guys, and even though you've never been to Spain, say, I like you. You'll sound smooth.

You'll be with her until about eight-thirty and then she will want to wash up. In the bathroom she will hum a song from the radio and her waist will keep the beat against the lip of the sink. Imagine her old lady coming to get her, what she would say if she knew her daughter had just lain under you and blown your name, pronounced with her eighth-grade Spanish, into your ear. While she's in the bathroom call one of your boys and say, Lo hice, loco. Or just sit back on the couch and smile.

But usually it won't work this way. Be prepared. She will not want to kiss you. Just cool it, she'll say. The halfie might lean back, breaking away from you. She will cross her arms, say, I hate my tits. Stroke her hair but she will pull away. I don't like anybody touching my hair, she will say. She will act like somebody you don't know. In school she is known for her attention-grabbing laugh, as high and far-ranging as a gull, but here she will worry you. You will not know what to say.

You're the only kind of guy who asks me out, she will say. Your neighbors will start their hyena calls, now that the alcohol is in them. You and the blackboys.

Say nothing. Let her button her shirt, let her comb her hair, the sound of it stretching like a sheet of fire between you. When her father pulls in and beeps, let her go without too much of a good-bye. She won't want it. During the next hour the phone will ring. You will be tempted to pick it up. Don't. Watch the shows you want to watch, without a family around to debate you. Don't go downstairs. Don't fall asleep. It won't help. Put the government cheese back in its place before your moms kills you.

GLOSSARY

malcriado (251): Spanish for bad-mannered.
government cheese (251): block cheese, usually a combination of three cheeses, provided to welfare and food stamp recipients during the Reagan era.
campo (251): unincorporated town (for example, in the Dominican Republic).
Bermúdez (253): Dominican rum.
Lo hice, loco (254): Spanish for "I did it, (you) crazy."

FROM *ORDINARY WOLVES*

by Seth Kantner

Part of growing up requires making decisions about who you are in relation to those you most admire and love. Another part involves either opting out of or adopting a particular community identity. Ten-year-old Cutuk must do both in this excerpt from Seth Kantner's episodic novel Ordinary Wolves. *Cutuk lives in the northern reaches of Alaska, in an igloo, fairly far from the nearest village and quite far from anything resembling a city. He is white, and though his loving older siblings have names like Jerry and Iris, Cutuk is known by his Iñupiaq name. In this excerpt, he engages in a struggle to identify himself as part of this family, which includes his remote artist-father, and also as a member of the indigenous culture.*

Living with their artist father is not easy for this motherless family. All of the children exhibit a high degree of independence and initiative, for when their father is painting, they are left completely on their own, cooking, cleaning, hunting for small animals to eat, even arranging baths and lessons. Cutuk's solitude and isolation can be felt in a number of ways. While his brother and sister fantasize about specific cars they want to drive when they are older and can escape this tundra world, Cutuk cannot really envision a car, having been born in a native hospital in Crotch Spit, a remote Alaskan village, and having never seen a "real" car. He also calls his father "Abe," and we sense that his understanding of who his father is and how much Cutuk does or does not resemble him is part of why Cutuk treats him more like a strange, exotic specimen than a parent.

Since occasional visitors—like a social worker named Wax Tiera, "Nippy" Skuq Sr., a drunken storyteller, and Enuk, an Iñupiaq trapper and hunter—are the only adults passing through Cutuk's landscape besides his father, he not only relies on them as role models but competes with his siblings for his share of attention from them, showing his frustration with how to define himself. While Cutuk fears that he has not inherited any of Abe's "specialness" that he observes in his siblings, Abe himself remains Cutuk's biggest challenge—not only how to make Abe aware of him, but also what to make of Abe, a man who burns his best canvasses and whose modesty about his excellent hunting, trapping, and tanning abilities borders on denial. Clearly, Abe is not interested in fame, treating the selling of his paintings the same way that he sells the furniture he makes. Abe also waits until absolutely necessary to hunt for meat and will not kill for the sake of killing; in fact, he values the conscious decision not to kill when you have the power to do so more than being the crack shot. All of this is confusing to a boy who wants desperately to kill his first wolf before he turns eleven.

What happens on a hunting trip with his father when "Two people pitched and clawed inside me," presents Cutuk with a choice that he does not feel ready to make. Will he always be an Outsider, like his father, or will he be like Enuk and define himself by killing a wolf? Kantner leaves us thinking that we are never entirely ready to make these decisions that demand a leap in the direction of an adult identity.

Like Cutuk, Seth Kantner was born and raised in an igloo in northern Alaska. He attended the University of Montana and received a degree in journalism. He has worked as a trapper, fisherman, gardener, mechanic, igloo builder, and adjunct professor. His writing and photography have appeared in such publications as Outside, Prairie Schooner, Alaska, *and* Reader's Digest.

Cutuk's attempt to work out his own identity with little in the way of traditional guidelines can be compared with Adiele's narrator in "Fire: An Origin Tale," Tucker's narrator in "How I Learned to Fly," and ZZ Packer's narrator in "Drinking Coffee Elsewhere."

When I was ten, on a night shortly after the sun returned, a pack of wolves raided our peoplefood pile. Along the bank to the east, beyond our pole cache, the wolves worked over it all except one frozen caribou—a skinny carcass that we too were leaving till last. Our dogs howled and barked in the dark. By first light at ten o'clock the pack had vanished, leaving a pawed circle of meat dust and cracked bone chips in the reddened snow, and tracks leading in too many directions onto the windblown tundra.

The faint scent of clean dog hung in the clawed holes. Abe hunched down, kneading his yellow beard, happier than if he'd discovered gold in the gravel at the bottom of our water hole. Snow clung behind his knees to the creases of his overpants. He examined a wolf turd, long and gray with twisted caribou hair. In his hand the shit looked as capable of magic as a tube of Van Gogh Basic White.

"Should have come out to check the barking," he muttered. "Like to have the scene in my mind." He stood and stared off north, spraying a square of his powerful imagination against the sky. He often leaned against trees, absorbed in the pastel glow of evening. "Been years since the wolves took much from us. Usually too wary. Hope we don't get people-company next couple days."

A raven flew overhead, heading north. We eyed it.

"We're low on meat." Jerry melted his cheek with a bare hand. Black hairs were sprouting on his jaw. I itched with distress when his hand wandered to the icicles on his downy mustache. "Wolves're always coming by. Why's it a big deal?"

I kicked the snow ground, embarrassed for both of them. I was ten years old, behind schedule on shooting my first wolf. "Let's go after 'em."

Abe didn't hear.

For the next two weeks Abe read on his bed. Suddenly his book would drop and he'd rise, practically walking through us to his easel. He worked in oil. The turpentine fumes left us breathless and lightheaded. Tubes of his paint had frosted to the wall under his workbench, and he swore. He glared over his shoulder at the dim light, paced, peered, his mouth puckered. At night he tossed on his *qaatchiaq*, lit candles, rose to sigh at his work, and one night he tore the canvas free and stuffed it in the stove.

The second painting became a staked dog team, witnessing a pack of wolves borrowing caribou. Each dog's face held a different expression. Some merely whined, sitting, suffering the thievery patiently. Others stood on their sinewy back legs, lunging against their chains. Their mouths were outraged barks. None of the dogs were of our team—they lived in Abe's past or in his imagination. A black dog closest to the wolves jumped so hard his chain flipped him upside down, and Abe painted his curled claws, hinted at the wiry gray hair between his toes. Nine wolves leaned over the meat, cracking bones in their triangle molars. The painting had a dark silvery feel, a feeling that the wolves were friends, with each other, and with the night. I thought Abe's paintings of wolves were better than his other paintings.

During those weeks the fire in the barrel stove often burnt down to ashes. The cold waiting beyond the door and walls hurried in. Our last caribou shrank to a backbone, neck, and one shoulder. We peeled the back sinew—for thread for sewing—and made frymeat out of the backstraps before boiling the backbones. Abe didn't care what was for dinner. He sipped his tea and answered some of our questions, not all of them. We asked few. He was in a place for artists; we didn't know the language. We kids simply knew Abe wouldn't hunt and kill meat until something changed. We were allowed the few .22 cartridges to shoot ptarmigan and rabbits and foxes—if we could find any—but not allowed to take the big rifle or its ammo.

Jerry and Iris and I sling-shot mice gnawing in the food shelves, and split wood and chipped five feet through the river ice and hauled buckets of water. We heated water on the stove and scrubbed our gray laundry in the galvanized washtub, mopping with a shirt at water that came out the leaks. The two windows steamed up. The black water we hauled outside and poured down the slop hole. Steam rose and the ice popped and crackled. The second week we splurged and hauled extra buckets and took baths in the washtub. It was my turn to use the water first. That meant I had less to kneel in because we kept the last kettle boiling to add as the tub cooled. Abe squatted in the tub last. His fingers and forearms were smeared with paint. The surface of the water grew oily. He stood naked by the fire and dried.

We studied our schoolbooks, administered exams to each other: spelling, phonics, math, English, biology. With his hands floury from making bread, Jerry drew circles, explaining cells and cell walls, mitochondria and osmosis. On the bearskin couch we read books out of the library box and flipped through *Harper's* magazines, scrutinizing glossy pictures advertising giraffe-legged women smoking cigarettes and sleek gray automobiles called Cougars.

"Someday I'm going to have a Chevy truck," Jerry declared.

"Don't be boring!" Iris bent his fingers off the page. "I'll have an ocean-blue convertible. And smoke Virginia Slims!"

"You never seen ocean. Except in Crotch Spit. That was frozen. It doesn't count."

I kept quiet. I was the one born in the native hospital in Crotch Spit. I'd never seen a real car—only the dead red jeep where kids in Takunak played tag and bounced on the burnt seat springs.

We put the magazines up and scraped caribou hides with the *ichuun*. You always scraped with another hide underneath, to pad the skin and keep the *ichuun* from tearing holes. We then spread on sourdough, folded the hides skin to skin, put them under Abe's *qaatchiaq* to let the sourdough soak in overnight, and later dried and scraped the skins again to finish tanning. The windows dripped condensation. Outside in the twilight, big snowflakes fell. We hauled in wood and kicked the door shut tight and stuffed a jacket at the base of the door to keep cold air out. Abe lit the Coleman light. He pumped it and hung the hissing lamp from a nail on the ridgepole. Shadows twirled and came to rest. We got out an early-fall hide that Iris had sourdoughed earlier. The hair was short, thinner, and soft. We scraped it and worked the skin in our hands until it was tanned and white. Jerry traced new insoles for all of our soft-bottom and *ugruk*-bottom *mukluks*. Iris cut them with Abe's razor. In silence we sewed ourselves caribou socks, then swept up the hairs. Abe hunched over his easel, silent. Caribou hairs clung to his sweater. Outside, the snow piled up.

"Should I boil meat?" Jerry murmured. Iris and I soundlessly raised our eyebrows, *yes* in Iñupiaq.

Jerry put leg bones and water into the cannibal pot. While it simmered, we used Abe's powder scale to measure 4832 gunpowder, and reload .30-06 ammo with the Lee Loader. Iris sighted down a completed cartridge. "Boy, fresh moose heart would be good, wouldn't it?" She covered a grin, swinging her gaze to Abe.

"Look!" Jerry said. "You forgot to prime this one. You're *wasting!*" We glanced at Abe. *Wasting* was the baddest word in our family. Jerry bit the lead. He pried the bullet out and dumped the gunpowder back in the scale. The bullet copper was dented but would still be good enough for finishing off a caribou if it was too alive to get with a knife. "Here! You're not supposed to get the inside of the primer sweaty, 'kay?"

I crossed my arms, checked my muscle. Actually, we had plenty of food: seasonings and sugar and fifty-pound sacks of flour, powdered milk, rice, and beans. Jars of rendered bear fat for shortening. Most of a quart of vanilla. And there was a keg of salted salmon bellies, and piles of *quaq* in the dogfood cache. We could eat that. It was good with seal oil, and in the seal oil were our prized *masru* and pink *tinnik* berries. We wouldn't go hungry.

In late January, Abe took his rifle off the peg behind the stove. We kids scattered for overpants and parkas. He blew dust off the bolt and scraped his thumbnail along the stock where frozen snot or dog spit had dried. His hair and beard were unruly. His turquiose eyes squinted with a grin. "Iris? Feel like coming along?" He nodded and laid the gun on the floor across his parka and mittens. Jerry and I slumped. Abe boiled water, filled his thermos, and slid it into the caribou-hide insulating tube. We fidgeted, out of the way, while Iris got bundled and ready.

They hitched the team and went east, hunting for an acquiescent moose to contribute both dog food and people food. The caribou herds were far south in their wintering grounds. It was cold—cold enough that the kerosene had jelled and wouldn't pour into the lamp—and the dogs did not lunge to run.

Afterward, Jerry wandered back inside to rewrite a letter to his pen pal in New Zealand, romancing her long distance. Mice rustled and scurried on the floor. His pen rustled the paper. He liked to write letters and poems. And his diary, too. I figured he was faking talent. We kids didn't say it—that would be bad luck—but we hoped we'd inherited a little of Abe's specialness. We grew up watching our dad; for months on end he was the only one to watch, to teach us about our world, and tidbits of the city world. We watched his left hand, the one with good genes, hoping to recognize the first twinges in our own hands.

I hauled armloads of wood. Jerry went out to cut meat for dinner. The house was quiet. The table and chairs and floorboards seemed gray, dingy, and bare with no one about. Curiosity pushed my honor aside— I slid a thumbnail in where the edges of his diary's pages were smudged. My eyes scrambled over the words . . . *only you who watched mothers fly away, after the cold will be my sisters and brothers.* . . . I dropped the book. Quickly I placed it back on the table. I laced my *mukluks*. Fumbled into my parka. Hurried out behind the woodpile and pretended to scan the tundra for life.

Jerry hung the bow saw on a nail. His *mukluks* squeaked on the snow. He carried sawed caribou ribs inside. They were skinny ribs, thin and with signs of wolf lips and shrew turds on them. He came outside, no jacket. His brown eyes looked rolled back like a village dog held down by its last six inches of iced-in chain. "That's mine." There was red meat sawdust between his fingers. Jerry's big square fist swung. My face seemed to crack open. Behind a snowbank I leaned over. Blood hung in coagulating red icicles off my nose. I tried to forget the words in the diary. And the jealousy that Jerry might have what I didn't—a share of Abe's gift.

Iris, too, had something. Something completely different, though. It wasn't something you could talk about. One spring a white-lady social

worker skied down the river towing a plastic sled. She was from the distant big city of Anchorage, and how she got upriver we didn't know. She
wore bright blue windbreakers and windpants, and had a black backpack, an orange aluminum foil space blanket, and dehydrated space
meals and Swiss chocolate bars. She was very beautiful and had heaps of
wavy brown hair and didn't seem to get cold. Her name was Wax Tiera,
and we adored her though we suspected her of being an alien. The odd
thing was, the day before she showed, Iris cleaned the entire igloo in a
way we had never before done. She swept away caribou hair and dust,
washed the floorboards with steaming soapy rags, organized Abe's
paints, used the splitting maul to knock down the spike that froze in the
outhouse. She had scrubbed all day, washing the outsides of mason jars,
laughing excitedly, squinting nearsightedly into corners.

Another time, two falls ago, before Freezeup, Napoleon Skuq Sr.
came upriver in his spruce-plank boat. Nippy had a big eighteen-horse
Evinrude. He was proud of it. He boated up every couple of years, his
fall trip. Sometimes he brought a cousin, sometimes his sons, Junior and
Caleb. Nippy wore a leather skullcap. His eyes around the edges were
bumpy and yellow. He arrived drunk, spent the evening telling Abe how
to hunt and trap, and traveled on in the morning. Within a few days he
came back downriver, his prop dinged, the boat weaving slow in the first
ice pans. Caribou legs poked over the gunnels of his boat. He spent the
night again, and this time Nippy's hands had a tremor as he pulled his
Bible out of a cotton sugar sack. He spread it soft and sagging on his
thigh and under the wick lamp preached about Jesus and sin and a bush
that you couldn't put out from burning. Then he told Abe some more
of his hunting stories. He bragged about his son graduating from Mt.
Edgecombe boarding school in Sitka.

"I thought your son died," Iris said softly. Nippy swung his wet eyes
on her. "Maybe you thinking somebody else." He was sitting on the
bearskin couch, on the shoulder end, where the hair had worn the least.
He glanced into the soup pot, served himself the tenderest fat short
brisket bones. He scooped a plop of cranberry sauce on his plate. Iris
stood up from the Standard Oil Co. wooden Blazo-box seat that
pinched your butt and squeaked. She scraped her gnawed bones into the

dog pot and went to fill kettles on the stove to heat water for dishes. After Freezeup, when the ice was thick enough to travel, word came that
Caleb Skuq had been stabbed behind a bar in Juneau and died. No one
told the whole story in front of Iris, though everyone in Takunak knew
it, and they glanced at her differently.

Abe had left the unruly puppies, Plato and Figment. They were interested
in my bloody nose. I hung around the dog yard, chopping out pissed-in
chains and the third-of-a-drum dogfood cooker. The top was sharp and
rusty where Abe had cut it with a sledgehammer and his piece of sharpened spring-steel. I ignored the bite of the cold and wandered in a fantasy
of myself shooting a charging moose. Jerry's pen pal wish-girl lay shriek-
ing in the trail. Broken leg. He couldn't get to her. Calmly I shot. The girl
blurred into the dark-haired woman on the front of the JCPenney catalog
and had no difficulty jumping up to kiss me repeatedly.

Suddenly Plato sniffed. She barked, and with a worried tail stared
north. A flock of redpolls shrilled up in the birch branches and vanished
in a gust of small wings. Off the high tundra west of Jesus Creek slid
the elongated black speck of a dog team. *Travelers!* It didn't matter who,
if we knew them or not, what they looked like. Or how much they ate,
snored, farted—even if they spoke only Iñupiaq, or Russian. Only that
they would talk and be *company!*

The speck separated into seven dogs and came across what we called
Outnorth Lake or Luck-a-Luck Lake or The Lake, depending on the
season and the conversation. Enuk mushed up the knife ridge that
formed a narrow bank separating the lake from the Kuguruk River. He
kicked his snow hook into an ice-hard drift. His dogs flopped down,
panting. I sank my hatchet into a dog stake and ran to his sled, gripping
the toprails.

"Hi, Enuk!"

He gazed stiffly out of the frosty silver circle of his wolf ruff. He
broke ice off his gray mustache and eyelashes. Then he grinned, as if
trying earlier might have pulled hairs. He smelled of campfire and coffee. He took off his rifle and hung it carefully off the handlebar of his

sled. His gaze flicked over the tracks left by Abe's team. I stayed respectfully silent while he rubbed the frosted faces of his dogs and bit the iceballs off from between their hairy toes. It was annoying and white to talk too much or ask questions, especially when a traveler first arrived. Shaking hands, also, was a sign of being an Outsider. Enuk wore new tan store-bought overpants. On one hem was the red chalk of frozen blood. His sled tarp was lashed down, too tight for me to poke under without being nosy. Sled tarps had always held secrets, brought packages, presents, fresh meat, store-bought cookies. Old and ratty didn't matter—sled tarps were the biggest wrapping paper of all.

"When you leavin', Enuk?" I asked finally.

"Pretty quick."

"How come? Spend the night."

Staring north, he pursed his lips thoughtfully. He nodded. "Maybe gonna I spen'a night."

"I wish!"

"If I know, I woulda' bring you-fellas' first class." His squinted eyes roamed the snow-covered river, willows, and tundra, probing for the tiniest movement of life. He swung back to me. "Anytime they could get you." I eyed his sled. What was he talking about? Bears? Spirits? "If they want you they get you, anytime." He noticed my eyes on his tarp. "Ha ha, Yellow-Hair!" He kicked a fast *mukluk* at me.

He unlashed the tarp and spread it open. "I get lucky." He nodded toward the mountains. "T'em wolves kill moose young one. Not too far." I didn't follow his eyes. The wolf was silver-gray and huge, twice the size of Enuk's huskies, its hair long and black-tipped. I petted the animal in wonder, feeling splinters of blood frozen deep in the fur. I recognized the clean dog odor. Broken ribs shone in a large bullet hole in the side of his chest. I saw the wolf stumbling, hearing his own bones grating, panting against death pouring into his lungs.

I shook my head to dislodge the pictures.

"Coulda have more, alright. Only thing, smart one in'a bunch. He let t'em others run." He looped his stringed overmitts behind his back. Barehanded, wary of the blood, he kneaded the wolf's thin lower legs.

"*Alappaa!* Freeze. Hard gonna for tat way ta skin. I bring tis wolf inside. Wait for your old man."

Abe and Iris returned without meat. We ate the skinny ribs Jerry had boiled. Skinny meat was a sign of a poor provider, but Enuk ate with relish. Afterward he skinned the wolf. When he finished, he folded the skin fur-out. On our floor the naked wolf grinned permanently in the weak lamplight, his teeth and tendons white against dark red muscles. The stomach was hard, and fetid smells were beginning to come out. Enuk had only a little blood on his fingertips. There was a slit in the wolf's throat. "Let his spirit go other wolf," Enuk said. "Gotta respect."

"Do you like wolves?" I asked.

Iris and Jerry peered over the tops of their schoolbooks. Their papers were spread on the wooden Blazo boxes that we made into desks—and also cupboards, shelves, seats, muskrat-stretching boards, and more.

"They got fam'ly. Smart. Careful. I like 'em best than all'a animal. Your dad know. He make tat good picture. Gonna ta white ladies buy tat one more than any kinda wolf skin. Ha! Ha!" Enuk opened the door. Cold-air fog rolled in. He flung the carcass into the dark. The furless animal slapped on the packed snow out under the chipped eyes of the stars. In the dog yard one of Enuk's dogs barked nervously at the thump in the still night. An echo rolled back lonesome from the timber across the river, and the dog challenged it with three quick barks.

"Yep, Yellow-Hair. Tomorrow you take your old man." Enuk grinned. "Go out back way, hunt moose." His eyes flicked to his knife, and I wondered what else he was thinking about and whether it was killing more wolves.

"We might." Abe smiled and looked shy about something. He wiped blood drips off the floor with a holey sock rag. His cheeks and nose burnt with red ovals from frostbite that day on the trail. Iris's face was marked red, too. They hadn't seen the right moose—a barren cow, a moose that would have fat meat and its hide fair for snowshoe *babiche*, sled washers, cold-weather *mukluk* bottoms.

"We might look again tomorrow." Abe folded the cardboard he had laid out for Enuk to work on. "You do a real nice job, Enuk." Abe sounded as if he would have an impossible time skinning even a caribou legging. Abe had taught me to skin and dry foxes, perfectly—better than any fox I'd ever seen skinned in Takunak. Their pelt was papery, difficult not to tear with the sharpened metal tube *ichuun*, difficult not to tear when turning the dried skin back fur-out. And though we often used only the thick warm fur for mittens, he made me skin to save the toenails, tail, eyelashes—out of respect to the animal whose life we'd taken.

Often, Abe helped me make birch and *babiche* snowshoes that few in Takunak remembered how to make. Or one time he helped write a letter to the substitute president, Gerald Ford. But he would never pick up an axe like he was tough. Never talk or hold a gun that way. Never brag, "I'm goin' after bear." Any bear we got walked up on its own and still Abe didn't want to kill it. Around travelers, Abe's modesty trimmed off too much of the fat. Apparently things started getting out of balance back with his dad. Tom Hawcly had been a sport hunter, a menacing species to have in any food chain. He left our grandmother in Chicago and roamed off to Barrow to be a pilot, the owner of two Super Cub airplanes, and a guide for polar bear hunters. The story was exciting enough, and romantic—up to the part where they found him smeared dead on the sea ice. People along the Kuguruk River hated sport hunters and guides as much as they did schoolteachers. Frequently they were one and the same. I was thankful that Barrow was a long way north. And that people thought of white people as having no relatives.

Enuk finished skinning out the paws. He talked of shooting his first wolf when he was ten. His dad had taken him to check a *tiktaaliq* fish trap. A lone wolf was there on the ice gnawing yesterday's frozen fish blood. The wind was behind the wolf. Enuk's father handed him the rifle.

I listened to Enuk's low voice and lusted to gun down a whole pack, to stockpile prestige. Somehow, I had to learn to stop worrying about wolf pain. Abe had to stop molding me into an unhero.

Abe slapped his pants, fumbled in his big pockets for tobacco and papers. He glanced over the table and workbench, and eventually gave up. To Iris he said, "Otter, boil water? When Enuk's washed up maybe you'll make a splash of tea?"

Iris set her math book on the wood box. She smiled at Enuk. The frostbite was pretty across her cheeks and nose. "Nine times eight, Cutuk!"

"Huh? Seventy-two."

"Twenty-one times eleven."

"Two hundred and thirty-one." My thoughts softened; I pictured happy otters playing, sliding along day-old ice, stopping to nuzzle each other.

Iris dripped the dipper on my head as she danced barefoot toward the water barrel. She peered close, to focus out of her weak eyes. "Cutuk? Why, Yellow-Hair Boy, you looked mad as a wolverine in a trap."

I flicked her leg. The religious poster—the one Abe tacked out in the outhouse, the one the Gospel Trippers had left when they passed through last winter—said a family was supposed to say it: "I love you," I whispered, at my hands, too softly, the only time in my life. Iris, with her black hair and surprising blue eyes, full of smiles where I had storms, she never heard. She was in her own thoughts. What were they? I should have asked, but kissing, saying the word *love*, and talking about feelings weren't what Hawclys did, and I was embarrassed and went outside for a few minutes in the dark, to stand barefoot on the snow and listen to the night beside the naked wolf.

The stove draft flickered orange lights on the peeled poles of the ceiling. The orange melted through my eyelids to clutter my dreams with flames. Pitch smoldered, sweet and resinous on top of the stove.

Enuk lay on his *qaatchiaq*. His legs stretched out of sight under the table. Iris's black hair curled across my face. I brushed it aside and pulled our pants and shirts under the covers to warm them. I gripped the corner of the sleeping bag tight to keep the chilly morning out. For years Abe had promised to order me my own sleeping bag. Like Iris's glasses, it was another thing we'd have to go out into the world and find for ourselves. Iris took up more room this winter. She was bigger. Her breasts were growing, disconcerting to me when I accidentally brushed them.

"You elbowed me really hard in the eye last night." Her voice was sleepy. She wore one of Abe's flannel shirts, faded and thin. She smelled of flannel, candle wax, and soft skin.

Jerry's bed was head to head with ours along the back wall. I wasn't sure if he was awake on his caribou skin. It was dark in the room, except for firelight. Abe banged the coffeepot on a round of firewood. He swore softly when a chunk of frozen grounds crumbled on the floor. He toed the grounds against the wood box. Iris leaned her chin on her wrists. "Daddy slobbest. What will he do without us?" Her words made me shiver. Firelight glowed on his broad white chest and arms. He crumpled a painting, stuffed it into the stove. The stiff paper caught and flared. For cash Abe made furniture to sell in Takunak, and occasionally he mailed one of his paintings to Anchorage. Never his best. I lay fantasizing; he was an outlaw artist with a notorious past, his name would be legend in the places I traveled.

His bare feet rasped on the cold boards. Outside darkness painted the windows black. The roar of the stove grew, and frost in the safety dripped and hissed. Kettles began to whine. Enuk yawned and rose. He wore jeans and a white T-shirt. His body was stout and muscular. The sun had never seen it, and his skin was smooth and pearly brown as a young man's, except on his thick hands and face where weather and time had stained their stories.

They sipped coffee. Abe lit the lamp. He took the cannibal pot off the stove and put it on the table. We knifed out hot meat and gravy and ate it with bread and the frozen sliced canned jam that Enuk brought. A fly buzzed, one wing frozen to the ice on the inside of the window. The door was frosty around the edges. It was still dark outside. The dogs howled.

Enuk put down his cup. "Today I get old."

Iris pattered her fingers on his shoulder, as unconcerned as if he were a shelf. "Are you a hundred?"

I watched her hand. Jerry was watching, too.

"Jan'wary twenty-one, nineteen hunnert an five. How many tat gonna? Seventy?"

"Seventy-one!"

"Not so many. I still hunt best than my son."

"My birthday was the fourth," I said, thinking how perfect it would have been to be born seventeen days later, on Enuk's birthday. "We're not sure we celebrated on the right day. That day was warm and it snowed sticky; you remember, was that the fourth?" I trailed off. The mouthful of numbers felt white.

Enuk ignored me and retrieved his frozen wolf skin from outside the door. Cold-air fog rolled in. He eyed the skin for shrew chews. His leather pouch lay beside his mug on the table. It had sounded heavy when he plunked it down. "You fellas have tat." He nodded at the can of jam. "Cutuk, t'em mooses waiting. You gonna hunt?"

I studied Abe's face for a sign.

"It could be cold." He sharpened his knife, three flicks on the pot, three flicks back. "Real cold."

"I'll put my face under the tarp when it freezes."

"Tat a boy!" Enuk said.

Down at the river it was minus a lot. My nose kept freezing shut on one side. The dogs uncurled and shook frost off their faces. They stood on three legs, melting one pad at a time while the other three quickly froze. Abe's leader, Farmer, stayed tight in a ball, melted into the packed snow. Her wide brown eyes peered out from under her tail. The hair on her feet was stained reddish brown. She was a gentle dog. I coaxed her to the front of the team where she shivered with her back arched, tail under her belly and pads freezing. Abe and Jerry harnessed the big, hard-to-handle dogs. The snaps were frozen. The harnesses were stiff and icy and hard to force into dog shapes. Our dogs weren't accustomed to company; even cold, they showed off to Enuk's dogs, tugging and barking, tangling the lines.

A quarter mile downriver, Abe waved a big wave good-bye to Enuk. Abe geed the dogs north, up the bank below the mouth of Jesus Creek. The snow on the tundra was ice hard, scooped and gouged into waves by wind. It creaked under the runners. Morning twilight bruised the southern sky. Shivers wandered my skin. I yanked off a mitten and warmed frozen patches on my cheeks. The cold burnt inside my nose.

My fingers started to freeze. I wondered what thoughts walked in Abe's mind. I felt as cumbersome and alone as a moon traveler, peering out the fur tunnel of my caribou hood, beaver hat, and wolf ruff.

Farmer led toward the Dog Die Mountains. They were steep mountains, the spawning grounds of brown bears, storms, and spirits. They beckoned like five giants, snowed in to their chins. Occasionally we crossed a line of willows that marked a buried slough or a pond shore, and a dog or two would heave against his neckline and mark a willow, claiming any stray females in the last ten thousand acres.

"Is that a moose?" I said.

The dogs glanced over their shoulders, faces frosty and alarmed at my shout.

"Might be a tree," Abe said softly.

My moose mutated into one of the lone low dark trees that grip the tundra, hunkered like a troll, gnarled arms thrust downwind. Abe had more careful eyes than I did; they grabbed details, touched textures, took apart colors. I slumped, cold on my caribou skin, stabbed by love for my dad. He didn't have to say "might be a tree" when he *knew*. Plenty of the dads in the village would holler, "Shudup. You try'na scare everything again?"

On a ridge, Abe whoa'd the dogs. He took out tobacco and papers. His bared hands tightened and turned red. I looked away, pretending for him that they were brown. He was too naive to know that red fingers were not the kind to have. The smoke smelled sharp in the smell-robbed air, comforting. The southern horizon glowed pink and for a few minutes a chunk of the sun flamed red through a dent in the Shield Mountains, like a giant flashlight with dying batteries. The snow glowed incandescent. I sprinted back and forth, melting fingers and toes. Abe glassed the land.

"Hmm. There she is."

Through the binoculars the moose stood silhouetted, black as open water. We mushed closer. A deep moan floated on the air. Abe braked the sled. He shushed the dogs. They held their breath, listening. Then the pups yowled and tugged, the scent stirring their blood.

"Must be that cow missing her calf," Abe said.

"They can sound like that?" I'd heard loons laughing manically, the woman-screams of lynx, ghoulish whimpering from porcupine, but I hadn't heard a mourning moose. I was proud of Abe, proud of his omniscient knowledge of the land.

"Never heard anything like it before," he said, pleased.

We jounced on.

"Abe, why do you think greatness is bad?" My question startled both of us. I stiffened, mortified. He snapped ice off his mustache. "I mean—Burning your best paintings. And acting like you don't know how to hunt when travelers are bragging."

When Abe spoke, he used his historical-problems-with-the-world voice. He had a degree in art and history; Iris often teased that his degree *was* history. "This book I'm reading, the author argues that our heroes aren't heroes at all and have traditionally—"

I stopped listening and watched frost-laden twigs pass. Abe liked to mull things over until he got them complicated. A discussion with him was like rolling a log uphill in sticky snow. Ideas glommed on. I started to offer ten-year-old facts, but the dogs sped up and we dropped into a slough and lost the trail of the conversation when the team piled up on the leftovers of the calf moose. Backbone, hair, hooves, and the head with the nose and eyes chewed down, all scattered in a red circle. Fine wolf trails and deep moose trenches mapped out the battle.

The dogs bit at the frozen blood and woody stomach contents. Abe bent, careful not to let go of the sled handlebar. He touched a clean wolf paw print. "Soft," he mused. "Been back to finish her up."

The dogs raced west, up a narrow slough. "Abe," I whispered, "should we maybe not shoot that ma moose? She's had enough bad luck. Didn't you want to shoot a barren cow, to be fatter?"

I wanted to get out of the overhanging willows before she charged. The snow was soft and deep. Anyone knew moose were more dangerous than bears. Especially on a dog team. As a child, I had been petrified during the night with fear of a moose dropping in our ground-level skylight. The thrashing black hooves would crack our skulls. The wind would sift the igloo full of snow. Shrews would tunnel under our skin and hollow us out, and when travelers found our bodies we'd be weightless as dried seagulls. Abe nourished the nightmare, shrugging, conveying the impression that, sure, given time, my prophecy was bound to come true. Abe was that way. Realistic, he called it.

He ran behind the runners, dodging willows that tried to slap his eyes. He panted over my hood. "Might be the only moose in fifty miles that doesn't care either way."

I knew I could argue with him, and he'd leave the animal. He'd welcome the discussion—and the chance not to kill. I shut my stiff lips. Willows whipped past. Abe climbed on the runners and rode. He cleared his throat and whistled encouragements to the dogs. I squinted in frustration, thinking, *Now I'm definitely not going to get to shoot.*

"My parents split up after the war," Abe said. "People didn't do that back then. That-a-girl, Farmer. Haw. Haw over. I was thirteen then."

In the sled I stared at my *mukluks*. Shocked—not that his parents divorced, but that he was telling me. His past was always as distant as the cities.

"I came home from school one day, in trouble with Sister Abigail for saying I trusted animals more than people. Dad's flannel shirts were all gone from the floor and the backs of chairs. I knew without those shirts, he was gone. He went off hunting fame or fortune, I guess." Abe sounded like he was telling himself the story, too. I stayed silent, pretending indifference. Those seemed to be the manners I'd been taught; I just couldn't remember learning them.

"Even in Barrow, I usually drew animals instead of shooting them. I would've liked to be a hero. Of course I wanted to be one. It just felt . . . phony. Wearing the clothes. Strutting and flexing. Shooting some poor creature. It just wasn't me."

Had he told Iris this yesterday? Probably not; she didn't have my mouth that had always wanted to know how to be someone else.

"I propped the Super Cub for my dad, the day he crashed. Kind of a heroic thing to do?"

Willows slapped my face and the crook of his arm. Snow sifted down my neck.

"The engine sounded funny. I could have said something but Dad would have hollered to stand clear. Guess life's like shooting a caribou, huh? You want a fat one, but if you end up with a skinny one, you don't waste it."

"People leave a skinny caribou, Abe. Or feed it to the dogs and shoot a sledload more."

"You kids!"

We plowed out of the willows, onto a lake. I saw her across the ice; she stood on long graceful legs, huge black shoulders. The backs of her ankles were pale yellow; along her flank stretched a white gash in the hair. Figment hollered and lunged, cheering the other dogs on. The moose cantered into low brush. The brake ripped furrows in the snow. The sled slid across the ice.

"Stand on the snow hook!"

I jumped out with the hook. It bit into the packed snow. I held it down with knees and palms. The moose waded in deep snow, disappearing into the willows. Abe raised the gun and shot. The moose went down, and WHOMP—the bullet hit sounded like an air-dropped box of nails. Fresh meat! I forgot my frozen cheeks. But not that I wanted to be the one to shoot. Abe wasn't going to change. He didn't believe it made any difference which hunter pulled the trigger. Since he was already an expert, of course he always shot.

A few yards from the dogs, I stood beside the steaming gut pile. Under the snow, the lake was solid six feet down, and I pictured lethargic pike and whitefish squeezed in the dark silence between mud and ice, waiting with cold-blooded thoughts for winter to go away. I felt strong withstanding the cold.

Up close the moose was alarmingly big. Abe and I loaded the huge hindquarters and butt on the basket sled. He hurried off to break willows, the springy sticks shattering like glass in the cold.

"Making stick towers to scare the ravens?"

"Get dry wood. I'll start a fire."

I discovered with dismay that one of us was staying with the remaining meat. Abe stepped away from the newborn fire and cut snow to clean his bloody knife.

I pretended to break the ice off my eyelashes. I peered about nervously. A couple of the dogs whined and tugged at the anchored sled, their feet and noses freezing, their hearts anxious to run toward home and dinner. The rest had curled up, conserving warmth. I longed to go, tented between the companionship of my father behind on the runners and the huskies panting faithful in front.

"I'll try to make it back 'fore too late." Abe planted the .30-06 stock-first in the snow. He stepped carefully, keeping his moosehide-bottom *mukluks* out of the circle of blood around the kill. "At home I'll have to lash on the gee-pole. And my skis." The gee-pole tied onto the front of the sled and Abe skied behind the wheel dogs—in front of the sled—and used the pole to steer when the load was heavy or the trail deep. I hefted the gun. The weight was powerful. The cold steel seared my bloody fingers and I knelt and thawed them in the pool of blood coagulated in the moose's chest. I wiped my hands on the coarse fur, slid my mittens on.

Suddenly all the dogs held their breath. Nine pairs of ears swiveled north. Abe and I turned. Across the distance floated shivers of sound: wolves howling. Abe straightened up bareheaded. His hair, aged gray with frost, slapped me with a glimpse of the future. We scanned the horizons. Finally, he took off his mittens and cinched the sled rope. Abe hated loose loads the way he hated whiny kids. "Nice to hear the wolves," he murmured. "Country's poor without them. Cutuk, it means there's other animals around."

I shifted, uncomfortable with him using my name. Abe had heard and seen hundreds of wolves over the years since he'd been a teenager in Barrow. He didn't shoot them; why did he care so much to see more?

Plato raised her muzzle and poured a perfect howl into the frozen sky. The other dogs joined in a cacophony of yips and howls that swelled out over the tundra. "Shudup!" Abe growled. He whipped the billowy gut pile with a willow. It made a hollow crack. We'd empty the rumen and take it and the fat intestines home for dog food, second load. We'd leave the lungs, windpipe, stomach contents, and some blood that the dogs didn't gnaw off the snow. The team sat, rolling their eyes apologetically.

"Don't hurry," I mumbled, casual. I glanced down at the gun. Already loneliness was settling like outer space pushing down the sky. The arctic twilight would fade and Abe would be under the stars before he slid into our dog yard.

He threw a caribou skin to me to lie on. Handed over dried meat and a chunk of pemmican with currants, dried cranberries, and caribou fat. "You don't need to shoot any wolves. You hear? We still have a piece of a wolf skin in the cache." His face twitched with sudden guilt for leaving. I opened my mouth to encourage the feeling, but he'd stridden back to the runners.

"Okay! Getup there! Hike!" Away they went, the sled heavy and the dogs heaving with their hips out to the sides and their tails stiff with effort. In minutes they had disappeared to a black dot on the tundra, silhouetted by the orange horizon that lay along the south pretending the sun had been up half the day and burnt that strip of fire.

I held my breath. Listened to the silence. The land at cold temperatures waited in molecular stillness; sound traveled far, though very little of it lived here anymore. My heart boomed. My ears filled with a waterfall of ringing. The land's thousand eyes watched. I knelt and tried to concentrate on the fire and the smoke, sweet with the smell of warmth and company. A noise startled me.

From a lone spruce on the far side of the lake a raven cawed. "Caaawk," I answered. I glanced behind. The watchful bird cawed again, urging me to leave the fat meat to him. I saw him standing on my face, feasting on my eyes. I saw him on Abe's face and I hummed quickly and fed the fire.

The pastel sky had darkened. In the south a last strip of orange and greenish blue lingered. The walls of blackness grew and leaned close over my head and joined. An icy east breeze thinned the smoke. The night cold was a monster now, merciless, pinching my face with pliers, sneaking fingers under my parka. It didn't seem possible to keep my cheeks thawed, and they froze over and over again. The flames sizzled the two-foot-long moose ribs I speared on a stick, burning the crisp fat while the ends froze.

In the flickering light my pile of dry willow shrank. I scratched my neck to steal glances behind. The raven had gone.

When the ribs were nicely burnt, I gnawed on the meat pressed between my mittens. I worked a bone clean, tossed it into the dark. Back home it was Jerry's day to bake bread; probably he was sliding loaves out of our oven box in the bottom of the barrel stove, rapping the brown bottoms to hear the hollow done sound. I wished for a hot slice, and walls behind my shoulders, and Iris's teasing squeezes.

Jaws crunched a bone.

I dropped the rib and snatched the rifle. The dark was made of dots, walls of eyes. A scream tore the night.

A fox! Was it rabid? I hissed out a hoarse fox bark. Silence rang back. I barked again. To the left I heard a soft thump. Then running feet and the quick sounds of a chase. My stomach tightened. The wolves had come!

If the fox was crippled the wolves would eat him. I wished bad luck on him until I remembered that Enuk would say he could wish the same on me. Above, aurora wavered, green smoke ghosting in the dark, quick pale brush strokes, the bottoms tinted pink, twinging up in the black. The fire had sunk, hissing and steaming down on the lake ice. I knelt forward to salvage some coals. Smoke stung my eyes. Snow squeaked. The darkness moved into shapes. Slowly, I turned my head. Behind stood more.

The *chik-chunk* of the rifle loading sounded as loud as river ice booming. I aimed over the dark shaking sights. My thoughts scattered down terrified trails. The pack couldn't have forgotten that a man had shot one of them yesterday. Now I would never get to be Eskimo, or see a 747, or know for how many years President Nixon had to go to jail. I tried to place myself in a future story to milk heroism out of my bad luck, but all I saw were clumps of bones and yellow hair. A voice I hadn't heard whispered, "Shoot! *Shoot!*" I gripped the gun. I was ten. My chance to be Enuk! People in the village would know it the next time they teased, "Catch any weasel in your trap, Cutuk?"

The steel trigger froze through my fox mitten liner. I yanked back. The gun lurched. The black wolf I'd aimed at sniffed his paw.

The safety. I flipped the lever. Now Abe's disappointed face floated in the way. I looked over the barrel, tried to aim. The northern lights had dimmed. It was harder to make out shapes. Abe wouldn't cuss or even kick things around. He would help skin the wolf. That was the thing about Abe, he'd help someone else before he helped himself. The thing about me was I couldn't accept that all people were not like that. I saw Abe as a boy, searching for his dad's shirts. I clicked the safety back. The wolf lifted his nose and howled. The pack joined.

Fear and elation skated on my skin. Were they cheering? Or voting? I felt cruel for lusting to kill one. I had eaten; I had a warm wolf ruff on my hood—but the gnawing inside was jittery and big, a hunger to kill and be great for it. It wasn't good, it was mean, but it felt glued all over inside me.

The harmony ceased. The wolves stood, listening. Finally, miles east, upwind, across the tundra, I heard the snap of branches, and fainter still, runners squeaking on cold snow; eventually came a low mumble that I knew as Abe's encouraging "Atta boys. Good girl, Farmer. Haw over now. Haw over."

The wolves circled, their claws tacking the hard snow. I aimed, bare-handed now, my fingers burning on the metal. Under the green luminescence from the sky the wolf pack fanned out north across the lake. The animals I'd wanted to kill mingled and faded. That wolf—how many miles and years had he walked under this smoky green light? Walked cold, hungry in storms, wet under summer rain; walking on this land I'd always called *my* home. He knew every mountain, every trail along every knoll so much better than I ever would. And the wolf, I only knew him dead. I didn't want to be an Outsider. Not here, too. How was it that I'd never considered carefully that an animal would know infinitely more about something than I could?

The whisper of their feet disappeared under the sounds of the coming dog team. Two people pitched and clawed inside me. One whispered in awe: "They were so close." The other mocked: "You dummy! Ten years old, same age as Enuk, and *you* didn't shoot." My fingers screamed in the pain of warming. I hunched over them, humming to hide the anguish. Abe had said to watch, but he was a painter. He read books and watched the sky too much. Enuk said to respect the wolves, but he'd have shot as many as he could. Even the last one. Under my skin, so well I knew, in the village "could have" meant nothing without the mantle of a dead animal. I wanted the stars to drop some silver stranger, an alluring alien like Wax Tiera, to tell me what I should think. But there was only the dark, the cold, the miles and miles of snow.

GLOSSARY

caribou (257): artic and subartic reindeer.

qaatchiaq (258): skin mattress, traditionally caribou hide.

ptarmigan (258): gamebird in grouse family, also known as the snow chicken; it breeds across artic and subartic North America and Europe on tundra and rocky mountainsides.

ichuun (259): skin scraper used in tanning.

ugruk-bottom mukluks (260): bearded-seal-bottom-skin boots.

quaq (260): frozen meat or fish, often aged or fermented.

masru (260): roots; Eskimo potato.

tinnik (260): bearberry.

splitting maul (262): wood-splitting axe.

Evinrude (262): brand of outboard motor.

dinged (262): to have minor damage.

Sitka (262): the fourth largest Alaskan city located on the west side of Baranof Island; part of the Alaskan Panhandle.

redpolls (263): small birds in the finch family that breed in the north and are associated with birch trees.

Iñupiaq (263): group of dialects of the Inuit language spoken in northern and northwestern Alaska.

Alappaa! (265): It is cold!

babiche (265): rawhide strips.

Super Cub airplanes (266): small, single-engine/propeller airplanes.

Barrow (266): northernmost Alaskan city and settlement in the United States.

tiktaaliq (266): mudshark.

geed (269): directional command to sled dogs

tundra (270): treeless plain of artic and subartic regions.

glommed (271): seized or latched on to, probably from Scots "glam," to snatch.

shrew (271): mouse-like mammals with high metabolic rates, requiring them to eat 80–90 percent of their own body weight daily.

gee-pole (274): sturdy pole lashed to a sled at one end and held for skiing support and steering purposes.

rumen (274): the first compartment of the stomach of a ruminant, such as a moose.

FROM *BURNT BREAD AND CHUTNEY: GROWING UP BETWEEN CULTURES—A MEMOIR OF AN INDIAN JEWISH GIRL*

by Carmit Delman

Every chapter of this memoir starts with a quote from the diary of Nana-bai, Delman's maternal grandmother, who casts a giant shadow over the Delman household. This excerpt begins with Nana-bai's recipe for chapati bread, a staple of Indian cuisine. Chapatis are tricky to make; if the frying pan is too hot, they will burn, and a burned chapati will never be served to the men of the Delman family, as young Carmit discovers. But she also discovers that a burnt chapati can bring forth pleasures "sometimes wrapped up in the larger principles of our household," offering culinary delight as well as unexpected insights into her family hierarchy.

Despite living in the United States, Nana-bai cannot change the way she thinks about men and women. Delman's status as second in a family of three daughters and one son means that she will have her share of household chores to do, while her younger brother Tzvi roams freely through the household. He is even adoringly trailed by the baby, Batsheva, who can be given the painful task of ferreting out a ball from the rose bushes, if Tzvi so designates, thorns notwithstanding. When Delman complains to her grandmother about her lot, demanding to know why Tzvi is exempt from his share of chores and even from the responsibility of making sure that no harm comes to his baby sister, the response from Nana-bai is always the same: "He is the boy." The excerpt examines the significance of this response—how Delman's mother and sisters have adjusted to Nana-bai's bias; how her father and Tzvi accept their elevated positions without gloating but also without question. Her parents rely on Nana-bai for the stability that her presence provides, and they respect her even if they don't agree with her.

As this excerpt oscillates between Delman's past and her present assessment of that past, we are given the benefit of Delman's mature understanding of how much even she absorbs from Nana-bai. She notes that she once worried incessantly about propriety; junior high karate lessons designed to make her more assertive only serve to reinforce Delman's perception of gender stereotypes. She observes that she always returns to her grandmother, who once offered her half of a burnt chapati smeared with chutney, not good enough for her father's or brother's portion, but not to be wasted; that it is good seems to both surprise and annoy Delman.

Delman's understanding of her grandmother's stubborn refusal to allow geographic displacement to compromise her values grows over time. So too does her perception that her mother, though appearing to be more modern and American, also purposely chooses the "most browned, most crusty, the most imperfect and raggedly shaped chapati in the stack" for her own meal. Some traditions and modes of thinking die hard—or perhaps insidiously infiltrate even our unconscious actions and thoughts.

Carmit Delman is descended from the Bene Israel, an ancient community of Indian Jews. India's Jewish community is made up of three groups: the ancient Jews of Cochin (now called Kochi), the Baghdadi Jews, and the Bene Israel, with the most obscure and shrouded history of all. Since the Bene Israel were said to have migrated from the ancient kingdom of Israel, they were among the most active of the Indian Jews in working toward creating the modern state of Israel, even though, ironically, they faced more discrimination in Israel than they ever encountered in India, owing to the darker color of their skin. Delman's mother went to live, study, and work in Israel, where she met and married Delman's father, an American Jew of Ashkenazi (Eastern European) descent.

American-born, Delman grew up bouncing back and forth be-
tween the United States and Israel, finally settling in the United
States, an amalgam of her Jewish, Indian, American, and Israeli
heritage. She studied literature and anthropology at Brandeis Uni-
versity and received an MFA in creative writing from Emerson
College. She currently lives, teaches, and writes in Boston.

This piece, with its emphasis on the separate and unequal lives
of women, might be compared to Villanueva's "La Llorona/Weep-
ing Woman," though Delman's memoir deals with the lives of
women more gently than Villanueva's story does. It might also be
read with Yamanaka's "Obituary" and Diaz's "How to Date a
Browngirl, Blackgirl, Whitegirl, or Halfie" for their examination
of how implied or explicit expectations affect the way that we
think about ourselves.

Chapatis:
Take 3 pounds whole wheat flour, mix 1-½ pounds flour
with flat tablespoon salt, some water and two tablespoons butter.
Knead it and after one hour take a small ball of dough,
and roll it on board.
With palm, apply butter on it, sprinkle slightly with flour.
Fold it and again to the other side.
Roll dough in round shape of 10 inches in breadth.
Keep pan on stove. Let it get hot. Put bread on, then turn
on other side. Fry in teaspoonful butter.
—NANA-BAI'S DIARY, PAGE 23

Pleasures—and the bar on them—were sometimes wrapped up in the larger principles of our household. More often, though, our pleasures lay in disguise, in things we could lay our hands on, and in small, unexpected moments.

It was Sunday, and while I lazily tried to avoid my chores, Nana-bai was making chapati bread in the kitchen. Some days I washed the dishes, other days I dusted. That particular day, while Mommy and Daddy were running errands, I was supposed to fold laundry. The afternoon stretched before me endlessly as I thought about the laundry that awaited, and the many starchy static shocks that lay in ambush among the clothes. What could be more tiresome than wrestling with the unmanageable elastic corners of fitted sheets and hunting for pairs in a mountain of single socks?

Straddling the basket of clean clothes still tangled, warm, and smelling of soap from the dryer, I sat in the doorway joining kitchen and den, watching Nana-bai work the dough, listing for her all my reasons why I shouldn't have to work. "I'm sick. I'm hungry. I'm tired. I folded clothes yesterday. I'm gonna fold clothes tomorrow." She said nothing and only pulled off a dough ball in her fingers. She formed it up, then smacked it down lightly against the wooden board, dusting the checkered table cloth around her and rolling it out. "I could be reading instead. I could be doing homework." I emphasized the word *homework* making it long and pointed, so she would understand that my very education was at stake here. Perhaps, I hoped, if I talked long enough, she would finally fold the clothes herself, with the brisk efficiency adults used when fed up with a child's inability to, say, find the jacket hanging quite obviously in the closet. But, it seemed, Nana-bai was not about to cave in.

I grasped for other ideas, other able bodies at hand, scrolling through the qualifications of my siblings. Batsheva was too young, still a baby, so that was not even a possibility. What if I offered up Gertie? She was older than me, fit, strong-willed, skilled at folding, maybe a laundry prodigy. A very reasonable option. "What about Gertie?" I asked decidedly, certain I had hit upon something. "Why can't *she* fold the clothes?"

"She is arranging all the beds upstairs. And then she is going to come down here and wash the pots and pans." Gertie had already been put to work. My plan was ruined.

"What about Tzvi then?" I suggested, trying to pin it on my younger brother.

"He is outside playing."

"Playing? Why does he get to play and I have to work?" I asked, indignant, but I already knew the answer.

With a firm splat of dough to wooden board, Nana-bai said matter-of-factly, "He's the boy."

"That's so unfair. All these clothes in here, they're his clothes, too."

"But you're his sister. You should respect him and do things for him."

No matter how many times I heard this, still my mind reeled with its injustice. "This isn't India," I said angrily. "Things are different here in America. Just 'cause he's a boy, it doesn't make him better. It doesn't mean I have to be his slave." In the good ol' U.S.-of-A.-world outside our house, women expected to be every bit as powerful as men. So I knew that all of American ideology backed me up on this point. And I held it over her, feeling myself to be an angry ambassador, a superhero, even. Nana-bai stood up and washed her hands at the sink. Pulling a pan out of the cupboard, she turned on the gas and set it on the stove to heat. "You favor him," I told her accusingly. "Can't you see you favor him?"

"Aiaa. I love all you kids." She dug into her pocket and pulled out a sesame candy for me. "Here," she pressed it into my hand. I toyed with the plastic wrapper, debating whether or not to accept this peace offering. Finally I unfolded it and popped it into my mouth, begrudgingly, enjoying the way ground sesame turned to a peanut taste between my teeth.

"But you do favor him," I said, unwilling to let go of my stance. "You would have given him three candies if he were here this moment." Nana-bai always kept sesame candies and nuts and dried fruits in her pockets. Every now and then, at odd times, on car trips or after dinner, she took us aside and pulled these out, trying to slip the gifts into our hands on the sly. If we politely refused, she insisted and forced the treats into our knapsacks anyway, shushing us so that we would feel special and no one else in the family would know what had just taken place. Of course, despite her best efforts, these exchanges were usually very obvious. And I could not help but notice that she always gave Tzvi more than she gave us girls. Soniia, she called him. My gold.

"You favor him. Admit it," I demanded.

"He is the boy," she told me simply. "Come, while the pan heats up, I will get you started with the laundry." Reluctantly, I allowed her to take my arm and stand me up. Then she overturned the basket of laundry onto the couch, making a deal with me: "If you finish all the other clothes, then I'll come and help you with the big things, the sheets and towels. Haa?" I agreed and got busy folding, watching her fry the chapati while I worked.

Gertie came downstairs a few minutes later, rolling her round eyes and fuming about her own chores. She and Nana-bai exchanged a few bickering words, then I heard her pound around the kitchen for a bit. Finally she dragged a chair to the sink, climbed up it, and turned on the tap to wash the dishes. Tzvi walked through the room just then, a skinny, barefoot brown boy with glasses. He had a good heart. But when he did not get what he wanted, he threw a tantrum and screamed until the veins on his neck popped out, and Nana-bai, trying to appease him, worried. "It's going to kill him, G–d forbid." Tzvi led a toddling Batsheva out into the backyard with him, her plastic diaper dragging heavy behind her. She adored him.

"Where are you taking her?" I demanded, nosy, and suspicious of the look on his face.

"Outside."

"Why outside?"

"My ball got stuck somewhere, so I need someone small to get it back."

"Where? Back in the rose bushes? Are you sending her into the prickles again?"

"Yeah, so?" he said, quickly pushing her through the door to outside and following in the next step. "She *is* smaller so the thorns won't get to *her*." He closed the door behind them.

I shook out a pair of Daddy's jeans broodingly. This was all because of Nana-bai, I decided. Unabashedly a tattletale, a worrier, and a goody-goody, I knew I would have to make a point of reporting all this to Mommy and Daddy later that night—even though last time it was no help at all. "She's so old-fashioned," I had told them. "She always fills

Tzvi's plate first and takes his side in arguments. And she never makes him do any work."

"You have to try and understand her," Daddy had said. Academically, he knew the history involved. He could tell me all about the culture that raised Nana-bai, could compare it to the cultures in Japan and China where he once lived himself. He started to, even, saying, "Picture life in India almost a century ago, under British rule. . . ."

But I had cut in. "What do you know about this, Daddy? She always fills your plate first, too. And she tells Mommy to never argue with you." His life was only made easier by this culture.

"Well, you should count yourself lucky," Mommy had told me. "Gertie is the oldest, so Nana-bai tries to give her most of the work, anyway."

"You kids should be happy to help out in the house. We all have to pitch in and work together here. Even Tzvi helps me out when I fix the car and shovel the snow," Daddy had pointed out.

"Well, can't you say something to her?"

"No, she's an elderly woman and we can't insult her like that," Mommy had said.

It amazed my classmates that Nana-bai had such influence in our home. Their elderly relatives had their own condominiums and lives. They visited for the holidays or my classmates flew down to Florida to be with them for a vacation, meeting for meals and to swim in the pool, then retreating to their separate rooms. The rest of the year they sent holiday cards with twenty-dollar checks. Even when Grandpa from Daddy's side came by, it was only for an afternoon of cake and coffee. He presented us with small noisemakers or illicit Hershey bars and we told him about what was going on at school, then he went home and that was it.

But Nana-bai lived with us all the time. Her values and experiences inhabited our household every day. Her freshly-washed petticoats hung over our bathtub and the house smelled like her spices. While Mommy and Daddy came in and out of our playroom between outside jobs and running the household and errands and budgets, Nana-bai was a constant presence with us, as she cooked and cleaned and involved herself in our every move. Sometimes, if I was scared at night, I even slept in her bed. In her culture, that generational overlap was natural. "Just respect her and help out and don't pay attention to the old-fashioned part of it," Mommy told me. Not so easy.

I knew intellectually that girls and boys should be equal, but the reality around me—dictated and accepted by people I loved, who loved me—was, in fact, otherwise, and therefore more true than abstractions could ever be. I made a fuss, for the principle of my frustrations, but on a deeper level, I resigned myself to it. Still, I could have processed that culture in any number of ways, like my siblings.

Gertie, my big sister, was already bossy and protective of me. My parents insisted that I play with her friends and that I wear her hand-me-downs so I was, inevitably, a reflection of her. Confident in this responsibility, in their trust and in my devotion, she glowed with charisma, and always drew people to her without effort. Nana-bai's traditions only fired her up in reaction, made her more vocal, more assertive.

Batsheva, the baby of the family, who even as a child was stunningly beautiful, managed to grow up wearing Nana-bai's way of life with proportion, with easy, classic grace. Like a feathered boa around her neck. Without vanities or airs in her perfect skin and coloring, she floated breezily, coolly through such cultural heaviness. And instead she became independent and self-assured in response to it.

Tzvi, the only boy, the remarkable product of a diverse genetic combination—artistic, athletic, musical, a doctor in the making—was expected to fulfill all our family's worldly ambitions. But from the heights of small kingliness, where once just about every demand and tantrum was soothed (my parents even seriously considered adoption when he begged for a brother to play with), he eventually learned to see his role as the boy with a balanced, gentlemanly perspective.

But for me, with my own particular shy chemistry and relationship to the world, I grew up understanding myself firstly by the traditional, often backward, differences between girls and boys. Boys could make the decisions. Girls could only support these decisions. Boys could wander around in public, meeting lots of people. Girls had to stay safely and modestly in the house. Boys could fart and burp. Girls couldn't; they had to be dainty. Boys could whistle. Girls shouldn't, because if they did, I was told, they would grow a moustache. Boys were loud. Girls must be quiet. Just to be near boys or men was inherently dangerous. Women who were violated had often brought it upon themselves from that sort of thing, from going somewhere alone at night with a man, from laughing too freely. If ever I went to play at the neighbors', I was warned repeatedly about the brothers and fathers. What terrible, perverted, and strange things could the brothers and father possibly do to me, I wondered, almost curiously. Also, I was told to guard my womb. To lift something too heavy might rip me inside, make me infertile. So many people in my family, it seemed, were invested in this part of me. And so I walked around worried, from an ache or a cramp, that somehow I had doomed myself to being barren. And all these ideas infiltrated my mind and bearing. When I went outside our home, I clutched the corners of my dress timidly and spoke in a painfully soft voice. I tried to be clean, safe, agreeable, odorless, and blend into the background.

Years later, by the time I reached junior high, propriety had seeped inside me too deeply. My parents themselves decided I needed to be more assertive, so they enrolled me in karate classes. Entering the studio, I found empowering paraphernalia at my fingertips. Punching bags. Mouth guards. Athletic cups. Sports bras. Donning these, our white-uniformed bodies became almost sexless amidst the grunting and yelling and boxing. I worked my way up to a green belt, kicked in blocks of wood, sparred in tournaments, and won several tall trophies. But still I did not learn to be a fighter or even an artist. Instead, again, I was conscientiously the girl. I tied my ponytail back with gold elastic and wore Chapstick on my lips at practices. I started shaving my legs solely for the moments when I kicked and my uniform slid up my calf. Inevitably, in the exercises we did, my body strove for grace, not power.

There were several middle-aged men in our class who had apparently one day reached age forty-five, looked down over their potbellies, and decided in a moment of revelation to reclaim their manhood. Gathering at the studio, they lounged around in their dungarees. They guffawed about football and snots and what chores their wives had them do last weekend. But a few minutes later, they stepped into the locker room to put on their uniforms. And suddenly they emerged as part of a Kung Fu movie world inhabited by honorable life-and-death battles, hard discipline, and soulful inner balance. It was the grandeur of their boyhood games revived, and they took this code seriously.

With these men, of all men, there might have been an exchange of equals. They might have honored the skill and talent demanded by my green belt, and come at me forcefully, awakening the force in my own body. But in the end, sparring with them, as we paired up then bowed and started circling each other, they held back—and I expected them to—because I was petite and smiled sweetly. Every so often they humored me, allowing me a clear opening to their ribs. And I took it, with a grateful, gentle, backhand jab.

Attaching to the power around me, I adored my karate instructor, Jim. One day Jim came over to me during class to correct my sparring stance. I held my breath as he tugged my knee one way, chucked at my chin, and barked, "Let's feel the strength here." The strength was supposed to be in my stomach, in the sharpness of my moves, in the depth of my voice when I yelled my battle cry and attacked. But the core of this strength instead concentrated on wondering, Had I forgotten to put on deodorant that morning? Did I stink of sweat? Would he notice? He leaned over me, to adjust my arm, and I breathed in his closeness, felt, almost deliriously, the force in his hands as he told me, "Tighten up, that's where the strength is. Try this." Then he leaned closer to impart some ancient words of wisdom which, finally, I was lucky enough to merit. "It should be like you're trying really, really hard to take a shit." As he said this, thousands of years of majestic karate tradition seemed to crash around me, and I stood there for a moment, mouth quivering, utterly bewildered to find I had nothing girly or delicate left to hide behind. Afterward, I could not meet his eyes again, feeling we had done something shameful together.

Gertie finished washing the dishes and escaped back upstairs, snatching a fresh, hot chapati to take with her. When I had finished folding most of the laundry, Nana-bai left another chapati cooking on the stove and came in from the kitchen, as she'd promised, to help me fold the big things. "Here. We'll do it together," she said, holding a sprawling king-size sheet in a pile in her hands. I picked up two corners of it and she picked up the other two corners. Pinching the ends and holding them taut, we walked backwards in opposite directions, stretching the expanse of the flowered sheet between us. We smoothed it and came back together, folding it in half. Then each of us selected two more of the newly formed corners, stepping backward again. Moving out, and in, and out again with the petal-strewn cloth drifting and shape-changing in a maypole dance, we must have taken a moment too long in our reverie because soon the smell of burnt chapati hit us. Hastily Nana-bai set the sheet aside and I followed her as she hurried back into the kitchen to pull a half-charred chapati out of the pan.

"Look what we did!" I gasped, scared from just the smell of burning in our house. But Nana-bai just put a thick spoon of butter in the pan and set a new piece of flattened dough on to cook. I relaxed a little. "Well, at least it's only one lost," I breathed.

"Lost? Nai."

"Well, who's gonna want to eat that one?"

She nodded, looking at the chapati lying limp on a plate and blackened with smoky stripes. "It's certainly not fine enough to put on the table for your brother and father—we'll have to be more careful. But this should not go to waste." Scraping a crumbly layer of the bitter blackness off with a knife, she took an almost-empty jar of homemade mango chutney from the refrigerator and tore the chapati in half. "Here. You and I will just eat this ourselves with a bit of chutney. You'll see it's quite tasty." Digging the spoon inside the jar till the sides shone clean of orange, she emerged, clanking with a heaping teaspoonful. She rolled one-half with chutney, then the other half also and said, "One for me. One for you. Try a piece now. I want you to always remember how it tastes."

Wordless and distrustful of what she offered, I took the burnt bread and chutney from her anyway. Then I ate it, and I was pleased to find that it was good.

Mommy and Daddy came back from running errands late that afternoon. While Mommy put away the groceries, I worked my way through the many overflowing bags covering the floor, chock-full of boxes and cartons and bottles, so I could sit down at the table and tell her all about that day. I told her about Nana-bai, listing everything for her. How I had to fold the laundry and Gertie had to wash dishes and arrange the beds. How she let Tzvi play outside, and even how he dragged Batsheva to do his dirty work, to pull a ball out from the thorns. I *definitely* saw a scratch or two on her leg later, I informed Mommy primly.

She had heard this kind of thing many times before. So now she only sighed, exasperated, and continued stocking fruit in the refrigerator. "Can I tell you a secret?" Then she continued, before I said yes or no. "Every month Nana-bai gives me money for each of you to put into your savings accounts. Not a lot, but some. She'll give me five dollars each for you and Batsheva and Gertie. Then she'll give me ten dollars for Tzvi, the boy." Mommy paused to let this sink in. "Each month I tell her, Nana-bai, I'm not going to do that, be unfair to my children like that. And I tell her I'm going to divide the money up equally between them. And I do that. Each month, it happens the same way." Mommy began folding the empty grocery bags away, to save and reuse.

"So you see?" I said, hopping up. "That proves it. She does love him more."

"No," she told me. "That proves she loves you all the *same*. Look, she's an old woman and she is stuck in her ways and you can't expect her to change too much. Who knows what she is thinking? That the boy will need money when he grows up and that after the dowry, the girls will be taken care of when they're married? I don't know," she paused. "Anyhow, sure, she divides up the money unevenly, because that's the only way she can do it. But in the end she knows I will equally distribute it among you four. And, if you ask me, I think that is why she continues to do this every month. She can't be fair herself, but she knows I *will* be."

Mommy finished restoring the kitchen to order silently then, while I sat back down at the table, thinking about this, gnawing on a piece of chapati. Eventually, once she was done, Mommy dished herself a plate of leftover cauliflower curry with a dollop of chutney on the side. Then she chose a chapati to warm up on the stove. I watched her and without even knowing about the burnt bread Nana-bai and I had shared that very day, Mommy also purposely weeded out the most browned, the most crusty, the most imperfect and raggedly shaped chapati in the stack. And that was the one she took for herself.

DRINKING COFFEE ELSEWHERE

by ZZ Packer

Never feeling at home even when she is home describes Dina, the narrator in "Drinking Coffee Elsewhere." It also refers to what Dina does when she imagines herself away from a reality too painful to experience or too complicated to examine. Not really the right type for the rough black Baltimore neighborhood where she grows up, Dina reads her way into Yale, where, no surprise, she finds, as a black student, that she is in equally hostile territory—only here, she has to deal with politically correct patronage rather than the taunts of gossipy store cashiers who consider reading outside of school antisocial. By the time she arrives at Yale, she has already lost her mother to kidney failure, though she blames her father's abusive behavior for this loss. Reading a lot and being black are not the only alienating factors in Dina's life.

At Yale, Dina immediately exhibits how alienated she feels when, during orientation game-playing, she is asked what inanimate object she wants to be and she chooses a revolver. Packer makes us feel Dina's anger through this obviously aggressive expression and through the resulting interviews with the dean and the psychiatrist to whom she is assigned. Only after Dina meets Heidi—white, overweight, quoting a Frank O'Hara poem about a lonely, misanthropic child "as though she had thought it up herself"—does she encounter someone who seems even more unhappy than she. Heidi

*becomes her companion, despite Dina's concern that Heidi is a les-
bian; they read books together, work together as dishwashers, and
sleep in the same bed. They are a couple, though Dina refuses to
acknowledge this; in fact, in her sessions with Dr. Raeburn, she designs a whole other life for herself, where she was once kissed by an
attractive boy from an upscale neighborhood back home.*

*The reality, however, is that she has fallen in love with Heidi,
someone who asks for nothing but Dina's love—and that not ever
explicitly or demonstrably. Dina's inability to recognize why she is a
stranger to herself, why she fits nowhere but in "a pleasant trap of
silence" with Heidi, brings her to a turning point. Soon after a
weekend Dina spends at home with her father, Heidi comes out,
something that Dina cannot bring herself to think about. When
Heidi's mother dies, Dina refuses to be there for her. Even after Dr.
Raeburn's observation that Dina is pretending not to care, that she
has so accustomed herself to lying that she no longer notices her lies,
perhaps as a function of being "black living in a white world,"
Dina can think only of drinking coffee elsewhere. Her imagination
has become her cover, and that cover has become her shield—from
the grief she denies and from the love she discovers. While Heidi re-
treats to Vancouver for her mother's funeral, back in Baltimore
Dina dreams of a future time "for people like me, who realign past
events to suit themselves." Perhaps, just perhaps, that future will include a single room with only Heidi knocking on the door.*

*ZZ Packer was born in Chicago and raised in Atlanta and
Louisville. She attended Yale University, the Writing Seminar at
Johns Hopkins University, the Writers' Workshop at the University
of Iowa, and was a Stegner Fellow at Stanford. "Drinking Coffee
Elsewhere" first appeared in* The New Yorker's *Debut Fiction issue in 2000, before being published as part of the short story collection that bears its name.*

*This story might be compared with Senna's "Triad," three ac-
counts of the traumatic aftermath of a mother's death. It may also
be read in conjunction with stories about avoidance and denial,*

like Chang's "The Eve of the Spirit Festival" and Lowenthal's "Ordinary Pain."

Orientation games began the day I arrived at Yale from Baltimore. In my group we played heady, frustrating games for smart people. One game appeared to be charades reinterpreted by existentialists; another involved listening to rocks. Then a freshman counselor made everyone play Trust. The idea was that if you had the faith to fall backward and wait for four scrawny former high school geniuses to catch you, just before your head cracked on the slate sidewalk, then you might learn to trust your fellow students. Russian roulette sounded like a better way to go.

"No way," I said. The white boys were waiting for me to fall, holding their arms out for me, sincerely, gallantly. "No fucking way."

"It's all cool, it's all cool," the counselor said. Her hair was a shade of blond I'd seen only on *Playboy* covers, and she raised her hands as though backing away from a growling dog. "Sister," she said, in an I'm-down-with-the-struggle voice, "you don't have to play this game. As a person of color, you shouldn't have to fit into any white, patriarchal system."

I said, "It's a bit too late for that."

In the next game, all I had to do was wait in a circle until it was my turn to say what inanimate object I wanted to be. One guy said he'd like to be a gadfly, like Socrates. "Stop me if I wax Platonic," he said. I didn't bother mentioning that gadflies weren't inanimate—it didn't seem to make a difference. The girl next to him was eating a rice cake. She wanted to be the Earth, she said. Earth with a capital E.

There was one other black person in the circle. He wore an Exeter T-shirt and his overly elastic expressions resembled a series of facial exercises. At the end of each person's turn, he smiled and bobbed his head with unfettered enthusiasm. "Oh, that was good," he said, as if the game were an experiment he'd set up and the results were turning out better than he'd expected. "Good, good, good!"

When it was my turn I said, "My name is Dina, and if I had to be any object, I guess I'd be a revolver." The sunlight dulled as if on cue. Clouds passed rapidly overhead, presaging rain. I don't know why I said it. Until that moment I'd been good in all the ways that were meant to matter. I was an honor roll student—though I'd learned long ago not to mention it in the part of Baltimore where I lived. Suddenly I was hard-bitten and recalcitrant, the kind of kid who took pleasure in sticking pins into cats; the kind who chased down smart kids to spray them with Mace.

"A revolver," a counselor said, stroking his chin, as if it had grown a rabbinical beard. "Could you please elaborate?"

The black guy cocked his head and frowned, as if the beakers and Erlenmeyer flasks of his experiment had grown legs and scurried off.

"You were just kidding," the dean said, "about wiping out all of mankind. That, I suppose, was a joke." She squinted at me. One of her hands curved atop the other to form a pink, freckled molehill on her desk.

"Well," I said, "maybe I meant it at the time." I quickly saw that this was not the answer she wanted. "I don't know. I think it's the architecture."

Through the dimming light of the dean's office window, I could see the fortress of the old campus. On my ride from the bus station to the campus, I'd barely glimpsed New Haven—a flash of crumpled building here, a trio of straggly kids there. A lot like Baltimore. But everything had changed when we reached those streets hooded by gothic buildings. I imagined how the college must have looked when it was founded, when most of the students owned slaves. I pictured men wearing tights and knickers, smoking pipes.

"The architecture," the dean repeated. She bit her lip and seemed to be making a calculation of some sort. I noticed that she blinked less often than most people. I sat there, intrigued, waiting to see how long it would be before she blinked again.

My revolver comment won me a year's worth of psychiatric counseling, weekly meetings with Dean Guest, and—since the parents of the

roommate I'd never met weren't too hip on the idea of their Amy sharing a bunk bed with a budding homicidal loony—my very own room.

Shortly after getting my first C ever, I also received the first knock on
my door. The female counselors never knocked. The dean had spoken to
them; I was a priority. Every other day, right before dinnertime, they'd
look in on me, unannounced. "Just checking up," a counselor would say.
It was the voice of a suburban mother in training. By the second week, I
had made a point of sitting in a chair in front of the door, just when I expected a counselor to pop her head around. This was intended to startle
them. I also made a point of being naked. The unannounced visits ended.

The knocking persisted. Through the peephole I saw a white face,
distorted and balloonish.

"Let me in." The person looked like a boy but it sounded like a girl.
"Let me in," the voice repeated.

"Not a chance," I said. I had a suicide single, and I wanted to keep it
that way. No roommates, no visitors.

Then the person began to sob, and I heard a back slump against the
door. If I hadn't known the person was white from the peephole, I'd
have known it from a display like this. Black people didn't knock on
strangers' doors, crying. Not that I understood the black people at Yale.
Most of them were from New York and tried hard to pretend that they
hadn't gone to prep schools. And there was something pitiful in how
cool they were. Occasionally one would reach out to me with missionary zeal, but I'd rebuff the person with haughty silence.

"I don't have anyone to talk to!" the person on the other side of the
door cried.

"That is correct."

"When I was a child," the person said, "I played by myself in a corner of the schoolyard all alone. I hated dolls and I hated games, animals
were not friendly and birds flew away. If anyone was looking for me I
hid behind a tree and cried out 'I am an orphan—' "

I opened the door. It was a she.

"Plagiarist!" I yelled. She had just recited a Frank O'Hara poem as
though she'd thought it up herself. I knew the poem because it was one
of the few things I'd been forced to read that I wished I'd written myself.

The girl turned to face me, smiling weakly, as though her triumph
was not in getting me to open the door but in the fact that she was able
to smile at all when she was so accustomed to crying. She was large but
not obese, and crying had turned her face the color of raw chicken. She
blew her nose into the waist end of her T-shirt, revealing a pale belly.

"How do you know that poem?"

She sniffed. "I'm in your Contemporary Poetry class."

She said she was Canadian and her name was Heidi, although she
said she wanted people to call her Henrik. "That's a guy's name," I said.
"What do you want? A sex change?"

She looked at me with so little surprise that I suspected she hadn't
discounted this as an option. Then her story came out in teary, hiccup-
like bursts. She had sucked some "cute guy's dick" and he'd told everybody and now people thought she was "a slut."

"Why'd you suck his dick? Aren't you a lesbian?"

She fit the bill. Short hair, hard, roach-stomping shoes. Dressed like
an aspiring plumber. And then there was the name Henrik. The lesbians
I'd seen on TV were wiry, thin strips of muscle, but Heidi was round
and soft and had a moonlike face. Drab henna-colored hair. And lesbians had cats. "Do you have a cat?" I asked.

Her eyes turned glossy with new tears. "No," she said, her voice qua-
vering, "and I'm not a lesbian. Are you?"

"Do I look like one?" I said.

She didn't answer.

"O.K.," I said. "I could suck a guy's dick, too, if I wanted. But I
don't. The human penis is one of the most germ-ridden objects there is."
Heidi looked at me, unconvinced. "What I meant to say," I began again,
"is that I don't like anybody. Period. Guys or girls. I'm a misanthrope."

"I am, too."

"No," I said, guiding her back through my door and out into the
hallway. "You're not."

"Have you had dinner?" she asked. "Let's go to Commons."

I pointed to a pyramid of ramen noodle packages on my windowsill.
"See that? That means I never have to go to Commons. Aside from
class, I have contact with no one."

"I hate it here, too," she said. "I should have gone to McGill, eh."

"The way to feel better," I said, "is to get some ramen and lock yourself in your room. Everyone will forget about you and that guy's dick and you won't have to see anyone ever again. If anyone looks for you—"

"I'll hide behind a tree."

"A revolver?" Dr. Raeburn said, flipping through a manila folder. He looked up at me as if to ask another question, but he didn't.

Dr. Raeburn was the psychiatrist. He had the gray hair and whiskers of a Civil War general. He was also a chain smoker with beige teeth and a navy wool jacket smeared with ash. He asked about the revolver at the beginning of my first visit. When I was unable to explain myself, he smiled, as if this were perfectly reasonable.

"Tell me about your parents."

I wondered what he already had on file. The folder was thick, though I hadn't said a thing of significance since Day One.

"My father was a dick and my mother seemed to like him."

He patted his pockets for his cigarettes. "That's some heavy stuff," he said. "How do you feel about Dad?" The man couldn't say the word "father." "Is Dad someone you see often?"

"I hate my father almost as much as I hate the word 'Dad.' "

He started tapping his cigarette.

"You can't smoke in here."

"That's right," he said, and slipped the cigarette back into the packet. He smiled, widening his eyes brightly. "Don't ever start."

I thought that that first encounter would be the last of Heidi or Henrik, or whatever, but then her head appeared in a window of Linsly-Chit during my Chaucer class. A few days later, she swooped down a flight of stairs in Harkness, following me. She hailed me from across Elm Street and found me in the Sterling Library stacks. After one of my meetings with Dr. Raeburn, she was waiting for me outside Health Services, legs crossed, cleaning her fingernails.

"You know," she said, as we walked through Old Campus, "you've got to stop eating ramen. Not only does it lack a single nutrient but it's full of MSG."

I wondered why she even bothered, and was vaguely flattered she cared, but I said, "I like eating chemicals. It keeps the skin radiant."

"There's also hepatitis." She knew how to get my attention—mention a disease.

"You get hepatitis from unwashed lettuce," I said. "If there's anything safe from the perils of the food chain, it's ramen."

"But do you refrigerate what you don't eat? Each time you reheat it, you're killing good bacteria, which then can't keep the bad bacteria in check. A guy got sick from reheating Chinese noodles, and his son died from it. I read it in the *Times*." With this, she put a jovial arm around my neck. I continued walking, a little stunned. Then, just as quickly, she dropped her arm and stopped walking. I stopped, too.

"Did you notice that I put my arm around you?"

"Yes," I said. "Next time, I'll have to chop it off."

"I don't want you to get sick," she said. "Let's eat at Commons."

In the cold air, her arm had felt good.

The problem with Commons was that it was too big; its ceiling was as high as a cathedral's, but below it there were no awestruck worshippers, only eighteen-year-olds at heavy wooden tables, chatting over veal patties and Jell-O.

We got our food, tacos stuffed with meat substitute, and made our way through the maze of tables. The Koreans had a table. Each singing group had a table. The crew team sat at a long table of its own. We passed the black table. Heidi was so plump and moonfaced that the sheer quantity of her flesh accentuated just how white she was. The black students gave me a long, hard stare.

"How you doing, sista?" a guy asked, his voice full of accusation, eyeballing me as though I were clad in a Klansman's sheet and hood. "I guess we won't see you till graduation."

"If," I said, "you graduate."

The remark was not well received. As I walked past, I heard protests, angry and loud as if they'd discovered a cheat at their poker game. Heidi and I found an unoccupied table along the periphery, which was isolated and dark. We sat down. Heidi prayed over her tacos.

"I thought you didn't believe in God," I said.

"Not in the God depicted in the Judeo-Christian Bible, but I do believe that nature's essence is a spirit that—"

"All right," I said. I had begun to eat, and cubes of diced tomato fell from my mouth when I spoke. "Stop right there. Tacos and spirits don't mix."

"You've always got to be so flip," she said. "I'm going to apply for another friend."

"There's always Mr. Dick," I said. "Slurp, slurp."

"You are so lame. So unbelievably lame. I'm going out with Mr. Dick. Thursday night at Atticus. His name is Keith."

Heidi hadn't mentioned Mr. Dick since the day I'd met her. That was more than a month ago and we'd spent a lot of that time together. I checked for signs that she was lying; her habit of smiling too much, her eyes bright and cheeks full so that she looked like a chipmunk. But she looked normal. Pleased, even, to see me so flustered.

"You're insane! What are you going to do this time?" I asked. "Sleep with him? Then when he makes fun of you, what? Come pound your head on my door reciting the collected poems of Sylvia Plath?"

"He's going to apologize for before. And don't call me insane. You're the one going to the psychiatrist."

"Well, I'm not going to suck his dick, that's for sure."

She put her arm around me in mock comfort, but I pushed it off, and ignored her. She touched my shoulder again, and I turned, annoyed, but it wasn't Heidi after all; a sepia-toned boy dressed in khakis and a crisp plaid shirt was standing behind me. He thrust a hot-pink square of paper toward me without a word, then briskly made his way toward the other end of Commons, where the crowds blossomed. Heidi leaned over and read it: "Wear Black Leather—the Less, the Better."

"It's a gay party," I said, crumpling the card. "He thinks we're fuck-ing gay."

Heidi and I signed on to work at the Saybrook dining hall as dishwash-ers. The job consisted of dumping food from plates and trays into a vat of rushing water. It seemed straightforward, but then I learned better. You wouldn't believe what people could do with food until you worked in a dish room. Lettuce and crackers and soup would be bullied into a pulp in the bowl of some bored anorexic; ziti would be mixed with honey and granola; trays would appear heaped with mashed potato snow women with melted chocolate ice cream for hair. Frat boys arrived at the dish-room window, en masse. They liked to fill glasses with food, then seal them, airtight, onto their trays. If you tried to prize them off, milk, Worcestershire sauce, peas, chunks of bread vomited onto your dish-room uniform.

When this happened one day in the middle of the lunch rush, for what seemed like the hundredth time, I tipped the tray toward one of the frat boys as he turned to walk away, popping the glasses off so that the mess spurted onto his Shetland sweater.

He looked down at his sweater. "Lesbo bitch!"

"No," I said, "that would be your mother."

Heidi, next to me, clenched my arm in support, but I remained mo-tionless, waiting to see what the frat boy would do. He glared at me for a minute, then walked away.

"Let's take a smoke break," Heidi said.

I didn't smoke, but Heidi had begun to, because she thought it would help her lose weight. As I hefted a stack of glasses through the steamer, she lit up.

"Soft packs remind me of you," she said. "Just when you've smoked them all and you think there's none left, there's always one more, hiding in that little crushed corner." Before I could respond she said, "Oh, God. Not another mouse. You know whose job that is."

By the end of the rush, the floor mats got full and slippery with food. This was when mice tended to appear, scurrying over our shoes; more often than not, a mouse got caught in the grating that covered the drains in the floor. Sometimes the mouse was already dead by the time we noticed it. This one was alive.

"No way," I said. "This time you're going to help. Get some gloves and a trash bag."

"That's all I'm getting. I'm not getting that mouse out of there."

"Put on the gloves," I ordered. She winced, but put them on. "Reach down," I said. "At an angle, so you get at its middle. Otherwise, if you try to get it by its tail, the tail will break off."

"This is filthy, eh."

"That's why we're here," I said. "To clean up filth. Eh."

She reached down, but would not touch the mouse. I put my hand around her arm and pushed it till her hand made contact. The cries from the mouse were soft, songlike. "Oh, my God," she said. "Oh, my God, ohmigod." She wrestled it out of the grating and turned her head away.

"Don't you let it go," I said.

"Where's the food bag? It'll smother itself if I drop it in the food bag. Quick," she said, her head still turned away, her eyes closed. "Lead me to it."

"No. We are not going to smother this mouse. We've got to break its neck."

"You're one heartless bitch."

I wondered how to explain that if death is unavoidable it should be quick and painless. My mother had died slowly. At the hospital, they'd said it was kidney failure, but I knew, in the end, it was my father. He made her so scared to live in her own home that she was finally driven away from it in an ambulance.

"Breaking its neck will save it the pain of smothering," I said. "Breaking its neck is more humane. Take the trash bag and cover it so you won't get any blood on you, then crush."

The loud jets of the steamer had shut off automatically and the dish room grew quiet. Heidi breathed in deeply, then crushed the mouse. She shuddered, disgusted. "Now what?"

"What do you mean, 'now what?' Throw the little bastard in the trash."

At our third session, I told Dr. Raeburn I didn't mind if he smoked. He sat on the sill of his open window, smoking behind a jungle screen of office plants.

We spent the first ten minutes discussing the Iliad, and whether or not the text actually states that Achilles had been dipped in the River Styx. He said it did, and I said it didn't. After we'd finished with the Iliad, and with my new job in what he called "the scullery," he asked questions about my parents. I told him nothing. It was none of his business. Instead, I talked about Heidi. I told him about that day in Commons, Heidi's plan to go on a date with Mr. Dick, and the invitation we'd been given to the gay party.

"You seem preoccupied by this soirée." He arched his eyebrows at the word "soirée."

"Wouldn't you be?"

"Dina," he said slowly, in a way that made my name seem like a song title, "have you ever had a romantic interest?"

"You want to know if I've ever had a boyfriend?" I said. "Just go ahead and ask if I've ever fucked anybody."

This appeared to surprise him. "I think that you are having a crisis of identity," he said.

"Oh, is that what this is?"

His profession had taught him not to roll his eyes. Instead, his exasperation revealed itself in a tiny pursing of his lips, as though he'd just tasted something awful and was trying very hard not to offend the cook.

"It doesn't have to be, as you say, someone you've fucked, it doesn't have to be a boyfriend," he said.

"Well, what are you trying to say? If it's not a boy, then you're saying it's a girl—"

"Calm down. It could be a crush, Dina." He lit one cigarette off another. "A crush on a male teacher, a crush on a dog, for heaven's sake. An interest. Not necessarily a relationship."

It was sacrifice time. If I could spend the next half hour talking about some boy, then I'd have given him what he wanted.

So I told him about the boy with the nice shoes.

I was sixteen and had spent the last few coins in my pocket on bus fare to buy groceries. I didn't like going to the Super Fresh two blocks away from my house, plunking government food stamps into the hands of the cashiers.

"There she go reading," one of them once said, even though I was only carrying a book. "Don't your eyes get tired?"

On Greenmount Avenue you could read schoolbooks—that was understandable. The government and your teachers forced you to read them. But anything else was antisocial. It meant you'd rather submit to the words of some white dude than shoot the breeze with your neighbors.

I hated those cashiers, and I hated them seeing me with food stamps, so I took the bus and shopped elsewhere. That day, I got off the bus at Govans, and though the neighborhood was black like my own—hair salon after hair salon of airbrushed signs promising arabesque hair styles and inch-long fingernails—the houses were neat and orderly, nothing at all like Greenmount, where every other house had at least one shattered window. The store was well swept, and people quietly checked long grocery lists—no screaming kids, no loud cashier-customer altercations. I got the groceries and left the store.

I decided to walk back. It was a fall day, and I walked for blocks. Then I sensed someone following me. I walked more quickly, my arms around the sack, the leafy lettuce tickling my nose. I didn't want to hold the sack so close that it would break the eggs or squash the hamburger buns, but it was slipping, and as I looked behind me a boy my age, maybe older, rushed toward me.

"Let me help you," he said.

"That's all right." I set the bag on the sidewalk. Maybe I saw his face, maybe it was handsome enough, but what I noticed first, splayed on either side of the bag, were his shoes. They were nice shoes, real leather, a stitched design like a widow's peak on each one, or like birds' wings, and for the first time in my life I understood what people meant when they said "wing-tip shoes."

"I watched you carry them groceries out that store, then you look around, like you're lost, but like you liked being lost, then you walk down the sidewalk for blocks and blocks. Rearranging that bag, it almost gone to slip, then hefting it back up again."

"Uh-huh," I said.

"And then I passed my own house and was still following you. And then your bag really look like it was gone crash and everything. So I just thought I'd help." He sucked in his bottom lip, as if to keep it from making a smile. "What's your name?" When I told him, he said, "Dina, my name is Cecil." Then he said, "D comes right after C."

"Yes," I said, "it does, doesn't it."

Then, half question, half statement, he said, "I could carry your groceries for you? And walk you home?"

I stopped the story there. Dr. Raeburn kept looking at me. "Then what happened?"

I couldn't tell him the rest: that I had not wanted the boy to walk me home, that I didn't want someone with such nice shoes to see where I lived.

Dr. Raeburn would only have pitied me if I'd told him that I ran down the sidewalk after I told the boy no, that I fell, the bag slipped, and the eggs cracked, their yolks running all over the lettuce. Clear amniotic fluid coated the can of cinnamon rolls. I left the bag there on the sidewalk, the groceries spilled out randomly like cards loosed from a deck. When I returned home, I told my mother that I'd lost the food stamps.

"Lost?" she said. I'd expected her to get angry, I'd wanted her to get angry, but she hadn't. "Lost?" she repeated. Why had I been so clumsy and nervous around a harmless boy? I could have brought the groceries home and washed off the egg yolk, but instead I'd just left them there. "Come on," Mama said, snuffing her tears, pulling my arm, trying to get me to join her and start yanking cushions off the couch. "We'll find enough change here. We got to get something for dinner before your father gets back."

We'd already searched the couch for money the previous week, and I knew there'd be nothing now, but I began to push my fingers into the couch's boniest corners, pretending that it was only a matter of time before I'd find some change or a lost watch or an earring. Something pawnable, perhaps.

"What happened next?" Dr. Raeburn asked again. "Did you let the boy walk you home?"

"My house was far, so we went to his house instead." Though I was sure Dr. Raeburn knew that I was making this part up, I continued. "We made out on his sofa. He kissed me."

Dr. Raeburn lit his next cigarette like a detective. Cool, suspicious. "How did it feel?"

"You know," I said. "Like a kiss feels. It felt nice. The kiss felt very, very nice."

Raeburn smiled gently, though he seemed unconvinced. When he called time on our session, his cigarette had become one long pole of ash. I left his office, walking quickly down the corridor, afraid to look back. It would be like him to trot after me, his navy blazer flapping, just to get the truth out of me. *You never kissed anyone.* The words slid from my brain, and knotted in my stomach.

When I reached my dorm, I found an old record player blocking my door and a Charles Mingus LP propped beside it. I carried them inside and then, lying on the floor, I played the Mingus over and over again until I fell asleep. I slept feeling as though Dr. Raeburn had attached electrodes to my head, willing into my mind a dream about my mother. I saw the lemon meringue of her skin, the long bone of her arm as she reached down to clip her toenails. I'd come home from a school trip to an aquarium, and I was explaining the differences between baleen and sperm whales according to the size of their heads, the range of their habitats, their feeding patterns.

I awoke remembering the expression on her face after I'd finished my dizzying whale lecture. She looked like a tourist who'd asked for directions to a place she thought was simple enough to get to only to hear a series of hypothetical turns, alleys, one-way streets. Her response was to nod politely at the perilous elaborateness of it all; to nod and save herself from the knowledge that she would never be able to get where she wanted to go.

The dishwashers always closed down the dining hall. One night, after everyone else had punched out, Heidi and I took a break, and though I wasn't a smoker, we set two milk crates upside down on the floor and smoked cigarettes.

The dishwashing machines were off, but steam still rose from them like a jungle mist. Outside in the winter air, students were singing carols in their groomed and tailored singing-group voices. The Whiffenpoofs were back in New Haven after a tour around the world, and I guess their return was a huge deal. Heidi and I craned our necks to watch the year's first snow through an open window.

"What are you going to do when you're finished?" Heidi asked. Sexy question marks of smoke drifted up to the windows before vanishing.

"Take a bath."

She swatted me with her free hand. "No, silly. Three years from now. When you leave Yale."

"I don't know. Open up a library. Somewhere where no one comes in for books. A library in a desert."

She looked at me as though she'd expected this sort of answer and didn't know why she'd asked in the first place.

"What are you going to do?" I asked her.

"Open up a psych clinic. In a desert. And my only patient will be some wacko who runs a library."

"Ha," I said. "Whatever you do, don't work in a dish room ever again. You're no good." I got up from the crate. "C'mon. Let's hose the place down."

We put out our cigarettes on the floor, since it was our job to clean it anyway. We held squirt guns in one hand and used the other to douse the floors with the standard-issue, eye-burning cleaning solution. We hosed the dish room, the kitchen, the serving line, sending the water and crud and suds into the drains. Then we hosed them again so the solution

wouldn't eat holes in our shoes as we left. Then I had an idea. I unbuck-
led my belt.

"What the hell are you doing?" Heidi said.

"Listen, it's too cold to go outside with our uniforms all wet. We
could just take a shower right here. There's nobody but us."

"What the fuck, eh?"

I let my pants drop, then took off my shirt and panties. I didn't wear
a bra, since I didn't have much to fill one. I took off my shoes and hung
my clothes on the stepladder.

"You've flipped," Heidi said. "I mean, really, psych-ward flipped."

I soaped up with the liquid hand soap until I felt as glazed as a ham.
"Stand back and spray me."

"Oh, my God," she said. I didn't know whether she was confused or
delighted, but she picked up the squirt gun and sprayed me. She was
laughing. Then she got too close and the water started to sting.

"God damn it!" I said. "That hurt!"

"I was wondering what it would take to make you say that."

When all the soap had been rinsed off, I put on my regular clothes
and said, "O.K. You're up next."

"No way," she said.

"Yes way."

She started to take off her uniform shirt, then stopped.

"What?"

"I'm too fat."

"You goddam right." She always said she was fat. One time I'd told
her that she should shut up about it, that large black women wore their
fat like mink coats. "You're big as a house," I said now. "Frozen yogurt
may be low in calories, but not if you eat five tubs of it. Take your
clothes off. I want to get out of here."

She began taking off her uniform, then stood there, hands cupped
over her breasts, crouching at the pubic bone.

"Open up," I said, "or we'll never get done."

Her hands remained where they were. I threw the bottle of liquid
soap at her, and she had to catch it, revealing herself as she did.

I turned on the squirt gun, and she stood there, stiff, arms at her sides, eyes closed, as though awaiting mummification. I began with the water on low, and she turned around in a full circle, hesitantly, letting the droplets from the spray fall on her as if she were submitting to a death by stoning.

When I increased the water pressure, she slipped and fell on the sudsy floor. She stood up and then slipped again. This time she laughed and remained on the floor, rolling around on it as I sprayed.

I think I began to love Heidi that night in the dish room, but who is to say that I hadn't begun to love her the first time I met her? I sprayed her and sprayed her, and she turned over and over like a large beautiful dolphin, lolling about in the sun.

Heidi started sleeping at my place. Sometimes she slept on the floor; sometimes we slept sardinelike, my feet at her head, until she complained that my feet were "taunting" her. When we finally slept head to head, she said, "Much better." She was so close I could smell her toothpaste. "I like your hair," she told me, touching it through the darkness. "You should wear it out more often."

"White people always say that about black people's hair. The worse it looks, the more they say they like it."

I'd expected her to disagree, but she kept touching my hair, her hands passing through it till my scalp tingled. When she began to touch the hair around the edge of my face, I felt myself quake. Her fingertips stopped for a moment, as if checking my pulse, then resumed.

"I like how it feels right here. See, mine just starts with the same old texture as the rest of my hair." She found my hand under the blanket and brought it to her hairline. "See," she said.

It was dark. As I touched her hair, it seemed as though I could smell it, too. Not a shampoo smell. Something richer, murkier. A bit dead, but sweet, like the decaying wood of a ship. She guided my hand.

"I see," I said. The record she'd given me was playing in my mind, and I kept trying to shut it off. I could also hear my mother saying that this is what happens when you've been around white people: things get weird. So weird I could hear the stylus etching its way into the flat vinyl of the record. "Listen," I said finally, when the bass and saxes started up. I heard Heidi breathe deeply, but she said nothing.

We spent the winter and some of the spring in my room—never hers—missing tests, listening to music, looking out my window to comment on people who wouldn't have given us a second thought. We read books related to none of our classes. I got riled up by *The Autobiography of Malcolm X* and *The Chomsky Reader*; Heidi read aloud passages from *The Anxiety of Influence*. We guiltily read mysteries and *Clan of the Cave Bear*, then immediately threw them away. Once we looked up from our books at exactly the same moment, as though trapped at a dinner table with nothing to say. A pleasant trap of silence.

Then one weekend I went back to Baltimore and stayed with my father. He asked me how school was going, but besides that, we didn't talk much. He knew what I thought of him. I stopped by the Enoch Pratt Library, where my favorite librarian, Mrs. Ardelia, cornered me into giving a little talk to the after-school kids, telling them to stay in school. They just looked at me like I was crazy; they were only nine or ten, and it hadn't even occurred to them to bail.

When I returned to Yale—to a sleepy, tree-scented spring—a group of students were holding what was called "Coming Out Day." I watched it from my room.

The emcee was the sepia boy who'd given us the invitation months back. His speech was strident but still smooth and peppered with jokes. There was a speech about AIDS, with lots of statistics: nothing that seemed to make "coming out" worth it. Then the women spoke. One girl pronounced herself "out" as casually as if she'd announced the time. Another said nothing at all: she came to the microphone with a woman who began cutting off her waist-length, bleached-blond hair. The woman doing the cutting tossed the shorn hair in every direction as she cut. People were clapping and cheering and catching the locks of hair.

And then there was Heidi. She was proud that she liked girls, she said when she reached the microphone. She loved them, wanted to sleep with them. She was a dyke, she said repeatedly, stabbing her finger to her chest in case anyone was unsure to whom she was referring. She could not have seen me. I was across the street, three stories up. And yet, when everyone clapped for her, she seemed to be looking straight at me.

Heidi knocked. "Let me in."

It was like the first time I met her. The tears, the raw pink of her face.

We hadn't spoken in weeks. Outside, pink-and-white blossoms hung from the Old Campus trees. Students played Hacky Sack in T-shirts and shorts. Though I was the one who'd broken away after she went up to that podium, I still half expected her to poke her head out a window in Linsly-Chit, or tap on my back in Harkness, or even join me in the Commons dining hall, where I'd asked for my dish-room shift to be transferred. She did none of these.

"Well," I said, "what is it?"

She looked at me. "My mother," she said.

She continued to cry, but seemed to have grown so silent in my room I wondered if I could hear the numbers change on my digital clock.

"When my parents were getting divorced," she said, "my mother bought a car. A used one. An El Dorado. It was filthy. It looked like a huge crushed can coming up the street. She kept trying to clean it out. I mean—"

I nodded and tried to think what to say in the pause she left behind. Finally I said, "We had one of those," though I was sure ours was an Impala.

She looked at me, eyes steely from trying not to cry. "Anyway, she'd drive me around in it and although she didn't like me to eat in it, I always did. One day I was eating cantaloupe slices, spitting the seeds on the floor. Maybe a month later, I saw this little sprout, growing right up from the car floor. I just started laughing and she kept saying what, what? I was laughing and then I saw she was so—"

She didn't finish. So what? So sad? So awful? Heidi looked at me with what seemed to be a renewed vigor. "We could have gotten a better car, eh?"

"It's all right. It's not a big deal," I said.

Of course, that was the wrong thing to say. And I really didn't mean it to sound the way it had come out.

I told Dr. Raeburn about Heidi's mother having cancer and how I'd said it wasn't a big deal, though I'd wanted to say the opposite. I told Dr. Raeburn how I meant to tell Heidi that my mother had died, that I knew how one eventually accustoms oneself to the physical world's lack of sympathy: the buses that are still running late, the kids who still play in the street, the clocks that won't stop ticking for the person who's gone.

"You're pretending," Dr. Raeburn said, not sage or professional, but a little shocked by the discovery, as if I'd been trying to hide a pack of his cigarettes behind my back.

"I'm pretending?" I shook my head. "All those years of psych grad," I said. "And to tell me *that?*"

"What I mean is that you construct stories about yourself and dish them out—one for you, one for you—" Here he reenacted this process, showing me handing out lies as if they were apples.

"Pretending. I believe the professional name for it might be denial," I said. "Are you calling me gay?"

He pursed his lips noncommittally, then finally said, "No, Dina. I don't think you're gay."

I checked his eyes. I couldn't read them.

"No. Not at all," he said, sounding as if he were telling a subtle joke. "But maybe you'll finally understand."

"Understand what?"

"Oh, just that constantly saying what one doesn't mean accustoms the mouth to meaningless phrases." His eyes narrowed. "Maybe you'll understand that when you finally need to express something truly significant your mouth will revert to the insignificant nonsense it knows so well." He looked at me, his hands sputtering in the air in a gesture of defeat. "Who knows?" he asked with a glib, psychiatric smile I'd never seen before. "Maybe it's your survival mechanism. Black living in a white world."

I heard him, but only vaguely. I'd hooked on to that one word, pretending. Dr. Raeburn would never realize that "pretending" was what had got me this far. I remembered the morning of my mother's funeral. I'd been given milk to settle my stomach; I'd pretended it was coffee. I imagined I was drinking coffee elsewhere. Some Arabic-speaking country where the thick coffee served in little cups was so strong it could keep you awake for days.

Heidi wanted me to go with her to the funeral. She'd sent this message through the dean. "We'll pay for your ticket to Vancouver," the dean said.

These people wanted you to owe them for everything. "What about my return ticket?" I asked the dean. "Maybe the shrink will chip in for that."

The dean looked at me as though I were an insect she'd like to squash. "We'll pay for the whole thing. We might even pay for some lessons in manners."

So I packed my suitcase and walked from my suicide single dorm to Heidi's room. A thin wispy girl in ragged cutoffs and a shirt that read "LSBN!" answered the door. A group of short-haired girls in thick black leather jackets, bundled up despite the summer heat, encircled Heidi in a protective fairy ring. They looked at me critically, clearly wondering if Heidi was too fragile for my company.

"You've got our numbers," one said, holding on to Heidi's shoulder. "And Vancouver's got a great gay community."

"Oh, God," I said. "She's going to a funeral, not a Save the Dykes rally."

One of the girls stepped in front of me.

"It's O.K., Cynthia," Heidi said. Then she ushered me into her bedroom and closed the door. A suitcase was on her bed, half packed.

"I could just uninvite you," Heidi said. "How about that? You want that?" She folded a polka-dotted T-shirt that was wrong for any occasion and put it in her suitcase. "Why haven't you talked to me?" she said, looking at the shirt instead of me. "Why haven't you talked to me in two months?"

"I don't know," I said.

"You don't know," she said, each syllable steeped in sarcasm. "You don't know. Well, *I* know. You thought I was going to try to sleep with you."

"Try to? We slept together all winter!"

"If you call smelling your feet sleeping together, you've got a lot to learn." She seemed thinner and meaner; every line of her body held me at bay.

"So tell me," I said. "What can you show me that I need to learn?" But as soon as I said it I somehow knew she still hadn't slept with anyone. "Am I supposed to come over there and sweep your enraged self into my arms?" I said. "Like in the movies? Is this the part where we're both so mad we kiss each other?"

She shook her head and smiled weakly. "You don't get it," she said. "My mother is dead." She closed her suitcase, clicking shut the old-fashioned locks. "My mother is dead," she said again, this time reminding herself. She set her suitcase upright on the floor and sat on it. She looked like someone waiting for a train.

"Fine," I said. "And she's going to be dead for a long time." Though it sounded stupid, I felt good saying it. As though I had my own locks to click shut.

Heidi went to Vancouver for her mother's funeral. I didn't go with her. Instead, I went back to Baltimore and moved in with an aunt I barely knew. Every day was the same: I read and smoked outside my aunt's apartment, studying the row of hair salons across the street, where girls in denim cutoffs and tank tops would troop in and come out hours later, a flash of neon nails, coifs the color and sheen of patent leather. And every day I imagined Heidi's house in Vancouver. Her place would not be large, but it would be clean. Flowery shrubs would line the walks. The Canadian wind would whip us about like pennants. I'd be visiting her in some vague time in the future, deliberately vague, for people like me, who realign past events to suit themselves. In that future time, you always have a chance to catch the groceries before they fall; your words can always be rewound and erased, rewritten and revised.

Then I'd imagine Heidi visiting me. There are no psychiatrists or deans, no boys with nice shoes or flip cashiers. Just me in my single room. She knocks on the door and says, "Open up."

Permissions

Grateful acknowledgment is made for the permission to print or reprint the following copyrighted material:

"Fire: An Origin Tale," by Faith Adiele. Reprinted with the permission of the author.

"Casual Water," from *Yellow: Stories*, by Don Lee. Copyright © 2001 by Don Lee. Reprinted with the permission of W.W. Norton & Company, Inc.

"Shades," from *I Got Somebody in Staunton*, by William Henry Lewis. Copyright © 2005 by William Henry Lewis. Reprinted with the permission of HarperCollins Publishers.

"Mrs. Turner's Lawn Jockeys," by Emily Raboteau. Reprinted with the permission of the author.

"Knuckles," by Mary F. Chen-Johnson. Reprinted with the permission of the author.

"The Shawl," from *The New Yorker* (March 5, 2001), by Louise Erdrich.

CPSIA information can be obtained at www.ICGtesting.com
Printed in the USA
LVOW08n1906021014

406948LV00004B/8/P